PERFORMANCE ANALYSIS IN TEAM SPORTS

Filling an important gap in performance analysis literature, this book introduces the key concepts and practical applications of performance analysis for team sports. It draws on cutting-edge research to examine individual and collective behaviours across an array of international team sports. Evidencing the close relationship between coaching and performance analysis, it promotes a better understanding of the crucial role of performance analysis in team sports for achieving successful results.

This book not only presents a variety of different ways to analyse performance in team sports, but also demonstrates how scientific data can be used to enrich performance analysis. Part one delineates the main guidelines for research in performance analysis, discussing the characteristics of team sports, coaching processes, variables characterising performance and methods for team member interaction analysis. Part two drills down into performance analysis across a range of team sports including soccer, basketball, handball, ice hockey, volleyball and rugby.

Performance Analysis in Team Sports is an essential companion for any course or research project on sports performance analysis or sports coaching, and an invaluable reference for professional analysts.

Pedro Passos is an Assistant Professor in the Faculty of Human Kinetics, University of Lisbon, Portugal.

Duarte Araújo is the Director of the Laboratory of Sport Expertise in the Faculty of Human Kinetics, University of Lisbon, Portugal.

Anna Volossovitch is an Assistant Professor in the Faculty of Human Kinetics, University of Lisbon, Portugal.

Routledge Studies in Sports Performance Analysis

Series Editor
Peter O'Donoghue
Cardiff Metropolitan University

Routledge Studies in Sports Performance Analysis is designed to support students, lecturers and practitioners in all areas of this important and rapidly developing discipline. Books in the series are written by leading international experts in sports performance analysis and cover topics including match analysis, analysis of individual sports and team sports, technique analysis, data analytics, performance analysis for high-performance management, and various methodological areas. Drawing on the very latest research, and introducing key concepts and best practice, the series meets a need for accessible, up-to-date texts at all levels of study and work in performance analysis.

Available in this series:

An Introduction to Performance Analysis of Sport
Peter O'Donoghue

Data Analysis in Sport
Peter O'Donoghue and Lucy Holmes

Performance Analysis in Team Sports
Pedro Passos, Duarte Araújo and Anna Volossovitch

PERFORMANCE ANALYSIS IN TEAM SPORTS

PEDRO PASSOS, DUARTE ARAÚJO AND ANNA VOLOSSOVITCH

Routledge
Taylor & Francis Group

LONDON AND NEW YORK

First published 2017
by Routledge
2 Park Square, Milton Park, Abingdon, Oxon OX14 4RN

and by Routledge
711 Third Avenue, New York, NY 10017

Routledge is an imprint of the Taylor & Francis Group, an informa business

British Library Cataloguing in Publication Data
A catalogue record for this book is available from the British Library

Library of Congress Cataloging-in-Publication Data
Names: Passos, Pedro, author. | Araújo, Duarte, author. | Volossovitch, Anna,
    author.
Title: Performance analysis in team sports / Pedro Passos, Duarte Araújo and
    Anna Volossovitch.
Description: Abingdon, Oxon ; New York, NY : Routledge is an imprint of the
    Taylor & Francis Group, an Informa Business, [2017] | Series: Routledge
    studies in sports performance analysis | Includes bibliographical references
    and index.
Identifiers: LCCN 2016020496| ISBN 9781138825833 (hardback) |
    ISBN 9781138825840 (pbk.) | ISBN 9781315739687 (ebook)
Subjects: LCSH: Sports—Psychological aspects. | Sports—Physiological
    aspects. | Team sports—Psychological aspects. | Team sports—
    Physiological aspects. | Sports sciences. | Performance.
Classification: LCC GV706.4 .P366 2017 | DDC 796.01/9—dc23
LC record available at https://lccn.loc.gov/2016020496

ISBN: 978-1-138-82583-3 (hbk)
ISBN: 978-1-138-82584-0 (pbk)
ISBN: 978-1-315-73968-7 (ebk)

Typeset in Melior
by Apex CoVantage, LLC

MIX
Paper from
responsible sources
FSC   FSC® C013056
www.fsc.org

Printed and bound in Great Britain by
TJ International Ltd, Padstow, Cornwall

I dedicate this book to my students.

Pedro

I would like to thank my wife, Carla, and son, Vicente. Without their wholehearted support for my work, and their abundant creation of life affordances, the lucidity and the perseverance to write this book would not have been possible.

Duarte

CONTENTS

PART II

FOREWORD

Sports science is awash with data. Waves and waves of statistics to be used to enhance athlete performance. How can we avoid drowning in this ocean of information? This book, *Performance Analysis in Team Sports* by Pedro Passos, Duarte Araújo and Anna Volossovitch, is a timely and well-considered academic endeavour at precisely the moment when the power of digital technologies is advancing rapidly, providing opportunities to record, measure, assess and evaluate performance in many different sports, including team sports. In the past decades the focus within *sports science* has broadened in scope and turned to *sport and exercise science* due to massive socio-cultural changes, responding to the need to understand how to design environments that facilitate people's engagement in physical activity and exercise. Recently the wheels have turned again and sport science dovetails with *performance analysis*, this time due to the socio-cultural constraints exerted by technological advances. It is now possible to record and measure athlete performance and behaviours during competition, training, practice, recovery and, most recently due to a revolution in apps, at rest. Clearly, it is undeniable that information is needed on performance, learning, training and recovery in sport programmes. But what to do with all these data and, importantly, the opportunities to collect more data? What kind of data are needed by athletes and practitioners? How can we harness the power of large data sets and at the same time avoid the reduction of athletes to marionettes dancing to the tune of a thousand measurements during practice and performance? These, and other related questions, are increasingly being posed in academic circles and sports development programmes, based on concerns about the impact of 'big data' or 'datafication' or 'dataveillance' (Williams & Manley, 2014) on athlete behaviours during practice, training and competition, as well as pedagogical practice.

The authors of this book provide a comprehensive response to these concerns by showing that nothing less than an integration of theoretical knowledge, empirical data, and research methodology of a quantitative and qualitative nature, as well as information from pedagogical practice and application, will be needed by the sports pedagogists, practitioners and performance analysts of the future. For the past decade, in my opinion, their group from the faculty of Human Kinetics at the University of Lisboa in Portugal has led the world in enriching performance analysis, moving it from a fundamentally operational approach, dominated by statistical analysis of action frequencies, to a powerfully descriptive and explanatory endeavour in which rich detail is woven into the tapestry of team sports performance. The research programme at both laboratories essentially uses three main types of methodology: (i) experimentation by direct manipulation of constraints on participants and/or the contexts of action, (ii) computerised simulations, and (iii) systematic observations and analysis of behaviours in sports performance settings. Measured variables are typically eco-kinematic, psychophysical, physiological, neuroscientific and notational (in terms of individual and collective behaviours), and these can be mathematically modelled. The equipment used includes GPS, video-based motion analysis, ball projection machines and neurophysiological sensors, which support performance analysis in team sports environments. Additionally this group utilises methods such as interviews, questionnaires and documental analysis to access experiential knowledge of expert performers and coaches.

Consequently, the different chapters of the book illustrate convincingly how performance analysts will be required to be conversant in theory, research, measurement and application to practice to provide the type of support needed by elite, sub-elite and development programmes in high-performance sport. The material presented here shows that performance analysts will be required to work in teams with pedagogues, psychologists, skill acquisition specialists, physiologists, biomechanists and engineers to collect and verify, discard and retain, analyse and interpret data collected during different phases of competition, preparation and recovery. The book's main focus is on team sports and each chapter deals with different types of games to engage with specific task constraints encountered. This is important because it has been noted that each type of (sport) performance environment has a specific 'form of life' (as Wittgenstein noted, predicated on unique patterns of behaviour, knowledge and skills, as well as customs and cultural constraints) (Rietveld & Kiverstein, 2014). It is feasible that performance analysts of the future will need to have a good grasp of a theory explaining how behaviours during competition and practice are organised so that an athlete's relationship with a particular performance environment is made more functional as a result of the hours spent training. Two fundamental questions will be posed: What is the nature of the performance process, and how should we conceptualise the performer in sport? Answering these questions requires performance analysts to acquire and use a model of (sport) performance and of the performer because without these models (and the same applies for the learning process and the learner) practitioners will simply bob like corks between islands of dry land surrounded by oceans of data. Performance analysis will become very reactive, rather than prospective.

So, what precisely is novel and innovative in this comprehensive text on performance analysis? This book elucidates a powerful theoretical framework which can provide a 'life raft' for a performance analyst submerged by a sea of information. It also provides a rationale for coaches wanting to use the methods and the data referenced in the book. The theoretical framework proposed here identifies (cooperating and competing) attackers and defenders in team games as intricate components (degrees of freedom) of a self-organising system linked by informational fields which surround them – e.g., acoustic and visual. Thus, in team sports considered as *complex adaptive systems*, the individual performer is conceptualised as the base unit degree of freedom. Team sports are dynamic, complex performance environments because of the continuous changes in the location, positioning and movements of competing and cooperating players. Due to the highly interactive nature of the performance environment in team sports, opportunities for action are constrained in time and space. These *affordances* or invitations for action emerge from a process of co-adaptation among individuals. Co-adaptation can emerge in many different forms, including interpersonal coordination, which provides a platform for performance in all sports, at elite and sub-elite levels and even subconsciously (Varlet & Richardson, 2015). In team games, co-adaptation has been shown to result in the continuous emergence and dissolution of spontaneous pattern-forming dynamics among system degrees of freedom (athletes) during performance. Like organisms in other complex adaptive systems, such as schools of fish and flocks of birds, individual athletes in sports teams use fairly simple local behavioural rules to create rich structures and patterns at a collective level that are much more nuanced than the behaviour of any single individual playing in the team. This is known as the 'complexity from simplicity' model for understanding behaviours of complex adaptive system. Research has shown how local rules for interactions among single system components can lead to the emergence of sophisticated 'macro-states' of organisation in a global system. What is needed are non-linear methods of analysis of patterns of emerging behaviours among individual athletes. This book discusses a range of such methods for understanding how sophisticated attacking and defending patterns of play in team sports emerge from continuous attacker–defender interactions. It clarifies how the constraints of a competitive environment in team sports force performers to continuously co-adapt to behaviours of teammates and opponents, typically in close proximity to specific locations of a playing area (such as the goal or sidelines). Important performance variables like relative angles among competing individuals, values of interpersonal distances between an attacker and a defender, and the relative velocity of two moving competitors have been empirically verified as relevant variables for understanding interpersonal coordination tendencies of team sports players as agents in a complex adaptive system. Additionally, variables capturing the shape of attacking and defending sub-units or formations, such as team centroids (a variable showing the centre of performance gravity of a team) and surface areas, as well as width and length, provide information on the coherent patterns in sports teams during performance. These behaviours emerge from processes of co-adaptation in team sports performance, providing working materials for coaches, teachers and practitioners. Finally, the book proposes that a major task for pedagogues during practice is to create small-sided and conditioned games that provide informationally constrained dynamic interactions created in space and time by changes in the relative positioning of attackers and defenders in many different team sports.

In conclusion, the many chapters of this book outline in fine detail a rich mix of theory, as well as non-linear and other methodologies for analysing performance behaviours over time; data from well-controlled empirical investigations in studies of athlete behaviours during different sub-phases of team sports performance; and applications for coaches, teachers and sport scientists. This rich integration of necessary information hands a veritable 'life raft' to the reader, and I consider that it has the potential to take sport science and performance analysis in a new direction.

Keith Davids, Nether Edge, Sheffield, June 2015

REFERENCES

Rietveld, E., & Kiverstein, J. (2014). A rich landscape of affordances. *Ecological Psychology, 26*, 325–352.

Varlet, M., & Richardson, M. (2015). What would be Usain Bolt's 100-meter sprint world record without Tyson Gay? Unintentional interpersonal synchronization between the two sprinters. *Journal of Experimental Psychology: Human Perception and Performance, 41*(1), 36–41. doi: 10.1037/a0038640.

Williams, S., & Manley, A. (2014). Elite coaching and the technocratic engineer: Thanking the boys at Microsoft! *Sport, Education and Society.* doi: 10.1080/13573322.2014.958816

PART I

CHAPTER 1

PHYSICAL AND INFORMATIONAL CONSTRAINTS CHARACTERISE TEAM SPORTS

Leading author: Duarte Araújo

INTRODUCTION

Performance analysis is concerned with the analysis, design and evaluation of sport systems. These systems are complex, and the distinction between analysis, design and evaluation is an abstraction and does not capture the actual practice of sport scientists and coaches. If sport systems are to be built in an integral fashion, then all three activities must be intimately intertwined and mutually informing each other. A sport system is composed of several layers. Traditionally, many disciplines like physiology, biomechanics, psychology, pedagogy or sociology have viewed their technical core as comprising the entire system. For example, the definition of 'sport science' for the *Encyclopedia of International Sport Studies* (Bartlett et al., 2006) does not include sociology, whereas 'training science', in the same encyclopedia, is mainly derived from physiology, and the entries 'practice' and 'practice structure and organisation' are mainly informed by psychology. A new layer of complexity appears when the discussions around how technical and tactical aspects of a sport should go beyond task characteristics and considering the players constraints (e.g., Davids et al., 2008). But this is not the whole story. The social-organisational level also plays a crucial role in the sport system. For example, the management changes implemented in a Team Sport Club may have consequences in terms of the performance of the professional team. Finally, environment also affects a sport system. The national football championships in Europe and in Asia greatly differ in terms of the competitive level of the teams, audience participation, economic management and the physical environment.

Any analysis of performance in a given sport is based on a certain set of assumptions about the performance that is intended to be analysed. For example, counting frequencies of a certain event in a match assumes both that the event is relevant, and that counting frequencies is informative. Rather than making those assumptions implicitly, the design of information systems for performance analysis should be based on an explicit model of performance in a given team sport. Since performance analysis is not an end in itself but rather a means to derive implications for sport training and competition, it is important to have an explicit understanding of what a sport system is, such as a competitive match.

CHARACTERISTICS OF SPORTS

Sport is a human activity characterised by a particular organisation and functioning in a given context. The ecology of sport is not only distinguished by the physical characteristics, where the activity of the players happens, but also by its social and cultural aspects. Given all the physical and social constraints, the sport activities explore the competition of players. The factor of interest for the sport audience is precisely to observe which are the players or the teams that succeed in a competition, characterised by a complex interaction of physical (e.g., gravity) and social (e.g., rules) constraints specific to each team sport. Specifically, the aim of a team is to score more points/goals than the other team. This implies an initiative to score (attacking), and also prevent the other team from scoring (defending). This distinction between attacking and defending is an oversimplification because there are team sports where a team can be defending when in possession of the ball, and the team without the ball may be attacking the space and the ball carrier of the other team to re-gain ball possession. It may be more appropriate to talk about team offense and defence (Mateus, 2005). In any case, a specific feature of team ball sports is the flow of interactions between cooperating and competing players, with or without the ball, to achieve the aim of each team for the match (Mateus, 2005). The aims of the teams are thus mutually exclusive during a match. This way, each team tries to avoid the implementation of the strategic plans of the other team, as well as thwart their tactical actions (Davids et al., 2005). The result is a complex, emergent behaviour of players and teams.

Complexity is, in general, a multidimensional concept and sport matches are not an exception (Davids et al., 2014). Some complex sport systems

4

such as team games are characterised by direct interaction among players and their opponents (e.g., a volleyball match), or by collaborative interactions among players competing with another group of collaborative players (e.g., a basketball match). The following list of interrelated characteristics is intended to be broad enough to encompass the different types of complexity that we can find in a team sport system (see Vicente, 1999), such as a competitive match:

1   Large problem spaces. Sport matches tend to be composed of many different elements and forces (Gréhaigne et al., 2011; McGarry et al., 2002). As a result, the number of potentially relevant factors that coaches and players need to take into account can be enormous. For example, in a soccer game the possibilities of combinations of players' actions in a team are unlimited. Large problem spaces also create difficulties for coaches, who ensure that the training sessions they develop allow athletes to deal with the entire array of possibilities without exceeding their resource limitations.

2   Social complexity. Sport complex systems are usually composed of groups of people who must work together to make the overall system function properly. This creates a strong need for clear communication to effectively coordinate the actions of the various parties involved (Araújo et al., 2015; Mateus, 2005). For example, a rugby club can't provide the most effective care for its players unless there is good communication between directors, coaches, parents, sponsors, journalists, doctors, sport psychologists and other staff.

3   Heterogeneous perspectives. The people involved in a sport context frequently come from different cultural and social backgrounds and thus represent the potentially conflicting values of a diverse set of origins. Consequently, the social negotiation process becomes more difficult by the fact that different values have to be adjusted to achieve a common goal (Kleinert et al., 2012).

4   Distributed. The demands associated with social coordination can be complicated by the fact that the people involved may be located in different places (e.g., different areas of the football pitch). It is difficult to get people located in different places to communicate clearly and coordinate their actions and decisions when trying to achieve a goal (Duarte et al., 2012; McGarry, 2005).

5   Dynamic. Complex sport systems are usually dynamic and can have long-time constants: it can take seconds to score a goal and hours or days to overcome a negative result. In a team, because the effects of

players' actions in training are delayed, players have to anticipate the future state of the game and act accordingly (Davids et al., 2005, Mateus, 2005; McGarry, 2005).

6   Hazard. There is also a high degree of potential hazard in certain types of competitions because inappropriate beliefs or actions can have catastrophic consequences (e.g., an offensive gesture by a player to the opponent's spectators), jeopardise public safety (e.g., initiate violence among rival spectators outside the sports facilities), or have economic consequences (e.g., disinterest of the sponsors due to losing a major international competition). This is particularly critical in abnormal or unusual situations (Vicente, 1999); for example, an elimination match of a championship, or an international match played after the threat of a bomb. Moreover, coaches cannot afford to rely on trial-and-error approaches. Because of the potential hazard involved, there is very strong requirement to try to 'get it right the first time'.

7   Coupling. Complex sport systems also tend to be composed of many sub-systems that are highly coupled (i.e., interact). This makes it very difficult to predict all of the effects of an action, or to trace all the implications of a disturbance of the adversary because there are many, perhaps diverging, possible outcomes (Davids et al., 2014; Mateus, 2005). Acting in a highly coupled sport competition puts a great burden on all those who are involved because of all the factors that need to be considered at the same time.

8   Uncertainty. There tends to be uncertainty in the data that are available to players (i.e., imperfect evaluation of the performance of the other team, the contribution of the substitute players, the strategic moves of the opponent's coach). Because of this lack of total information, the actual state of the competition is never known with complete certainty (Davids et al., 2005; Mateus, 2005). Furthermore, players must distinguish changes that are caused by events in the match from those that are caused by random drift. Thus, there may be a need for problem solving and inference (i.e., to 'go beyond the information given') (Eccles, 2010).

9   Disturbances. Finally, athletes are also responsible for dealing with unanticipated events (e.g., two players with a red card; the other team scored in the first minutes of the game). They must improvise and adapt to an unanticipated event quickly to maintain team productivity. Therefore, players' training can't be solely based on expected or frequently encountered situations (McGarry, et al., 2002; Travassos et al., 2012). Instead, complex sport systems must also

6

operate effectively under idiosyncratic events – that is, events not anticipated by players or coaches.

It is important to emphasise that not all team sport matches rate high in all these dimensions. There are important differences across sports (e.g., football vs. volleyball), so some dimensions may not even be particularly relevant for some matches, and some may not be exclusive for team sports. Nevertheless, all team sport competitions will rate highly in at least some of these dimensions, and will also usually exhibit several other dimensions of complexity albeit to a lesser extent. These dimensions should be analysed in order to see how they constrain the effectiveness of the player or the team. Effectiveness criteria are of different kinds in different sports, but productivity (i.e., goal achievement), safety (i.e., not getting injured) and satisfaction (i.e., motivation to continue) should be considered.

PHYSICAL AND INFORMATIONAL CONSTRAINTS CHANNEL INDIVIDUAL AND TEAM BEHAVIOUR

As can be understood from these characteristics, team sport competitions can be considered as complex dynamic systems composed of many interacting parts (e.g., Davids et al., 2014). A dynamic systems approach to sport studies describes how patterns of coordinated movement come about ('emerge'), persist and change. It builds on the insight that social systems (e.g., teams) consist of a large number of interacting parts, endowing them with the capacity of spontaneous pattern formation or self-organisation. The spontaneous creation of coherent macroscopic patterns (e.g., team coordination) is important scientifically because it allows for studying the resulting macroscopic patterns in terms of the dynamics of one or a few collective variables (e.g., the centroid of a team), without having to know all the microscopic states of the individual parts (e.g., the movement of each player) (Kelso, 1995). Conversely, when the dynamics of macroscopic phenomena have been identified, the contributions of relevant dynamic components (e.g., the movement of certain players) to the overall dynamics may be investigated in a top-down fashion.

Performers can generate behavioural patterns that are tightly coordinated with the environment (e.g., the match configuration), in the service of achieving a specific goal. In team sports, athletes are surrounded by physical (e.g., gravity, altitude) and social (e.g., audience, rules of the game) constraints and continuously interact with each other to achieve performance goals. Successful performance in sport is predicated on an individual's perceptual and action capabilities, and is grounded in the information used for action selection and goal achievement (Araújo et al., 2006). The view of the performer–environment relationship is central to performance analysis, but it is here usually assumed to follow the post-Cartesian paradigm, whereby the performer is regarded as the active agent and the environment as something that only supports the actions of the individual or provides the source of stimuli (Araújo & Davids, 2011).

According to the view of the organism–environment system, the environment is not just a passive scene in the background of the acting players but an active part of the system making specific results of behaviour possible (Gibson, 1979; Järvilehto, 2009). This means that the structure and physics of the environment, the biomechanics of the body, perceptual information about the state of the performer–environment system, and the demands of the task all serve to constrain the performance (Turvey, 2009). One consequence of this account is that behaviour can be understood as self-organised, in contrast to organisation being imposed from the inside (e.g., the team captain) or the outside (e.g., the coach). Performance is not prescribed by internal or external structures, yet within the given constraints there are typically a limited number of stable solutions that achieve the desired outcome.

From the player's point of view, the task is to exploit physical (e.g., the pitch characteristics as determined by the rules) and informational (e.g., the movement of other players) constraints to stabilise the intended behaviour. Constraints have the effect of reducing the number of configurations available to a dynamic system at any instance. In a team sports match, coordinated patterns (individual or collective) emerge under constraints as less functional states of organisation are dissipated. In its most general meaning, a constraint can be defined as a limitation on the available states of a system being studied. Every team sport presents its own set of constraints, which helps define its functioning. For example, the offside rule in association football implies specific training tasks for the players as a whole be perceptually attuned to this physical constraint – i.e., this configuration of the match, which has tremendous impact on how attacking and defensive team actions can be played.

Aligned with these notions of physical and informational constraints, a Constraints-Led Approach has been promoted as a theoretical framework for understanding how players perform and learn in sport (see Davids

8

et al., 2008; Renshaw et al., 2015). Developing a sound theoretical understanding of the major constraints on performers in sport could provide a strong basis for performance analysis and coaching at introductory as well as advanced levels of training and practice.

CONSTRAINTS-LED APPROACH TO PERFORMANCE IN TEAM GAMES

Actions in sports differ in the nature of the constraints imposed on performers. The characteristics of each sport as indicated by the sport's rules and competition goals, the characteristics of the players, as well as the characteristics of the environment define the broad categories of constraints (Davids et al., 2008). Despite the huge variety of influential factors or constraints imposed by team sports, one thing they all share is a requirement for highly coordinated actions and perfectly timed movement sequences. A Constraints-Led Approach emphasises the study of coordination and how it changes with learning and development and attempts to categorise the many constraints of different sports, as well as the individual differences that each performer brings to practice and training environments (Davids et al., 2008). Importantly, coordination can be seen at an intra-individual level (e.g., during a basketball shot), between the performer and an external object (e.g., kicking a moving ball), or between two or more performers (e.g., playing football and basketball). Individual and team coordination are therefore a key issue in team sports, and they are highly sensitive to the characteristics of each sport – i.e., to the physical and informational constraints that channel the coordination pattern (behaviour).

Dynamic sport systems exhibit several important characteristics that are useful for our understanding of coordination. First, they have many independent degrees of freedom which are free to vary. The term 'degrees of freedom' refers to the number of potential configurations available to the many independent parts of a system (e.g., the players in a team). So, for example, a player is free to move in a pitch, but his/her degrees of freedom are reduced if he/she is marking, and therefore constraining, another player. A social system such as a competitive match has an abundance of degrees of freedom (e.g., players actions, trajectories of players and ball displacements, etc.), which is a rich resource to exploit in coordinating interpersonal actions to achieve a goal. Second, dynamic movement systems have many different levels (e.g., individual, intra-group, inter-group, social-organisational). The contribution of each level needs to be considered as coaches attempt to understand the constraints on behaviour. Third, the huge number of sport system degrees of freedom (e.g., players) has the potential to interact, resulting in non-linearity of behaviours emerging from the system (e.g., apparently unpredictable peaks and troughs in the performance, 'highs' and 'lows' of an inconsistent sports team). Finally, dynamic systems have the capacity for stable and unstable patterned relationships among system parts (e.g., stable and uns collective behaviours, such as attacking) to occur as the sport system components (such as players) spontaneously adjust and adapt to each other, a process called self-organisation.

What does the idea of self-organisation imply for our understanding of individual and team coordination? It appears that dynamic systems such as teams are able to exploit the constraints that surround them in order to allow functional patterns of behaviour to emerge in specific contexts. Large-scale coordination patterns (e.g., tactical configurations) occur among the vast number of small-scale degrees of freedom or component parts (e.g., players). Self-organisation of a particular system into different states occurs when the many micro-components (e.g., players) interact and begin to seriously influence each other's behaviour. These micro-level dynamics typically lead to no large-scale changes in system behaviours, merely a lot of underlying fluctuation, which mildly perturbs system stability – for instance, when defenders need to adjust relative positions due to attackers' attempts to get closer the goal. However, key events – for example, a defender breaking through the adversary defence with the ball – can alter the whole system structure, leading to macroscopic-level changes and reorganisation into a different state (Araújo et al., 2015). Self-organisation in dynamical systems is not a random or 'blind' process in which any pattern can result. Typically, a dynamic system only takes on very few states of organisation (e.g., having possession of the ball, not having possession of the ball, as well as transitions between these states). The type of order that emerges is dependent on initial conditions (existing match conditions) and the constraints that shape a system's collective behaviour (Davids et al., 2012).

Constraints and performance

These ideas of order emerging under constraints have some important implications for understanding how players learn coordination patterns.

10

Ecological dynamics views influential factors within the practice environment as constraints on performance development. It is proposed that performance emerges under interacting constraints, which harness the body's degrees of freedom during learning. Due to the abundance of mechanical degrees of freedom available in the human motor system, the main problem for the learner is to convert the complex human movements to a more controllable, stable system (Bernstein, 1967). What happens is that, with learning, functional groupings or coordinated states emerge from the available degrees of freedom, which stabilise the motor system from the random fluctuations that can occur between system components. The same process happens in a sports team. The difference is that while for the player the parts (e.g., limbs) are physically constrained (linked), in a team the parts (players) are linked by information (Schmidt et al., 1999).

According to Newell (1986), constraints can be classified into three distinct categories to provide a coherent framework for understanding how coordination patterns emerge during goal-directed behaviour (Figure 1.1). It is important to clarify that the constraints are not negative influences on behaviour, like 'oppressors' or 'punishers', which take away freedom. Instead, constraints are seen as the way the components of a system are linked, forming a specific type of organisation. It would be strange to consider that the wheels of a car have lost their freedom because they are constrained by the axis. A good driver is aware of these constraints and explores them, and he/she does not decry the absence of freedom of the wheels. Moreover, the particular ways the components of a car are linked (constrained) together comprise a vehicle. The separate unassembled components of a car do not constitute a vehicle.

Performer constraints

These constraints refer to characteristics of individual athletes, such as genes, height, weight, muscle–fat ratio, connective strength of synapses in the brain, skill level and readiness to learn, as well as psychological characteristics such as thoughts, motivations and emotions. Some of the most important constraints on motor performance involve the neuroanatomical design of the muscles and joints of the human body. For example, Carson and Kelso (2004) showed how flexor muscle groups have structural characteristics and cortical connections that provide greater stability in sensorimotor coordination compared to extensor muscle groups. It appears that performers can counteract this feature of neuroanatomical design by focusing attention on extension phases and through resistance training (Carroll et al., 2001). Understanding how intrinsic differences in neuroanatomical design of muscles and limb segments can constrain coordination will help coaches to design specific training and practice programmes to target areas of movement instability accordingly. The performer can view such unique characteristics as resources that can be used to solve a particular task problem or limitations that can lead to individual-specific adaptations.

Environmental constraints

These constraints can be physical in nature, such as ambient light, altitude or ambient temperature, all of which can affect players at different levels. Gravity is a key environmental constraint on performance in all tasks, as demonstrated by the example of a fall in a match. The ambient temperatures encountered in equatorial countries can affect the muscle properties of the players. Some environmental constraints are social rather than physical. Socio-cultural factors are key environmental constraints including family support networks, peer groups, societal expectations and values as well as cultural norms.

Task constraints

Task constraints are more specific than environmental constraints and include goals, rules of a specific sport, implements or tools used during an activity, pitches and boundary markings. The movements of player may vary, even within seemingly highly consistent activities such as a basketball free throw or a penalty kick in football because some task constraints differ among performance trials. An important task constraint to consider is the information available in specific performance contexts that players can use, and it is important to spend some time understanding the nature of informational constraints on action. It has been argued that biological organisms, including humans, are surrounded by huge arrays of energy flows that can act as information sources (e.g., optical, acoustic, proprioceptive) to support movement behaviour, including decision making, planning and organisation, during goal-directed activity (Araújo et al., 2013). For example, informational constraints can be used to continuously guide our actions as we navigate through a defensive formation on a basketball court. These ideas suggest that

12

practitioners need to understand the *nature* of the information that regulates movement and performance. The structure of energy in the surrounding environment carries information for a performer that is specific to certain contexts and that is available to be directly perceived. For example, light reaches the eyes of a basketball player after having been reflected off surfaces (i.e., the floor and backboard) and moving objects (i.e., other players and the ball) in the busy, cluttered environment which is the court. In order to pick up this information, a significant role is attributed to specific *movements* of the performer and/or objects to be acted upon. Movements cause changes to energy flows that provide specific information to organisms about the properties of a dynamic environment. It is argued that movement generates information that, in turn, supports further movements, leading to a direct and cyclical relationship between perception and movement (see Araújo et al., 2013).

The interaction among categories of constraints

Each of these categories does not act by itself on behaviour. Constraints from all three categories interact to influence performance. Thus, behaviour is not determined by these categories or by a specific constraint, since it

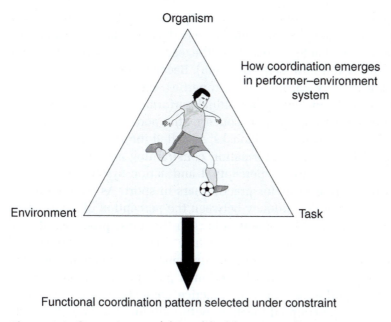

Functional coordination pattern selected under constraint

Figure 1.1 Constraints model (modified from Newell, 1986).

emerges at the level of the player–environment system, towards the task goal. Newell's (1986) model is an excellent conceptualisation to guide understanding of human performance (see also Davids et al., 2008). Interestingly, when the interacting constraints undergo specific levels of analysis, there are new ideas that can be raised based on such a framework. Team ball sports provide scenarios where both individual and team coordination are relevant. In such activities, a special category of constraints can be conceived. Each team acts as a system where its components (players) are organised in such a way that it can be considered as a super-organism (see Davids & Araújo, 2005; Duarte et al., 2012). Therefore, the team with its specific constraints (which are different from those of each individual) interacts with the environment to achieve the task goal. Each player undertakes a certain local function that is coordinated with the function of the next player and so on, leading to goal achievement at the team level. For example, it is not the player who scored a goal or saved a penalty who is winning, but the whole team. Therefore, it is important to recognise the role of inter-player coordination in the category of team constraints.

CONSTRAINTS-LED APPROACH TO THE DESIGN OF TRAINING TASKS

The implication of the Constraints-Led Approach (CLA) is that, in sport, performers need to become attuned to specific and relevant task properties that inform what to do to achieve the team goal (e.g., different match configurations and how to act on them). Because flow patterns are specific to particular environmental properties, they can act as information sources to be picked by individual performers to guide (constrain) their actions. Learning in sport concerns the perceptual attunement to information sources in specific tasks, so-called information–movement couplings. This view of information constraining action so that tight couplings emerge between perceptual and action systems provides a range of interesting ideas for practitioners in sport. As a consequence of the mutual interdependency between the perception of information and the generation of movement, it is clear that these processes should not be separated in practice by coaches. Practice conditions should be structured to maintain specific information–movement linkages. The smartness of evolutionarily designed perceptual mechanisms are exploited by performers only in practice contexts where perception and movement are coupled together, with individuals relatively free to

14

perform within sport environments (Chow et al., 2011; Van der Kamp, & Renshaw, 2015). But how to identify relevant constraints for designing tasks for training?

Identifying the characteristics of training tasks based on the characteristics of the match

Definitions of task vary according to the dimensions of the extent of factors considered in the categorisation and whether only criteria external to the subject are considered or whether performer's perceptions of the task are also defined. A proposal made by Newell (1986) considered the following: (i) the task goal; (ii) the rules constraining response possibilities; and (iii) implements or mechanisms constraining the response dynamics. The idea is that constraints to action have to be viewed from the functional perspective (i.e., the goal to be achieved by a performer in a given circumstance) rather than from reliance on the external physical description of the constraints.

Traditionally, motor behaviour tasks have been classified according to dimensions, such as continuous and discrete, referring to the extent to which the task demands movement with a definite beginning and end; or closed and open, referring to the extent to which the task is constant or changing (Schmidt & Lee, 2011). The outcome of movements in terms of the task goal has been measured essentially in terms of accuracy (and deviations to it) and speed. These measures of movement outcomes have been studied in a certain range of tasks. For example, the goal of accuracy can be a given force, distance, speed or time, where deviations (i.e., 'errors') of the players' performances with respect to the given target are measured. In these experiments, very simple tasks are generally conducted, mostly restricted to a single degree of freedom. For measuring speed the most used task is the discrete reaction time (RT), where the subject is given a warning signal, and after a randomly determined foreperiod, the stimulus is presented. According to Schmidt and Lee (2011) the tasks can be arbitrarily created in order to represent a motor performance novel to the subject, and the experimenter studies how the subject attempts to learn it or what variables influence that performance. The objection is that nowhere is there a consideration or justification of the origin and selection of the tasks. What general theory of performance insisted that these tasks should be used as markers of skilled performance? What theory of tasks led to the selection of these tasks?

The original basis for the choice of the tasks is defenceless; what should have been a coherent presentation of a series of ideas or concepts that provides the justification for 'Why these tasks?' is missing. Ironically, the task- and theory-makers can explain coherently the accuracy (or lack of it) of their participants, but are unable to explain their own accuracy when choosing the tasks. The consequence is that even if we try to explain the nature of performance those tasks, it remains performance on arbitrarily chosen tasks, tasks that lack theoretical justification.

Understanding the influence of constraints on performance from a Constraints-Led Approach is important because constraints can be viewed as another way to interpret the degrees of freedom in a given task situation. This realisation is important not only for defining the physical boundaries to action at various levels of analysis, but also for understanding the information available to the performer (Davids et al., 2012).

If we consider the specific constraints of a basketball as opposed to, say, those of a sailing task, they are very different. A possibility for identify the goal-relevant constraints in a sport task is the abstraction hierarchy of Rasmussen (1986). This is a hierarchy with several levels, where each level represents a normative model of the goal-relevant constraints in the world (see also Vicente, 1999). Each level below the top level describes the set of means that is available to achieve the ends at the level above. Each level deals with the same system, but different levels provide different descriptions for observing the system. Very important is the notion

Table 1.1 An example of an abstraction hierarchy analysis for identifying the specific characteristics of a basketball match

Abstraction hierarchy	Basketball game
Functional purpose or desired final state	Win the game, score a certain range of points or achieve a certain percentage of success in a certain function (e.g., assistances, rebounds)
Abstract functions or strategies	Plans for the organisation of the team previously presented by the coach (e.g., zone defence)
Generalised functions or tactics	Combinations of actions with other players that can implement a strategy (e.g., to block when the teammate attacks)
Basic functions	Local actions performed to fulfil tactics (i.e., to pass, to dribble or to throw)
Physical components of the competition	The characteristics and positions of the teammates and opponents on the court the referees, the audience, the court and ball characteristics

16

that understanding the system increases by crossing levels. By moving up the hierarchy, one obtains a deeper understanding of the system's significance with regard to the goals that are to be achieved; whereas in moving down the hierarchy, one obtains a more detailed explanation of the system's functioning in terms of how those goals can be carried out. One important property of the abstraction hierarchy is that higher levels are less detailed than lower levels. This allows people to deal with complex systems (e.g., the entire match) that would be unmanageable if they had to observe a whole system in full detail all at once (e.g., Eccles, Ward & Woodman, 2009; Vicente & Wang, 1998). In the examples of Table 1.1 it is clear that, even with similar labels, the detailed contents of the levels differ, showing that the constraints are very different among sports. However, Table 1.1 does not show the set of means–ends links among the different levels in the hierarchy. Each level of the hierarchy is nested within the context defined by the level above, and it is this nesting that provides the hierarchy with its behavioural value.

Principles for designing the training task based on the characteristics of a team game

Practice can be considered a form of exploratory behaviour, a continually evolving search for task solutions. Thus, even though there may be repetition in achieving a given task goal, there is no repetition to the process of achieving that goal. A usual statement about practice is that the number of practice attempts should be maximised. However, there is little research aimed at understanding the influence of the structure and quality of practice on sports performance. Practice is to be understood as a necessary, but not sufficient, condition for sports performance. It is the structure of practice and how it relates to the organismic, environmental and task constraints that determine the attainment of a potential solution to a task goal. While the amount of practice is an important concern for the coach, it is more important to consider how the amount of practice interacts with other variables, such as the contextual interference, contextual information and information–movement coupling which influence sports performance (Broadbent et al., 2015). These combine to channel and alter the structure of practice and the search through the task context towards some goal. The organisation of task structures, through a session or over sessions of directed practice, can extend to a larger scale over a broader time span (Kiely, 2012).

Practice and training cannot be isolated from the context where they occur; in fact, the organisational context matters significantly. According to Salas and Cannon-Bowers (2001), researchers are adopting a systems view of training and are more concerned with the organisational context. Thus, practice should consider a training-needs analysis – what should be trained, including organisation, task and person analysis; antecedent training conditions; pre-training variables – that may enhance or disrupt learning, training methods and instructional strategies; and post-training conditions – training evaluation and transfer of training. Because there is no single method to deliver training, researchers continue to address how to best present targeted information to trainees. In particular, researchers are seeking cost-effective, content-valid, easy-to-use, engaging and technology-based methods.

The issue of whether to address a whole task or parts of a task in practice has been a topic of discussion for a long time. Unfortunately, the research generated has led to confusion rather than understanding. Again, this confusion comes from the fact that different conclusions have been generated from different tasks. The basic assumption, when addressing a part of the whole task, is that learning one part of the task will transfer positively to performing the whole task. Therefore, the question becomes not whether part- or whole-task practice should occur, but which part-practice technique should be applied. Different techniques for achieving part practice have been proposed. The first of these is segmentation, which involves separating the skill into parts and then practicing the parts so that, after the learner practices one part, he/she then practices that part together with the next part, and so on. Fractionation involves practicing separate components of the whole skill, and simplification reduces the difficulty of the whole task or of different parts of the task. In serial tasks, learning transfer from part-practice can be enormous. However, the task should be reassembled because mere practice on a part isolated from the sequence does not appear to be useful for transfer. In continuous tasks (e.g., gait, and each phase of the upper and lower limb position during the gait) the parts must frequently be coordinated with each other, and it might seem that breaking this pattern of coordination to practice a part might not be effective. In general, the limitations of part-to-whole transfer methods will probably depend on the extent to which the parts of the task interact within the whole task. For discrete tasks, the findings suggest that practicing isolated components of the whole task produces hardly any transfer to the performance of the whole task (Lee et al., 2001). For example, in the volleyball serve decoupling the ball toss with

18

one arm from the hitting movement of the other arm results in a toss that is different from that when the movements are coupled (Handford, 2002, 2006).

The separation of parts has focused on subjective assessments of skills in terms of 'appropriate units of action' and their perceived relationships with one another. The problem is that researchers have never provided a theoretically coherent account for this common practice; consequently meaningful practical guidance has not been forthcoming. The result is that many practices in sport implement task decompositions with a tentative and unprincipled foundation. The CLA has shown that the movement system is a complex system that is capable of self-organising under constraint. Thus, instead of a tentative decomposition, the role for coaches is to identify the relevant constraints on movement system behaviour, and then manipulate them to enhance skilled performance. Therefore, the criteria for representative task design need to be fulfilled (Araújo et al., 2007; Pinder et al., 2011).

The representative sport task as a 'modified environment' implies a specific adaptation of the athlete, since both contexts (the representative task and the performance context) may have different affordances (i.e., action possibilities; Araújo et al., 2007). Importantly, instead of the commonly used term 'specificity', which implies an a priori definition of what the general is in order to define the specific, and can be applied in any science, 'representative design' is a technical term defined in behavioural terms (Araújo et al., 2007, for a discussion about the vagueness of concepts like specific, natural or typical behaviour). This implies a theoretical change, from understanding an environment that interacts with a performer (i.e., two separate systems that interact) to a more holistic view, which understands performer and environment as a single coherent system. The affordance-based design proposed by Araújo and Davids (2015) seeks to propose principles to demonstrate the correspondence between behaviour in a training setting and behaviour in the match. The interrelated criteria to test behavioural correspondence between contexts are as follows:

1   Selection of functional (i.e., relevant) affordances. Even though affordances can be empirically tested (see Fajen et al., 2009), their selection should be theoretically driven, even if the researcher is not adopting an ecological psychology standpoint. Functionality of affordances is also related to the actions they invite from performers,

as well as the performance success they support. The next two criteria test the adequacy of this selection.

2   Action fidelity. For Stoffregen et al. (2003) the key aspects of this concept are as follows: (i) perception is defined with respect to behaviour, and (ii), action fidelity does not mandate a concentration on 'stimulus fidelity', since the environment is defined in behavioural terms (i.e., affordances). Therefore, action fidelity concerns the degree to which actions performed in the experimental setting are related to the actions performed during competition. It can be measured in terms of task-related measures, such as variance in performance across trials, trials to criterion or spatiotemporal patterns of interaction with others, objects, surfaces, gaps, terrain, etc. (Araújo et al., 2007; Travassos et al., 2012).

3   Performance achievement. Achievement is the degree of success obtained when performing a task for a specific goal. It can be seen as a concept with similitudes with that of ecological rationality. For Gigerenzer, Todd and ABC research group (1999), behaviour is successful, if it is adapted to the structure of the information in the environment in which it is realised. That is, the ecology is the reference point for the observation of behaviour. This view is contrasted with traditional normative references, which define a priori what a classical movement technique is or the 'best' solution according to a social or 'expert' definition, even when it is not effective. Achievement can be assessed with output task measurements (ball entering the basket or distance of the drive/closeness to the green in golf).

Recently, Travassos and colleagues (2012) have tested the idea of behavioural correspondence among contexts by including affordances that are theory-relevant, spatiotemporal patterns of interaction to measure action fidelity and the criteria to define success (performance achievement). Travassos and colleagues (2012) required players of the team sport of futsal (small-sided indoor football) to perform a passing task in which the uncertainty of the passing direction for the player in possession of the ball was increased under four distinct conditions and compared with passing data observed during a competitive match. Higher levels of regularity were observed in predetermined passes (distance and direction of pass verified) compared to passes made under practice conditions, which included more uncertainty for performers (i.e., distance, angle and direction of pass varied). Importantly, passing speed regularity and accuracy were more similar

20

among practice tasks with higher levels of uncertainty and during competitive performance. The data convincingly demonstrated that only the design of the more uncertain passing tasks *represented* the speed, accuracy and success found in passing circumstances performed during a competitive match. These data show how the informational constraints of practice tasks can be designed to correspond to the informational constraints of a competitive performance environment in team sports.

CONCLUSION

Team sports games can be considered as complex dynamical systems composed of many interacting parts. Games are characterised by direct interaction between athletes and their opponents (e.g., inter-team interactions in a basketball match), or by collaborative interactions between athletes competing with another group of athletes (e.g., a volleyball match). Therefore, collaborative players interact with opposition players with the aim to score more than others, and express attacking and defensive behaviours. The environment is not just a passive scene in the background of the acting players, but an active part of the system that uniquely and specifically characterises team sports behaviour. From the point of view of the player (and the team), the task is to exploit physical and informational constraints to stabilise the intended behaviour. Constraints have the effect of reducing the number of configurations available to a team sports game at any instance. In competitive matches, coordination patterns (individual or collective) emerge under constraints as less functional states of organisation are dissipated. Developing a sound theoretical understanding of the major constraints on performers in sport (i.e., the Constraints-Led Approach) could provide a strong basis for performance analysis and coaching at introductory as well as advanced levels of training and practice. Moreover the notion of representative design (i.e., a rigorous conceptualisation of specificity) indicates how behaviour in one context (training) may correspond to behaviour in another context (competition). The suggestion is that modelling the 'behavioural correspondence between contexts' (e.g., from training to competition and vice-versa; see Araújo & Davids, 2015) ensures that such generalisations can be achieved, based on adherence to the intertwined criteria of selection of affordances, action fidelity and performance achievement.

REFERENCES

Araújo, D., & Davids, K. (2011). Talent development: From possessing gifts, to functional environmental interactions. *Talent Development & Excellence Interactions, 3*(1), 23–25.

Araújo, D., & Davids, K. (2015). Towards a theoretically driven model of correspondence between behaviours in one context to another: Implications for studying sport performance. *International Journal of Sport Psychology, 46*, 268–280.

Araújo, D., Davids, K., & Hristovski, R. (2006). The ecological dynamics of decision making in sport. *Psychology of Sport and Exercise, 7*, 653–676.

Araújo, D., Davids, K., & Passos, P. (2007). Ecological validity, representative design and correspondence between experimental task constraints and behavioural settings. *Ecological Psychology, 19*, 69–78.

Araújo, D., Davids, K., & Passos, P. (2013). The intending-perceiving-acting cycle in sports performance. In T. McGarry, P. O'Donoghue, & J. Sampaio (Eds.), *Routledge handbook of sports performance analysis* (pp. 32–41). London: Routledge Taylor & Francis Group.

Araújo, D., Passos, P., Esteves, P., Duarte, R., Lopes, J., Hristovski, R., & Davids, K. (2015). The micro-macro link in understanding sport tactical behaviours: Integrating information and action at different levels of system analysis in sport. *Science & Motricité, 89*, 53–63.

Araújo, D., Silva, P., & Davids, K. (2015). Capturing group tactical behaviors in expert team players. In J. Baker & D. Farrow (Eds.), *Routledge Handbook of Sport Expertise* (pp. 209–220). New York, NY: Routledge.

Bartlett, R., Gratton, C., & Rolf, C. (2006). *Encyclopedia of International Sport Studies*. London: Routledge.

Bernstein, N. (1967) The coordination and regulation of movement. London: Pergamon Press.

Broadbent, D., Causer, J., Williams, M. & Ford, P. (2015). Perceptual-cognitive skill training and its transfer to expert performance in the field: Future research directions. *European Journal of Sport Science, 15*(4), 322–331. DOI: 10.1080/17461391.2014.957727

Carroll, T. J., Barry, B., Riek, S., & Carson, R. G. (2001). Resistance training enhances stability of sensorimotor coordination. *Proceedings of Royal Society of London B, 268*, 221–227.

Carson, R. G., & Kelso, J. A. S. (2004). Governing coordination: Behavioural principles and neural correlates. *Experimental Brain Research, 154*, 267–274.

Chow, J. Y., Davids, K., Hristovski, R., Araújo, D., & Passos, P. (2011). Nonlinear pedagogy: Learning design for self-organizing neurobiological systems. *New Ideas in Psychology, 29*, 189–200.

Davids, K., & Araújo, D. (2005). A abordagem baseada nos constrangimentos para o treino desportivo. In D. Araújo (Ed.), *O Contexto da decisão: A acção táctica no desporto* (pp. 35–60). Lisbon, Portugal: Edições Visão e Contextos.

Davids, K., Araújo, D., Hristovski, R., Passos, P., & Chow, J. Y. (2012). Ecological dynamics and motor learning design in sport. In N. Hodges & M. Williams (Eds.), *Skill Acquisition in Sport: Research, Theory and Practice* (2nd ed., pp. 112–130). Abingdon, UK: Routledge.

22

Davids, K., Araújo, D., & Shuttleworth, R. (2005). Applications of dynamical systems theory to football. In T. Reilly, J. Cabri, & D. Araújo (Eds.), *Science and football V* (pp. 547–560). London: Routledge, Taylor & Francis.

Davids, K., Button, C., Araújo, D., Renshaw, I., & Hristovski, R. (2006). Movement models from sports provide representative task constraints for studying adaptive behaviour in human motor systems. *Adaptive Behavior, 14,* 73–95.

Davids, K., Button, C., & Bennett, S. (2008). *Dynamics of Skill Acquisition: A Constraints-led Approach.* Champaign, IL: Human Kinetics.

Davids, K., Hristovski, R., Araújo, D., Balague, N., Button, C., & Passos, P. (Eds.). (2014). *Complex systems in sport.* London: Routledge.

Duarte, R., Araújo, D., Correia, V., & Davids, K. (2012). Sport teams as superorganisms: Implications of sociobiological models of behaviour for research and practice in team sports performance analysis. *Sports Medicine, 42*(8), 633–642.

Eccles, D. W. (2010). The coordination of labour in sports teams. *International Review of Sport and Exercise Psychology, 3,* 154–170.

Eccles, D. W., Ward, P., & Woodman, T. (2009). The role of competition-specific preparation in expert sport performance. *Psychology of Sport and Exercise, 10,* 96–107

Fajen, B., Riley, M., & Turvey, M. (2009). Information, affordances and the control of action in sport. *International Journal of Sport Psychology, 40,* 79–107.

Gibson, J. J. (1979). *The ecological approach to visual perception.* Boston, MA: Houghton Mifflin.

Gigerenzer, G., Todd, P. M., & The-ABC-Research-Group (1999). *Simple heuristics that make us smart.* Oxford: Oxford University Press.

Gréhaigne, J. F., Godbout, P., & Zerai, Z. (2011). How the "rapport de forces" evolves in a soccer match: The dynamics of collective decisions in a complex system. *Revista de Psicología del Deporte, 20*(2), 747–765.

Handford, C. (2002). Strategy and practice for acquiring timing in discrete, self-paced interceptive actions. In K. Davids, G. J. P. Savelsbergh, S. J. Bennett, & J. van Der Kamp (Eds.), *Interceptive Actions in Sport* (pp. 288–300). London: Routledge, Taylor & Francis.

Handford, C. (2006). Serving up variability and stability. In K. Davids, S. Bennett, & K. Newell (Eds.), *Movement System Variability* (pp. 73–83). Champaign: Human Kinetics.

Järvilehto, T. (2009). The theory of the organism-environment system as a basis of experimental work in psychology. *Ecological Psychology, 21*(2), 112–120.

Kelso, J. A. S. (1995). *Dynamic Patterns.* Cambridge, MA MIT Press.

Kiely, J. (2012). Periodization paradigms in the 21st century: Evidence-led or tradition-driven?. *International Journal of Sports Physiology and Performance, 7,* 242–250. Champaign: Human Kinetics.

Kleinert, J., Ohlert, J., Carron, B., Eys, M., Feltz, D., Hardwood, C., . . . Sulprizio, M. (2012). Group dynamics in sport: An overview and recommendations on diagnostic and intervention. *The Sport Psychologist, 26,* 412–434.

Lee, T. D., Chamberlin, C. J., & Hodges, N. J. (2001). Practice. In R. N. Singer, H. A. Hausenblas, & C. M. Janelle (Eds.), *Handbook of Sport Psychology* (2nd ed., pp. 115–143). New York: John Wiley.

Mateus, J. (2005). In pursuit of an ecological and fractal approach to soccer coaching. In T. Reilly, J. Cabri, & D. Araújo (Eds.), *Science and Football V* (pp. 580–593). London: Routledge.

McGarry, T. (2005). Soccer as a dynamical system: Some theoretical considerations. In T. Reilly, J. Cabri & D. Araújo (Eds.), *Science and Football V: The Proceedings of the Fifth World Congress on Science and Football* (pp. 570–579). London: Routledge, Taylor & Francis.

McGarry, T., Anderson, D., Wallace, S., Hughes, M., & Franks, I. (2002). Sport competition as a dynamical self-organizing system. *Journal of Sports Sciences, 20,* 771–781.

Newell, K. M. (1986). Constraints on the development of coordination. In M. Wade & H. T. A. Whiting (Ed.), *Motor Development in Children: Aspects of Coordination and Control* (pp. 341–360). Dordrecht, Netherlands: Martinus Nijhoff.

Pinder, R. A., Davids, K., Renshaw, I., & Araújo, D. (2011). Representative learning design and functionality of research and practice in sport. *Journal of Sport & Exercise Psychology, 33,* 146–155.

Rasmussen, J. (1986). *Information Processing and Human-machine Interaction: An Approach to Cognitive Engineering.* Amsterdam: North-Holland.

Renshaw, I., Araújo, D., Button, C., Chow, J. Y., Davids, K., & Moy, B. (2015). Why the constraints-led approach is not teaching games for understanding: A clarification. *Physical Education and Sport Pedagogy, 10.* doi: 10.1080/17408989.2015.1095870

Salas, E., & Cannon-Bowers, J. (2001). The science of training: A decade of progress. *Annual Review of Psychology, 52,* 471–499.

Schmidt, R. A., & Lee, T. (2011). *Motor control and learning* (5th ed.). Champaign, IL: Human Kinetics.

Schmidt, R. C., O'Brien, B., Sysko*, R. (1999). Self-organization in between-person cooperative tasks and possible applications for sport. *International Journal of Sport Psychology, 30,* 558–579.

Stoffregen, T. A., Bardy, B. G. Smart, L. J., & Pagulayan, R. J. (2003). On the nature and evaluation of fidelity in virtual environments. In L. J. Hettinger & M. W. Haas (Ed.), *Virtual and Adaptive Environments: Applications, Implications, and Human Performance Issues* (pp. 111–128). Mahwah, NJ: Lawrence Erlbaum Associates, Inc.

Travassos, B., Duarte, R., Vilar, V., Davids, K., & Araújo, D. (2012). Practice task design in team sports: Representativeness enhanced by increasing opportunities for action. *Journal of Sports Sciences, 30,* 1447–1454.

Turvey, M. (2009). On the notion and implications of organism-environment system. *Ecological Psychology, 21,* 97–111.

Van der Kamp, J., & Renshaw, I. (2015). Information-movement couplings as a hallmark of sports expertise. In J. Baker & D. Farrow (Ed.), *Routledge Handbook of Sports Expertise* (pp. 50–63). London: Routledge.

Vicente, K. J. (1999). *Cognitive Work Analysis: Toward Safe, Productive, and healthy Computer-based Work.* Mahwah, NJ: Lawrence Erlbaum Associates, Inc.

Vicente, K. J., & Wang, J. H. (1998). An ecological theory of expertise effects in memory recall. *Psychological Review, 105,* 33–57.

24

CHAPTER 2

COACHING PROCESSES IN TEAM SPORTS – KEY DIFFERENCES TO COACHING IN OTHER SPORTS

Leading author: Pedro Passos

INTRODUCTION: THE NEED TO IDENTIFY AND CREATE RELEVANT INFORMATION THAT HELPS PLAYERS TO IMPROVE SPORTS PERFORMANCE

The amount and quality of the data that is captured by performance analysis systems provide significant information which may support coaches' decisions. A main issue is related with the kind of information that is useful for coaches – in other words, What kind of data really provides the coaches with information about the individual and collective performance of his/her players.

The main feature that distinguishes team sports from other sports is the interpersonal coordination. The need to relate with others within field boundaries, constrained by rules and influenced by the distance to the teammates and opponents, creates highly relevant information that sustains each player's performance. Therefore, one main issue is the presence of the 'others', which is a variable that is continuously changing because of the player's own presence. Like every other social interaction, interpersonal interactions in team sports are characterised by non-linearity, which means that it is not possible to predict in advance (and with high accuracy) what the other will do in a near future (Strogatz, 2004). However, players have the ability to anticipate, which means that, despite the non-linearity that characterised social interactions, there is information that players explore actively that helps them to be attuned – that allows them to anticipate some behaviour and in a certain way predict what the others will do. This information is paramount for coaches' decisions. For instance, with this knowledge coaches can design appropriate learning environments to enhance players' performance.

Performance analysis and relevant information

One way to assess what the relevant information is for a player's performance is to use performance analysis methods. Thus, the first question is: Given the huge amount of information that is created and becomes available in a performance context, what is the most relevant to consider in order for players to succeed? How can we measure this information, and what variables can be considered? After answering this first set of questions the second question is: How can coaches create learning environments which make this relevant information emerge?

To answer the first set of questions previous research on interpersonal coordination in team sports suggest kinematic variables as good predictors to help players to act. However, this is not the main issue to be discussed in this chapter. A set of variables usually used to capture interpersonal coordination in team sports is presented on chapter 5.

This chapter's focus is on the information concerning the tools that allow coaches to identify the most relevant information that enhance players' individual and team performance. This information may help to create learning environments that lead players to success. Learning environments must be representative[1] with respect to the environments that players face in competitive situations. This means that coaches and the technical staff must be capable of analysing and identifying key features, which allow them to 'replicate' the general components of competitive situations in practice settings. That is why performance analysis occupies a key role in the cyclical process of coaching and mastering team players' performances (Figure 2.1).

Some of the relevant information that feeds this coaching cycle is provided by performance analysis. Observation methods that capture team and individual behaviours provide databases for quantitative (e.g., notational, statistics, kinematic) and qualitative analysis of performance (e.g., match reconstruction, video recorded).

Synthesising, the coaching processes in team games are mainly concerned with three cyclical phases: (i) observing, analysing and evaluating performance; (ii) planning practice; (iii) and conducting practice. These coaching phases include a wide variety of coaching skills, which will be described in the next section as the components of the Coach's Instructional Model (CIM) (Figure 2.2).

26

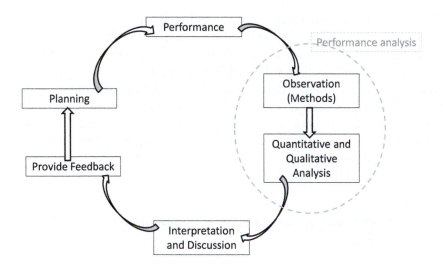

Figure 2.1 The role of performance analysis in the cyclical processes of coaching (adapted from Carling, Williams & Reilly, 2005).

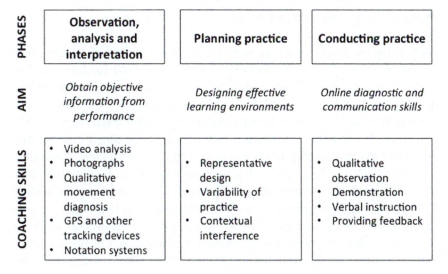

Figure 2.2 Coach's Instructional Model (adapted with the support of Maslovat & Franks, 2008; Williams & Hodges, 2005).

Nested within the three phases aforementioned, there are several skills influencing the coaching process and its effectiveness. It is very important to master each of these skills, and the coach and technical staff need to integrate them to enhance the performance of their players and teams. Next is described in more detail some of the coaching skills in order to clarify the coach's utility, main procedures and key points. The coaching skills from the Coaching Instructional Model are powerful tools to capture the most relevant information, which supports the design of effective learning environments, as well as to develop coach's communication skills, a paramount issue to succeed.

Tools to identify and create the relevant information and to act upon

This section describes methods and tools that help coaches to identify, create and manipulate critical information in practice and competition. Observational tools and qualitative and quantitative analysis methods must be included in the cyclical coaching process to create systematic procedures on how coaches and the coaching staff observe, evaluate and obtain feedback to plan the preparation phase.

Video analysis and GPS systems

Technological devices such as high-definition cameras and Global Positioning Systems (GPS) are nowadays commonly used for team performance analysis. In the last decade we can observe an increase in the development and use of GPS devices in team sports. For instance, several professional teams of the rugby union, the rugby league and Australian football use GPS to capture players positioning along competitive matches (see www.catapultsports.com; http://statsports.ie/). Currently GPS (Black & Gabbett, 2014; Hulin et al., 2014) and accelerometers (Chandler et al., 2014) are being used to calculate the player's physical load in training and competition. From these data it is possible to calculate a ratio of training/match load, which provides powerful (critical) information for periodisation, allowing for adjustments in the intensity and/or volume of the practice sessions and also for creating training drills grounded in objective (measurable) information. Moreover, these combined GPS+accelerometer+gyroscope systems also provide online

28

data (i.e., during practice), with relevant information for coaches' tactical decisions and instant feedback for players. Using the data of the physical load, it is possible to calculate the odds of a player getting injured, which is important for planning the season.

The video record of a team's previous matches is currently used for retrospective analysis. Usually the video record is coupled to time-motion analysis software, which provides the technical staff with accurate information regarding their team and the opponents (for a few examples see http://www.inmotio.eu/en-GB/22/analysis-software.html; http://www.sportvu.com/football_coaching.asp; http://www.prozonesports.com/product/team-profile/). Through the automatic capture of the coordinates (x, y and z) of each player during a competitive situation, it becomes possible to calculate the variables of each player's position at any given time: the interpersonal distances among players; the interpersonal angles among players; and players' relative velocities.[2] Therefore, video and time-motion analysis can work as feedback systems and can be used for two purposes: i) to provide technical and tactical information for the players; and ii) to provide information that will motivate or inspire the players' enthusiasm for an upcoming match.

This tool has to address two major issues that performance analysts have to deal with: (i) analysis of individual skills, mainly focused on the frequency of the technical skills that were performed during a match (e.g., notational analysis); and (ii) a focus on how each player interacts with the others in the area over time and how this task constraint influences individual performance – that is, a dynamical analysis that aims to identify patterns of interaction with the others. This second issue is the major concern when using tools like video analysis or GPS, especially because coordinative variables, which describe the collective behaviour of a set of players, remain under research and testing (Bourbousson et al., 2010; Frencken et al., 2011; Grehaigne et al., 1997; Passos, et al., 2009; Passos, et al., 2011; Travassos et al., 2011; Vilar et al., 2012).

The trends of research in collective behaviours in team games over the last decade points out that the analysis of collective behaviours in team sports will be a paramount research issue for the next decade. As stated on the preceding section, previous research on team sports focused on the interaction between attackers and defenders and provided some relevant information regarding opponent players' interpersonal distances and relative velocities, which is crucial for success (Passos et al., 2008; Passos et al., 2011).

With the advances in video technology and software systems, analysts and coaches have available some highly accurate technology (but also highly expensive) that uses several high-definition cameras that capture the displacements of each player and the ball during an entire match (e.g., Prozone, SportVU). Nevertheless, there is also freeware, which is very user friendly and can be downloaded from the Web. For example, Kinovea (available at www.kinovea.org) can be used to digitise players' positions in sub-phases of a match (e.g., 3v3) based on the images recorded by a single video camera. With the data set provided by these systems, performance analysts and technical staff can easily describe, identify and act upon critical information, from their own players, the opponents and most important from the interaction among them. The basis to create learning environments that support players to succeed is created; we just need to work on it.

Coaches' communication skills

We would like to start this section with a question: Are communication skills a tool that coaches use to transmit knowledge (through specific instructions regarding how the players must perform) or to provide conditions that allow players to acquire knowledge? This is not an easy question to address, but we will provide some clues aiming to get an answer.

The first clue is grounded in a feature of playing team sports: every player must learn to play with others, teammates and opponents. As stated in the Introduction section of this chapter, social interactions are non-linear, meaning there is no direct relationship between the initial conditions and the outcome. Notwithstanding, players develop the ability to anticipate what the others will do, which helps to prevent disadvantaged situations. Learning to anticipate what the others will do (especially the opponents) within a context characterised by non-linear behaviours demands that each player can 'read' what is occurring in the performance environment. Thus, the decisions and actions that characterise anticipative behaviours are grounded in information that is locally created (Fajen et al., 2009; Schmidt et al., 1998).

The second clue is related to adaptive behaviours. Due to the non-linearity that characterises social interactions, players need to continuously adapt to the behaviours of their colleagues and opponents. These adaptive

30

behaviours are mainly supported by the information that is created locally, when two players face each other, and less by the information that was previously defined, due to video analysis or coaches instructions (Passos et al., 2012). So, to succeed players need to learn how to attune to the most relevant information, which is locally created due to player interactions. Sustained on the two clues presented, it has been suggested that the non-linearity and adaptive behaviours that characterise team sports reinforce the suggestion that coaches' communication should be mainly driven to create circumstances that constrain the learning environments that drive players to search for the best solution, and not to provide those solutions.

Nevertheless, coaches' technical and tactical instructions should not be neglected, because they create boundaries that channel players' performance. A balance in the contents and focus of coaches' communication is required for the successful performance in team games. Therefore, our second question is: What should the coaches' communication be focused on? In other words, when does the coach need to direct his/her communication to technical skills and when to tactical skills? What are the implications of each one of these directions? What will be the relationship with performance analysis?

The main message here is that both focuses are important. What coaches need to be aware of is what the consequences of focusing on technical skills or focusing on tactical skills are. The improvement of technical skills will lead the players to explore the environment differently. A rugby player who improves his/her passing ability and can place the ball with a support player at 25 m distance, for sure he/she can now explore affordances (i.e., possibilities of action) that he/she wasn't able to identify or use before, which then leads to this outstanding passing skill. This example highlights how the improvement of technical skills influences changes in players' tactical skills, conditioning the way in which players explore the context when interacting with each other. On the other side, tactical instructions are focused on players' interactions, highlighting key aspects such as players' running line trajectories, interpersonal distances and angles, relative velocities, ball flight paths, etc., which require technical skills in order to be successful. The improvement of technical skills results in changes on player's tactical abilities. This player evolution directly influences the planning and periodisation of season and also the variables selected to be used in performance analysis. For instance, it would be noteworthy to analyse the interactive behaviour among teammates before and after their technical skill improvement: Did the players alter their interpersonal distance creating more difficulties for defenders? If so how fast are they in changing their relative positions? This is just an example of the challenges for performance analysts in response to the improvements in player's technical and tactical abilities. Consequently, the data provided by performance analysis have a direct influence on the cyclical processes of coaches' planning and communication. Thus, we would like to reinforce the reciprocal causality that exists between technical and tactical skills, a crucial issue that coaches should be aware when communicating with the players.

Feedback

Coaches need to identify, act upon and create relevant information that help players to improve (O'Donoghue & Mayes, 2013). Providing feedback is an essential part of the coaching process. The feedback is crucial for learning and has to provide additional and significant information for the player. Due to the influence of environmental constraints (e.g., coaches position on the pitch), individual constraints (e.g., emotional and cognitive states, limited capacity of the human memory and observation skewed by expectations), coaches frequently demonstrate a limited accuracy in their feedback regarding players' performances. As a consequence, coaches miss recalling close to half of the critical events that happen in a game (Laird & Waters, 2008; Maslovat & Franks, 2008).

Augmented feedback is additional information provided for players to improve. The accuracy of augmented feedback could be enhanced with the advances in technology used in performance analysis, creating quantitative analysis grounded in statistics, but also a qualitative interactive analysis supported by video analysis and virtual reality environments, where players can test possible solutions with immediate feedback regarding their performance.

In order to provide precise and informative feedback, professional teams already use the most advanced technological supports (such as Super HD cameras). However, for amateur teams with limited budgets, these tools are not always accessible. The improvements and easy-to-use profile of the most technological devices under development make us think that in the next decades the way that coaches provide additional

32

information to the players will be strongly supported by online data, making use of tablets and apps. These improvements in technological devices allow easier and faster access to relevant information regarding team and individual performances. As a consequence, coaches will have access to the most up-to-date information, which can be used during important periods of the game. This information, which is available in apps, may help to ensure a *sandwich* approach during a time out or other critical moments of the game. Basically a *sandwich* approach divides a communication on three layers: (i) a positive statement to get players' attentions; (ii) objective information, which aids the players in improving performance – it is in this middle layer that the use of apps, tablets and PCs might be a very useful tool for coaches to transmit in a fast and objective way the most relevant information; and finally (iii) the final layer, again a positive statement with the aim of placing the players enthusiasm at an optimal, functional level (Figure 2.3).

Additionally the evolution of technological devices and Internet services provide for the storage of considerable amounts of information, which can be used for remote analysis.

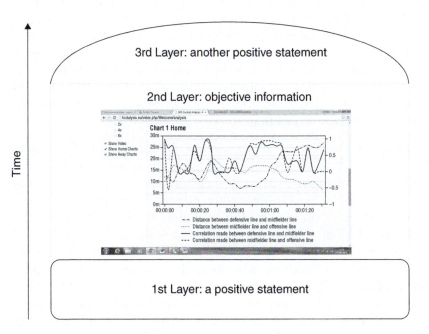

Figure 2.3 An example of the *sandwich* approach using apps.

Planning and designing learning environments

The way that coaches plan and create learning environments, where players acquire and develop the ability to solve problems (i.e., achieve goals) and display different task solutions (rather than specifying a single solution), is a crucial issue regarding players' adaptive behaviour learning.

The Constraints-Based Approach is one of the theoretical supports to design and create learning environments that encourage players to explore what different task solutions for the same outcome (e.g., to dribble past a defender, shoot a goal) can be (Araújo et al., 2002; Davids et al., 1994; Davids et al., 2008; Passos et al., 2008; Passos et al., 2010). The main guideline of this approach for coaching is that planning is supported by the manipulation of three types of constraints, which bind the perceptive motor workspace, channelling players' performances : (i) *individual* constraints (e.g., technical and tactical skills); (ii) *task* constraints (e.g., interpersonal distances between opponents, attacker–defender relative velocities; angles between the ball carrier and the closest defenders); and (iii) *environmental* constraints (e.g., weather, the presence of significant others). These constraints display a mutual and reciprocal interaction (for further information, see Newell, 1986). Thus, decreasing attacker–defender interpersonal distances (which consequently decrease the time for decisions and actions) will constrain, for instance, the ball carrier's decisions and actions concerning the technical skill to be used: to pass to the support player; to shoot towards the goal; or to dribble past the defender. The solution to be adopted is based on information that is created due to players' interaction.

Regarding the planning of training sessions, the adoption of a Constraints-Based Approach raises the following question: When should the task constraints be changed? While this question remains open in the literature, our suggestion is as follows: when players' behaviour becomes 'too' stable – that is, when players do not explore different solutions. This might be a further challenge to performance analysis: describe when players' interactive behaviours became stable. If we can describe the stability of players' interactive behaviours then we set the conditions to assess under which task constraints stability becomes 'variable'. Thus, a first step is to find out or create coordinative variables that accurately describe players' interactive behaviours (chapter 5 presents some suggestions about dealing with this issue).

34

In sum a contribution of coaching processes to performance analysis should be focused on how players solve game problems. This requires identifying typical situations that occur during a game and characterising how players usually deal with those sorts of situations (e.g., characterise what the defenders do when their team lose ball possession; characterise what the attackers do when their team regains ball possession). This does not mean that performance analysis should avoid or stop recording the player's actions; it simply means that in team sports there are other features that are crucial to characterise a team behaviour that goes beyond discrete events registered during notational analysis.

CONCLUSIONS AND SUGGESTIONS

Coaches cannot identify and remember more than a half of the crucial events that occur during a game. The advances in technology can help to fill this gap. Further work needs to be done to develop user-friendly software to collect and analyse the collective variables proposed and tested over the last decade. These variables should be linked to players' behaviours constrained by coaches' instructions.

Moreover, current literature emphasises the complementarity between notational analysis and dynamical analysis. When the former became more sophisticated, better known and less time consuming due to enhancing technology and software development, this complementarity will provide additional insights for coaching, particularly in planning and design of training sessions.

Another improvement might be the use of online data, which is collected and becomes available for coaches to use during a game. How will this data influence coaches' decisions? The quick and easy access to large amounts of information will influence coaches' communications skills and feedback. Further work should bring the answer to this question.

ACKNOWLEDGEMENT

I would like to thank Ricardo Duarte, my colleague at Faculdade de Motricidade Humana, Universidade de Lisboa, Portugal, for the help in reviewing this chapter.

REFERENCES

Araújo, D., Davids, K., Sainhas, J., & Fernandes, O. (2002). *Emergent decision-making in sport: A constraints-led approach*. Paper presented at the International congress 'movement, attention & perception' Poitiers, France; Université de Poitiers.

Black, G. M., & Gabbett, T. J. (2014). Repeated high-intensity effort activity in elite and semi-elite rugby league match-play. *International Journal of Sports Physiology, 10*(6), 711–717.

Bourbousson, J., Seve, C., & McGarry, T. (2010). Space-time coordination dynamics in basketball: Part 2. The interaction between the two teams. *Journal of Sports Science, 28*(3), 349–358.

Carling, C., Williams, A.M., and Reilly, T. (2005). *The Handbook of Soccer Match Analysis*. London, UK: Routledge.

Chandler, P. T., Pinder, S. J., Curran, J. D., & Gabbett, T. J. (2014). Physical demands of training and competition in collegiate netball players. *Journal of Strength & Conditioning Research, 28*(10), 2732–2737.

Davids, K., Button, C., & Bennett, S. (2008). *Dynamics of Skill Acquisition. A Constraints-Led Approach*. Champaign: Human Kinetics.

Davids, K., Handforf, C., & Williams, A. M. (1994). The natural physical alternative to cognitive theories of motor behaviour: An invitation for interdisciplinary research in sports science? *Journal of Sport Sciences, 12*(6), 495–528.

Fajen, B. R., Riley, M. A., & Turvey, M. T. (2009). Information, affordances, and the control of action in sport. *International Journal of Sport Psychology, 40*(1), 79–107.

Frencken, W., Lemmink, K., Delleman, N., & Visscher, C. (2011). Oscillations of centroid position and surface area of soccer teams in small-sided games. *European Journal of Sport Science, 11*, 215–223.

Grehaigne, J. F., Bouthier, D., & David, B. (1997). Dynamic-system analysis of opponent relationships in collective actions in soccer. *Journal of Sports Sciences, 15*(2), 137–149.

Hulin, B. T., Gabbett, T. J., Kearney, S., & Corvo, A. (2014). Physical demands of match-play in successful and less-successful elite rugby league teams. *International Journal of Sports Physiology and Performance, 10*(6), 703–710.

Laird, P., & Waters, L. (2008). Eyewitness recollection of sport coaches. *International Journal of Performance Analysis in Sport, 8*(1), 76–84.

Maslovat, D., & Franks, I. M. (2008). The need for feedback. In M. Hughes & I. M. Franks (Eds.), *The Essentials of Performance Analysis: An Introduction* (pp. 1–7). London: Taylor and Francis.

Newell, K. M. (1986). Constraints on the development of coordination. In M. W. H. T. A.Whiting (Ed.), *Motor Development in Children: Aspects of Coordination and Control* (pp. 341–360). Dordrecht, Netherlands: Martinus Nijhoff.

O'Donoghue, P., & Mayes, A. (2013). Performance analysis, feedback and communication in coaching. In T. McGarry, P. O'Donoghue, & J. Sampaio (Eds.), *Routledge Handbook of Sports Performance Analysis* (pp. 165–175). London: Routledge.

Passos, P., Araújo, D., Davids, K., Gouveia, L., Milho, J., & Serpa, S. (2008). Information-governing dynamics of attacker-defender interactions in youth rugby union. *Journal of Sports Sciences, 26*(13), 1421–1429.

Passos, P., Araújo, D., Davids, K., Gouveia, L., Serpa, S., Milho, J., & Fonseca, S. (2009). Interpersonal pattern dynamics and adaptive behavior in multiagent neurobiological systems: Conceptual model and data. *Journal of Motor Behavior, 41*(5), 445–459.

Passos, P., Araújo, D., Davids, K., & Shuttleworth, R. (2008). Manipulating constraints to train decision making in rugby union. *International Journal of Sports Science & Coaching, 3*(1), 125–140.

Passos, P., Araújo, D., Davids, K., & Shuttleworth, R. (2010). Manipulating tasks constraints to improve tactical knowledge and collective decision making in rugby union. In K. Davids, G. Salvesbergh, & I. Renshaw (Eds.), *Motor Learning in Practice: A Constraints-Led Approach* (pp. 120–130). Oxford: Routledge.

Passos, P., Cordovil, R., Fernandes, O., & Barreiros, J. (2012). Perceiving affordances in rugby union. *Journal of Sports Science, 30*(11), 1175–1182.

Passos, P., Milho, J., Fonseca, S., Borges, J., Araújo, D., & Davids, K. (2011). Interpersonal distance regulates functional grouping tendencies of agents in team sports. *Journal of Motor Behavior, 43*(2), 155–163.

Schmidt, R. C., Bienvenu, M., Fitzpatrick, P. A., & Amazeen, P. G. (1998). A comparison of intra- and interpersonal interlimb coordination: Coordination breakdowns and coupling strength. *The Journal of Experimental Psychology: Human Perception and Performance, 24*(3), 884–900.

Strogatz, S. (2004). *Sync: The Emerging Science of Spontaneous Order.* London: Penguin Press Science.

Travassos, B., Araújo, D., Vilar, L., & McGarry, T. (2011). Interpersonal coordination and ball dynamics in futsal (indoor football). *Human Movement Science, 30*(6), 1245–1259.

Vilar, L., Araújo, D., Davids, K., Travassos, B., Duarte, R., & Parreira, J. (2012). Interpersonal coordination tendencies supporting the creation/prevention of goal scoring opportunities in futsal. *European Journal of Sport Science, 14*(1), 28–35.

Williams, A. M., & Hodges, N. J. (2005). Practice, instruction and skill acquisition in soccer: Challenging tradition. *Journal of Sports Science, 23*(6), 637–650.

CHAPTER 3

VARIABLES CHARACTERISING PERFORMANCE AND PERFORMANCE INDICATORS IN TEAM SPORTS

Leading author: Duarte Araújo

INTRODUCTION

Sports performance is influenced by several sources of constraint (Davids et al., 2008). Performers prepare themselves to be in a state of performance readiness at a specific future date. In order to assess such a state of readiness and to describe some aspects of sports performance many variables, metrics, indicators,[3] or indices have been developed by sport scientists (Hughes & Bartlett, 2002; Sampaio & Leite, 2013). Applied sport scientists and coaches use these indicators, often complemented with images and video footage, to make decisions about diagnostics and interventions. More specifically, the main applications for performance indicators have been on educational use, for coaches and players, movement analysis, modelling and creation of databases for statistical compilation (Alamar, 2013; Hughes & Franks, 2008).

Recently Sampaio and Leite (2013) wrote an in-depth discussion on the issues related to normalisation and validity of performance indicators in team sports. In the present chapter we take a complementary approach by describing empirical findings and theoretically discuss the properties of performance that these indicators are capturing. For example, Hughes and Bartlett (2002) proposed that these indices could be categorised according to the type of sport and then sub-categorised into general match indicators, tactical indicators, technical indicators, and biomechanical indicators. Other conceptions exist according to how performance is conceived (e.g., Carling et al., 2009; Morrow et al., 2000; Sanders, 1998; Schmidt & Lee, 2014). In the next section we will discuss how performance has been conceived in sports sciences.

38

SPORTS PERFORMANCE AND PERFORMANCE ANALYSIS

Performance is the behavioural process of accomplishing a task. In sport, there have been two predominant approaches to understand performance: (i) the 'human performance model' (Weldford, 1968) tries to answer to the question: 'How is performance realised by a certain population?'; (ii) the differential approach, which is mainly related to contrasting successful and unsuccessful performances (e.g., winners vs. losers, experts vs. non-experts, males vs. females, etc.), tries to capture the differences in performances between groups of players. Both of these approaches developed several metrics to capture performance.

The systematic search for performance indicators grew up in the last decade in the field of sports sciences, and has been associated with the research work developed in experimental sciences like biomechanics, physiology and motor learning, and the differential approach defended by notational analysis and psychology (Glazier, 2010; Hughes & Bartlett, 2002). However, more recently the technological progress has allowed for an automatic and computerised register of performance that initially was made manually and was very time consuming. The result of the increase in computing power and the availability of massive amounts of data to both teams and the public is that more relevant information is available. Nowadays, advanced statistics and analytic predictive models, data management, data visualisation and information systems, as well as several other tools, are used to gain a competitive advantage (Alamar, 2013).

The metrics following the differential approach tend to focus on scoring indicators (e.g., goals, winners, errors, the ratios of winners to errors and goals to shots) or on performance indicators (e.g., turnovers, tackles, passes/possession, etc.) (Hughes & Bartlett, 2002). These variables are typically recorded in a discrete sequential fashion to operationalise sports behaviours (Bush et al., 2015). Each action in a number of games is recorded in a 'Who (did)–What–Where–When' sequence, together with any associated outcomes (i.e., winner, error or neutral outcome) (McGarry, 2009). An important criticism of notational analysis research is that it tends to omit the reference to the 'Why' and 'How' of performance, which underlie the structure of recorded behaviours and would define their functional utility (McGarry, 2009; Vilar et al., 2012a). More to the point, the interactions among the many independent parts that compose human movement sub-systems (e.g., metabolic, locomotor, neural), the interactions among the players and the teams, make clear that social systems like team sports need theoretical guidance (Davids et al, 2014). These interactions are mainly non-linear and can be exemplified by a single event like, say, the injury (microscopic level) of a basketball player, which can produce a large-scale impact on his/her performance (e.g., stop playing for the rest of the season), and an even greater influence on team coordination and performance (the micro–macro link; see Araújo et al., 2015).

On the other hand, research following the experimental approach to the human performance model derives from deterministic or hierarchical models of performance (Lees, 2002), isolating effects of specific factors that potentially influence performance. The interactive effect of these factors or its time-evolution (in a match or between matches) tends not to be considered (Bartlett et al., 2012; Dutt-Mazumder et al., 2011; Vilar et al., 2012a). Next, we discuss the differential approach as highlighted by notational analysis, and then we return to the human performance model to finalise with a complementary view of how performance and performance indicators could be conceived.

METRICS FOR ACTIONS IN PERFORMANCE CONTEXTS

Performance analysis has studied team sports performance by seeking to record the type of actions that are performed in a competitive game. This approach has been commonly operationalised by discrete measures of actions and their consequences (e.g., goals, winners, errors, turnovers, tackles, passes/possession, dribbles) (Hughes & Bartlett, 2002). The aim has typically been to catalogue which actions are performed, *who* performs them and *where* those actions took place, defining coordination patterns through the summary of discrete categories of actions recorded in a sequential fashion. These measures, whether considered over time (as in sequential analysis studies) or not, have been categorised to describe successful or unsuccessful performance behaviours in sport.

Researchers have described goals scored in football by relating this outcome measure to each team's 'style of play' – that is, with data from passing sequences in different matches (Hughes & Franks, 2005). Jones et al. (2004) examined teams' 'ball possession' in soccer as a function of

40

the evolving match status (i.e., winning, losing or drawing) (for research on evolving match status, see also, e.g., Lago & Martin, 2007). Results showed that successful teams displayed significantly longer periods of ball possession than unsuccessful teams. However, when match status was not considered, both groups displayed longer periods of possession when *losing* than when *winning*. Other research on match performance has focused on distinct aspects of performers' actions, either at an individual or team level, such as players' movement displacement trajectories during competitive performance (e.g., Carling et al., 2008; O'Donoghue, 2008), patterns of events (e.g., Dawson et al., 2004), occupation of different spatial areas of the field by individuals or teams (e.g., Gréhaigne et al., 1997), and effects of game venue on performance outcomes (e.g., Jones et al., 2004; Lago & Martin, 2007).

In sum, since the introduction of the term performance indicators in sport (Hughes & Bartlett, 2002) there has been a research effort into defining valid performance indicators in team games. Various approaches have been proposed to identify the key performance indicators to characterise the different aspects of team sports performance such as coach opinion, literature review, relationship to outcome success and discrimination of different levels of performance. Performance indicators tend to be compared to norms for the level of opposition faced in the match. However, there are no generalisable variables, nor standard performance indicators, nor even results. The only common points among researches tend to be the analysis methods themselves (e.g., regression analysis, artificial neural networks, principal component analysis) (see O'Donoghue, 2010 for a discussion).

In general, the measurement of sports actions has described performance by recording the patterned frequency of discrete or sequential actions in association with key events. Current technological developments (such as the increased capacity of different match analysis software packages and remote sensing technology) may facilitate data collection and online analysis of performers' actions on a massive scale. Whilst a large number of descriptive studies have created awareness among athletes and coaches of how individual players can influence team patterns, research using these data has paid little attention to how actions emerge from the continuous interactions between performers and the environment – that is, what the circumstances were (i.e., information and constraints) that made a particular action possible.

CAPTURING THE INFORMATION UNDERLYING ACTIONS

Fitts and Posner's (1967) human performance model aimed 'to analyze complex tasks into their simpler components and to establish quantitative estimates of man's abilities in each of the basic functions' (p.1). This model aims to predict performers' capability for performing complex skills and follows the information-processing paradigm (Schmidt & Lee, 2014). Indeed, Weldford (1968) described the human performance model as a means to specify how the information processing activities result in a movement that is 'coordinated to the demands of the environment' (Marteniuk, 1976, p. 5). Contrasting with the differential approach, which is focused in actions and their consequences, the human performance model is mainly focused on the study of human's ability to detect and store information (Fitts & Posner, 1967).

Some of the models of information processing focus on the temporal aspects of information processing, concentrating on the duration of these various processes. This basic chronometric approach, as it is termed (Posner, 1978, after Donders, 1868/1969), makes considerable use of the reaction-time (RT) method, whereby the key measure of the subject's behaviour is the interval between the presentation of a stimulus and the beginning of the response (i.e., RT). The paradigm is built on the premise that many different information processes occur during RT. Therefore, if the experiment is designed properly, so that the durations of most other processes are held constant, one can infer that an increase in RT, caused by some experimental variable, was caused by the lengthening of the duration of a particular process – that is, some activity in one of the information-processing stages (i.e., stimulus identification, response selection, response programming) (Schmidt & Lee, 2014). The application of the RT tasks to common skills (like dribbling in basketball) is possible under the assumption that the processes within the individual are the same in RT laboratory tasks and in sport context tasks.

SPORT EXPERTS USE DIFFERENT INFORMATION THAN NOVICES

Some researchers focus specifically on sports related tasks trying to understand which processes performers may use to organise effective performance. For example, some research has claimed to demonstrate

42

how schemata or action rules (basketball and handball; Fruchart et al., 2010), and information processing and memory interface processes (association football; Zoudji et al., 2010), allowed participants to plan and program actions before performing. Concerning visual perception in sport, experimenters have relied on temporal and/or spatial occlusion paradigms and eye movement registration techniques for analysing the performance of participants differing in skill levels (for a review see, e.g., Williams & Ericsson, 2005). Temporal occlusion methods include filmed action sequences during determined time periods requiring participants to verbally report what they believe would happen next. Moreover, these methods usually involve a discrete action response to choose between alternatives (e.g., a button press). Results from this body of work have suggested that experts outperform novices by having the ability to detect 'cues' at an earlier time point in an action sequence (Müller & Abernethy, 2006). Spatial occlusion methods omit information components during the preparation and execution of an action image displayed on a screen (Williams & Ericsson, 2005), examining how the loss of that particular arrangement of information constrains perception and decision-making efficacy. Eye movement registration techniques assess the specific locations on an image where participants fixate, presumably to gain information from the display (Panchuk & Vickers, 2006). With these techniques, discrete eye movement measures such as search rate, latency of saccade, fixation location, fixation duration, number of fixations and fixation order are assumed to indicate how sources of information are picked up by participants to support judgments about actions. For example, Vaeyens and colleagues (Vaeyens et al., 2007) combined visual gaze and occlusion analysis to investigate the relationships among visual search behaviours, decision-making, skill and experience level. Results led the investigators to assume that the memory of skilled participants supports their greater ability to pick up and interpret the consequences of perceptual information for action when compared to less skilled participants.

Experimental control is suggested to be important to draw conclusions about the effects of different variables on performance. However, these variables have been generally examined in designs that have decoupled perceptual processes from actions on relevant external objects and events (Fajen et al., 2009). Moreover, performance outcome measures are often discrete (e.g., response time, response accuracy, response consistency), describing how actors use 'cues' to conduct specific actions or to report judgments on possible actions. Importantly, most studies have tended to examine *where* and *when* athletes detect 'cues', but there is little systematic research about *how* performers use information throughout the course of action during goal-directed performance.

THE NEED TO LINK INFORMATION AND ACTION WHEN MEASURING PERFORMANCE

The metrics identified in the previous sections can help inform and reduce the risk around a given diagnostic or intervention decision. Alamar (2013) suggested that, when a sport analyst presents a given analysis, he/she should clarify what the circumstances were that made a particular performance indicator possible, how much that indicator is related to success, and, if is it possible, to obtain more and better information. Indeed, to better understand performance in team sports, it is important to comprehend how individuals *use* information sources to guide ongoing goal-directed behaviours during practice and performance (Araújo et al., 2013; Correia et al., 2013). However, in most prevalent methodological approaches in the literature, perception of information sources and observed actions are not considered as being linked.

THE LINK OF INFORMATION WITH NON-SPORT ACTION

Traditional research on perception in sport focuses essentially on the use of information for verbal judgments or micro-movements with a joystick or button pressing. Conversely, when research is action centred and unpaired movement is considered, performance measures are recorded in a discrete fashion, often studied in isolation of sports performance contexts (e.g., number of passes, missing what made a particular pass possible, and distinct from the relevant functional behaviours in those contexts) (Correia et al., 2013). Investigations rarely examine ongoing goal-directed interactions of participants with key performance constraints. For instance, gaze behaviour analysis has some notable weaknesses, particularly the fact that an ocular fixation on a specific location of a visual display is not necessarily related to the use of that environmental property as a source of information to regulate action (Huys et al., 2009; Nougier et al., 1992).

Another issue to consider is related to the generalisation of results (Araújo & Davids, 2015). Although investigators have been increasing

44

the involvement of action in virtual reality simulation studies, they often still do not allow performers to undertake unhampered functional movement behaviours (Dicks et al., 2010). Consequently, different behaviours of participants have been reported when studied under simulation and in situ experimental task constraints (Dicks et al., 2010).

An important consideration is how local interaction rules among players shape global system outcomes. From this perspective it is necessary to identify the relevant variables at a macro (e.g., match) and micro (e.g., 1vs1 sub-phase) levels that express the interactions among players and teams, and influence emergent actions (Araújo et al., 2015). Analysis of stable and unstable patterns of coordination reveal exploratory behaviours of players – that is, actions to detect and create information about what actions are possible, to achieve specific performance goals. Perceiving these action possibilities for oneself, as well as teammates and opponents, is a key feature of skilled performance in team sports (Araújo et al., 2015; Fajen et al., 2009). Furthermore, the performance of players and teams may be considered as being 'conditionally coupled' (Araújo et al., 2015). That is, one discrete measurement of an action at one point in time is dependent on previous observations of that action, signifying that it should not be studied in isolation. To tackle this issue, some research is studying sports performance from a complex system approach (Davids et al., 2014).

THE INFORMATION AND THE CONSTRAINTS THAT CHANNEL SPORTS ACTION

Some key contributions of a complex and dynamical approach to sports were the coupled oscillator paradigm applied by McGarry and colleagues to squash (McGarry & Franks, 1996; McGarry et al., 1999) and then by other researchers to tennis (Lames, 2006; Palut & Zanone, 2005) and to football (Duarte et al., 2012). The properties of coupled oscillators, such as two pendulums moving at the same time, were extended to players. The movement of one in relation to the other indicates their coordination, as it happens in a team. These studies concluded that the players' behaviour exhibit properties of self-organised coupled oscillators (for reviews, see Glazier & Robins, 2013; McGarry, 2013). In general, the collective variables (collective because it quantifies in a single measure the spatial and temporal details of the two movements) used captured the coordination patterns that were expressed between the two entities (players or groups of players). The most used collective variables were cross correlation functions, and continuous and discrete relative phases (Bartlett et al., 2012). However, a different strategy is needed when three or more entities are involved, as is exemplified by the metrics used in cluster phase computations (Duarte et al., 2013) or by complex social networks (Duch et al., 2010; Grund, 2012; Passos et al., 2011).

As Araújo et al. (2013) argued, for a given sports task, a performer and the performance environment need to be treated as a pair of dynamical sub-systems that are coupled and interact mechanically and informationally. Following this ecological dynamics rational (Araújo et al., 2006), manipulation of task constraints (information) and motion analyses methods have been used to collect time series data on the displacement coordinates (x, y) of players and ball. By showing statistical relationships between the information of the performance environment and behavioural outcome measures, researchers have provided evidence on how players support successful performance through the use of that information. Motion analysis methods help to identify players' performances in a *continuum* and transitions in their course of action during competitive performances. For example, Correia and colleagues (Correia et al., 2011) used motion analysis techniques to show that the time for the gap between the ball carrier and the defender to close (time-to-contact) constrained the type of pass (short or long) performed in a rugby union match. Likewise, during competitive performances, other recent studies have shown, for instance, how players perform successful passes (Travassos et al., 2012) or shape opportunities for goal scoring (Vilar et al., 2012b) in the team sport of futsal.

Also using process-tracing methods, Araújo and colleagues (Araújo et al., 2006; Davids et al., 2006) examined 1vs1 sub-phases in basketball and showed that a phase transition in the players' distance to the basket precipitated a dribble. Functional actions were suggested to emerge, as previous stable patterns became unstable, forcing the dyadic system to adopt a different pattern of coordination. In rugby union it has been demonstrated that the collective behaviours of attacker–defender dyads could also be explained by the dynamics of an angle defined by an attacker, his direct defender and the try line (Passos et al., 2009). In that study, data verified that the relative velocity of the ball carrier and a marking defender, nested within a specific value of the interpersonal distance between the performers, indicated the critical threshold beyond which a phase transition in the dyadic system could occur (Passos et al., 2008)

46

(for similar findings in soccer, see Duarte et al., 2010). These studies provided understanding of how players interact with the performance environment to create and use information to support successful performances (Correia et al., 2013).

THE ADAPTATION OF ACTION IS SPECIFIC TO THE CIRCUMSTANCES

The highlighted research designs are aimed to assess how performers adapt their ongoing actions according to their own action capabilities, contextual constraints and performance goals (Araújo et al., 2013). Action adaptations allow performers to explore and perceive what actions are possible in their unfolding interactions with key aspects of the performance environment (including key events, significant others and spatial locations of the playing area). It is important to note that the perception of these action possibilities (also known as affordances, Gibson, 1979) is also dynamic (for examples, see Fajen et al., 2011; Weast et al., 2011).

Performer–environment interactions are analysed with process-tracing methods to examine the emergent dynamics of performance behaviours, their transitions and their relation with performance efficacy (Duarte et al. 2010; Esteves et al., 2011; Passos et al., 2008; Passos et al., 2009). Nevertheless, the studies following identification of relevant informational constraints on sports performance have typically not attempted to actually manipulate these biophysical (spatiotemporal) informational variables. This limitation should be overcome by future research, manipulating, for example, potential informational variables through the use of immersive and interactive virtual reality simulations of performance environments (e.g., Correia et al., 2012). The use of this type of interactive technology allows for the precise control of the informational layout of the simulated performance environment, ensuring reproducibility/ manipulation of informational variables between trials (see, e.g., Correia et al., 2014).

CONCLUSION

Overall, to describe successful performance it seems most important to focus on the link between information and action and to avoid simply a focus on information sources or on discrete actions. An important challenge is to investigate the dynamics of ongoing goal-directed (inter) actions of performers in sports, considering their context-dependency and concurrently assessing what information is being used to support functional behaviours. An interesting development for future research would be to not only investigate how collective variables that describe the state of the performer–environment system in a given sports task contextualise or govern the components (e.g., players) of the system (e.g., a game or game sub-phase), but also how these are constrained by the orderly behaviour of the system components. Additionally, researchers could progressively attempt to manipulate a possible key constraint of this system, identifying features of stability, instability and phase transitions.

REFERENCES

Alamar, B. (2013). *Sports Analytics: A Guide for Coaches, Managers, and other Decision Makers*. New York: Columbia University Press.

Araújo, D., & Davids, K. (2015). Towards a theoretically – driven model of correspondence between behaviours in one context to another: Implications for studying sport performance. *International Journal of Sport Psychology, 46*, 268–280.

Araújo, D., Davids, K., Diniz, A., Rocha, L., Santos, J. C., Dias, G., . . . Fernandes, O. (2015). Ecological dynamics of continuous and categorical decision-making: The regatta start in sailing. *European Journal of Sport Science, 15*, 195–202.

Araújo, D., Davids, K., & Hristovski, R. (2006). The ecological dynamics of decision making in sport. *Psychology of Sport & Exercise, 7*, 653–676.

Araújo, D., Davids, K., & Passos, P. (2013). The intending-perceiving-acting cycle in sports performance. In T. McGarry, P. O'Donoghue, & J. Sampaio (Eds.), *Routledge Handbook of Sports Performance Analysis* (pp. 32–41). London: Routledge Taylor & Francis Group.

Araújo, D., Passos, P., Esteves, P., Duarte, R., Lopes, J., Hristovski, R., & Davids, K. (2015). The micro-macro link in understanding sport tactical behaviours: Integrating information and action at different levels of system analysis in sport. *Science & Motricité, 89*, 53–63.

Araújo, D., Silva, P., & Davids, K. (2015). Capturing group tactical behaviors in expert team players. In J. Baker & D. Farrow (Eds.), *Routledge Handbook of Sport Expertise* (pp. 209–220). New York, NY: Routledge.

Bartlett, R., Button, C., Robins, M., Dutt-Mazumder, A., & Kennedy, G. (2012). Analysing team coordination patterns from player movement trajectories in soccer: Methodological considerations. *International Journal of Performance Analysis in Sport, 12*, 398–424.

Bush, M., Barnes, C., Archer, D., Hogg, B., & Dradley, P. (2015). Evolution of match performance parameters for various playing positions in the English premier league. *Human Movement Science, 39*, 1–11.

48

Carling, C., Bloomfield, J., Nelsen, L., & Reilly, T. (2008). The role of motion analysis in elite soccer: Contemporary performance measurement techniques and work rate data. *Sports Medicine, 38*(10), 839–862.

Carling, C., Reilly, T., & Williams, A. M. (2009). *Performance Assessment for Field Sports.* London, UK: Routledge.

Correia, V., Araújo, D., Craig, C., & Passos, P. (2011). Prospective information for pass decisional behaviour in rugby union. *Human Movement Science, 30*, 984–997. doi:10.1016/j.humov.2010.07.008

Correia, V., Araújo, D., Cummins, A., & Craig, C. (2012). Perceiving and acting upon spaces in a VR rugby task: Expertise effects in affordance detection and task achievement. *Journal of Sport & Exercise Psychology, 34*, 305–321.

Correia, V., Araújo, D., Vilar, L., & Davids, K. (2013). From recording discrete actions to studying continuous goal-directed behaviours in team sports. *Journal of Sports Sciences, 31*(5), 546–553.

Correia, V., Araújo, D., Watson, G., & Craig, C. (2014). Using Virtual environments to study interactions in sport performance. In K. Davids, R. Hristovski, D. Araújo, N. Balague, C. Button, & P. Passos (Eds.), *Complex Systems in Sport* (pp. 175–189). London: Routledge.

Davids, K., Button, C., Araújo, D., Renshaw, I., & Hristovski, R. (2006). Movement models from sports provide representative task constraints for studying adaptive behaviour in human motor systems. *Adaptive Behavior, 14*, 73–95.

Davids, K., Button, C., & Bennett, S. J. (2008). *Dynamics of Skill Acquisition: A Constraints-Led Approach.* Champaign: Human Kinetics.

Davids, K., Hristovski, R., Araújo, D., Balague, N., Button, C., & Passos, P. (Eds.). (2014). *Complex Systems in Sport.* London: Routledge.

Dawson, B., Hopkinson, R., Appleby, B., Stewart, G., & Roberts, C. (2004). Player movement patterns and game activities in the Australian football league. *Journal of Science and Medicine in Sport, 7*(3), 278–291.

Dicks, M., Button, C., & Davids, K. (2010). Examination of gaze behaviors under in situ and video simulation task constraints reveals differences in information pickup for perception and action. *Attention, Perception, & Psychophysics, 72*(3), 706–720. doi:10.3758/App.72.3.706

Donders, F. (1868/1969). On the speed of mental process. *Acta Psychologica, 30*, 412–443.

Duarte, R., Araújo, D., Correia, V., Davids, K., Marques, P., & Richardson, M. (2013). Competing together: Assessing the dynamics of team-team and player-team synchrony in professional football. *Human Movement Science, 2*, 555–566.

Duarte, R., Araújo, D., Freire, L., Folgado, H., Fernandes, O., & Davids, K. (2012). Intra- and inter-group coordination patterns reveal collective behaviours of football players near the scoring zone. *Human Movement Science.* doi:10.1016/j.humov.2012.03.001

Duarte, R., Araújo, D., Gazimba, V., Fernandes, O., Folgado, H., Marmeleira, J., . . . Davids, K. (2010). The ecological dynamics of 1v1 sub-phases in association football. *Open Sports Sciences Journal, 3*, 16–18.

Duch, J., Waitzman, J. S., & Amaral, L. A. N. (2010). Quantifying the performance of individual players in a team activity. *PLoS ONE, 5*(6), e10937. doi: 10.1371/journal.pone.0010937

Dutt-Mazumder, A., Button, C., Robins, A., & Bartlett, R. (2011). Neural network modelling and dynamical system theory: Are they relevant to study the governing dynamics of association football players? *Sports Medicine.* doi: 10.2165/11593950–000000000–00000

Esteves, P. T., de Oliveira, R. F., & Araújo, D. (2011). Posture-related affordances guide attacks in basketball. *Psychology of Sport and Exercise, 12,* 639–644. doi:10.1016/j.psychsport.2011.06.007

Fajen, B., Riley, M., & Turvey, M. (2009). Information, affordances, and the control of action in sport. *International Journal of Sport Psychology, 40*(1), 79–107.

Fajen, B. R., Diaz, G., & Cramer, C. (2011). Reconsidering the role of movement in perceiving action-scaled affordances. *Human Movement Science, 30,* 504–533. doi:10.1016/j.humov.2010.07.016

Fitts, P., & Posner, M. (1967). *Human Performance.* Belmont, CA: Brooks/Cole.

Fruchart, E., Pâques, P., & Mullet, E. (2010). Decision-making in basketball and handball games: A developmental perspective. *Revue européenne de psychologie appliquée, 60,* 27–34. doi:10.1016/j.erap.2009.10.003

Gibson, J. J. (1979). *An ecological approach to visual perception.* Boston, MA: Houghton-Mifflin.

Glazier, P., & Robins, M. (2013). Self-organization and constraints in sport performance. In T. McGarry, P. O'Donoghue, & J. Sampaio (Eds.), *Routledge Handbook of Sports Performance Analysis* (pp. 42–51). London: Routledge Taylor & Francis Group.

Glazier, P. S. (2010). Game, set and match? Substantive issues and future directions in performance analysis. *Sports Medicine, 40*(8), 625–634. doi: 10.2165/11534970–000000000–00000

Gréhaigne, J. F., Bouthier, D., & David, B. (1997). Dynamic-system analysis of opponent relationships in collective actions in soccer. *Journal of Sport Sciences, 15*(2), 137–149.

Grund, T. U. (2012). Network structure and team performance: The case of English premier league soccer teams. *Social Networks, 34*(4), 682–690. doi: 10.1016/j.socnet.2012.08.004

Hughes, M., & Franks, I. (2005). Analysis of passing sequences, shots goals in soccer. *Journal of Sport Sciences, 23*(5), 509–514. doi: 10.1080/02640410410001716779

Hughes, M., & Franks, I. M. (2008). *The Essentials of Performance Analysis: An Introduction.* London & New York: Routledge.

Hughes, M. D., & Bartlett, R. M. (2002). The use of performance indicators in performance analysis. *Journal of Sport Sciences, 20*(10), 739–754. doi: 10.1080/026404102320675602

Huys, R., Cañal-Bruland, R., Hagemann, N., Beek, P. J., Smeeton, N. J., & Williams, A. M. (2009). Global information pickup underpins anticipation of tennis shot direction. *Journal of Motor Behavior, 41*(2), 158–170.

Jones, P. D., James, N., & Mellalieu, S. D. (2004). Possession as a performance indicator in soccer. *International Journal of Performance Analysis in Sport, 4*(1), 98–102(5).

Lago, C., & Martín, R. (2007). Determinants of possession of the ball in soccer. *Journal of Sport Sciences, 25*, 969–974.

Lames, M. (2006). Modelling the interaction in game sports – relative phase and moving correlations. *Journal of Sports Science and Medicine, 5*, 556–560.

Lees, A., (2002). Technique analysis in sports: A critical review. *Journal of Sport Sciences, 20*, 813–828.

Marteniuk, R. (1976). *Information Processing in Motor Skills.* New York: Holt, Rinehart & Winston.

McGarry, T. (2009). Applied and theoretical perspectives of performance analysis in sport: Scientific issues and challenges. *International Journal of Performance Analysis in Sport, 9*, 128–140.

McGarry, T. (2013). Sport competition as a dynamical self-organizing system: Coupled oscillator dynamics of players and teams underscores game rhythm behaviors of different sports. In T. McGarry, P. O'Donoghue, & J. Sampaio (Eds.), *Routledge Handbook of Sports Performance Analysis* (pp. 52–63). London: Routledge Taylor & Francis Group.

McGarry, T., & Franks, I. (1996). Development, application, and limitation of a stochastic Markov model in explaining championship squash performance. *Research Quarterly for Exercise and Sport, 67*(4), 406–415.

McGarry, T., Khan, M., & Franks, I. (1999). On the presence and absence of behavioural traits in sport: An example from championship squash matchplay. *Journal of Sports Sciences, 17*, 297–311.

Morrow, J., Jackson, A., Dish, J., & Mood, D. (2000). *Measurement and Evaluation in Human Performance* (2nd ed.). Champaign: Human kinetics.

Müller, S., & Abernethy, B. (2006). Batting with occluded vision: An in situ examination of the information pick-up and interceptive skills of high- and low-skilled cricket batsmen. *Journal of Science and Medicine in Sport, 9*(6), 446–58.

Nougier, V., Azemar, G., Stein, J-F., & Ripoll, H. (1992). Covert orienting to central visual cues and sport practice relations in the development of visual attention. *Journal of Experimental Child Psychology, 54*(3), 315–333.

O'Donoghue, P. (2008). Time-motion analysis. In M. Hughes & I. Franks (Eds.), *The Essentials of Performance Analysis: An Introduction* (180–205). London: Routledge.

O'Donoghue, P. (2010). *Research Methods for Sports Performance Analysis.* London: Routledge.

Palut, Y., & Zanone, P. G. (2005). A dynamical analysis of tennis: Concepts and data. *Journal of Sports Essentials Sciences, 23*, 1021–1032.

Panchuk, D., & Vickers, J. N. (2006). Gaze behaviors of goaltenders under spatial–temporal constraints. *Human Movement Science, 25*, 733–752

Passos, P., Araújo, D., Davids, K., Gouveia, L. F., Milho, J., & Serpa, S. (2008). Information-governing dynamics of attacker-defender interactions in youth rugby union. *Journal of Sport Sciences, 26*, 1421–1429.

Passos, P., Araújo, D., Davids, K., Gouveia, L., Serpa, S., Milho, J., & Fonseca, S. (2009). Interpersonal pattern dynamics and adaptive behaviour in multi-agent neurobiological systems: A conceptual model and data. *Journal of Motor Behavior, 41*, 445–459.

Passos, P., Milho, J., Fonseca, S., Borges, J., Araújo, D., & Davids, K. (2011). Interpersonal distance regulates functional grouping tendencies of agents in team sports. *Journal of Motor Behavior, 43*(2), 155–163.

Posner, M. (1978). *Chronometric Explorations of Mind.* Hillsdale, NJ: Lawrence Erlbaum Associates.

Sampaio, J., & Leite, N. (2013). Performance Indicators in game sports. In T. McGarry, P. O'Donoghue, & J. Sampaio (Eds.), *Routledge Handbook of Sports Performance Analysis* (pp. 115–126). London: Routledge Taylor & Francis Group.

Sanders, A. F. (1998). *Elements of human performance.* Mahwah, NJ: Lawrence Erlbaum Associates

Schmidt, R. A., & Lee, T. (2014). *Motor Control and Learning* (5th ed.). Champaign, IL: Human Kinetics.

Travassos, B., Araújo, D., Davids, K., Vilar, L., Esteves, P., & Correia, V. (2012). Informational constraints shape emergent functional behaviors during performance of interceptive actions in team sports. *Psychology of Sport & Exercise, 13*, 216–223.

Vaeyens, R., Lenoir, M., Williams, A. M., Mazyn, L., & Philippaerts, R. M. (2007). The effects of task constraints on visual search behaviour and decision-making skill in youth soccer players. *Journal of Sport Exercise Psychology, 29*, 147–169.

Vilar, L., Araújo, D., Davids, K., & Button, C. (2012a). The role of ecological dynamics in analysing performance in team sports. *Sports Medicine, 42*(1), 1–10.

Vilar, L., Araújo, D., Davids, K., & Travassos, B. (2012b). Constraints on competitive performance of attacker-defender dyads in team sports. *Journal of Sports Sciences, 30*, 459–469.

Weast, J. A., Shockley, K., & Riley, M. A., (2011). The influence of athletic experience and kinematic information on skill-relevant affordance perception. *The Quarterly Journal of Experimental Psychology, 64*(4). doi: http://dx.doi.org/10.1080/17470218.2010.523474

Weldford, A. T. (1968). *Fundamentals of Skill.* London: Methuen.

Williams, A. M., & Ericsson, K. A. (2005). Perceptual–cognitive expertise in sport: Some considerations when applying the expert performance approach. *Human Movement Science, 24*, 287–307.

Zoudji, B., Thon, B., & Debu, B. (2010). Efficiency of the mnemonic system of expert soccer players under overload of the working memory in a simulated decision-making task. *Psychology of Sport and Exercise, 11*, 18–26. doi:10.1016/j.psychsport.2009.05.006

CHAPTER 4

PERFORMANCE-RELATED ISSUES IN TEAM SPORTS

Leading author: Pedro Passos

INTRODUCTION

This chapter focuses on several issues that arose from research and applied fields in the last decades. Due to the huge amount of variables which influence players' behaviour and also to the dynamics of these variables which mutually and reciprocally interact with each other, team sports are usually described as complex dynamic systems. This understanding of team sports takes players' individual and collective performance away from being an explanation where linear cause–effect relationships are the rule. Instead the rules of the game, the field width and depth, the goal location, the proximity and number of the teammates and opponent players are a few examples of task constraints which create the boundaries of a perceptual-motor workspace from where player's behaviours emerge in time and space (Araújo et al., 2004; Araújo et al., 2006; Davids et al., 2008; Glazier, 2010). The term 'emerge' means that it is not possible to predict (beyond a probabilistic basis) *where* and *when* each player's next movement will occur. Moreover it is not possible to predict behaviour from the individual properties of each of the elements of the system. Team sports performance is highly influenced by the interactive behaviour among players, which means that players' decisions and actions are constrained by the information that surrounds them, which is continuously changing. Thus ecological dynamics is an appropriate rationale for performance-related issues in team sports (Araújo et al., 2006) and sets a common ground for concepts as task representativeness, creativity and behavioural self-organisation.

Task representativeness

The task representativeness is a 'hot topic'. Modern training methods are highlighting tasks that in some way 'represent' match sub-phases. *Representative task design* was conceived by Egon Brunswick (Brunswik, 1956) to strengthen the correspondence between experimental task constraints and the daily settings to where research results are intended to apply. In the last decade the concept of *representativeness* was imported to sports sciences to highlight the importance of creating and developing practice sessions which are representative of the competitive settings (Araújo et al., 2005). Applying this concept to practice environments in team sports implies the need to create *representative learning designs* (Pinder et al., 2011).

Players' movement interactions with teammates and opposing players are regulated by perceptual information (Dicks et al., 2008). Tasks constraints are crucial for this circular relationship between perceptual information and movement. In practice sessions, practicing under different task constraints than those that players will face on competitive settings, this means that coaches are promoting that players become attuned to other perceptual information than that which is found on a competitive match. To enhance players' perceptual attunement to affordances found in the competition, practice learning designs should include task constraints which are representative of competitive settings.

The consequence of practice without a representative learning design, is the emergence of different (and perhaps less functional) patterns of interpersonal coordination among players (Pinder et al., 2011). A key issue to creating a representative learning design is to consider how affordances designed into practice environments can correspond to those affordances that exist in competitive environments (Araújo & Davids, in press; Passos & Davids, 2015).

Methods to measure representativeness

There is a key concern about how to measure the degree of representativeness between two (or even more) different environments as team sports training exercises and game sub-phases. This association between practice and competitive contexts has been proposed through the *action fidelity* concept, which aims to analyse the similarity of behavioural responses between different environments (e.g., practice vs competition) (Araújo et al., 2007; Dicks et al., 2008; Pinder et al., 2011; Stoffregen et al., 2003).

A previous study on the task of diving from springboards aimed to measure the action fidelity between diving in a dry-land practice context and diving into the water (Barris et al., 2013). The hypotheses was sustained on the existence of kinematic differences, due to changes on interlimb coordination patterns and also on differences in performance indicators such as step lengths and jump heights on the springboard. The methods used to measure *action fidelity* were based on the qualitative analysis of plot diagrams of joint kinematics (e.g., angle–angle) of the same key events performed in the aquatic and dry-land environment. To be considered as similar, the diagram shapes of joint kinematics needed to be 'stretched' to fit each other. And, shape similarity was based on the diagrams equivalent topology. The authors hypothesised that differences in topological patterns of the diagrams correspond to differences in coordination patterns when performing diving in dry-land or in aquatic environments (Barris et al., 2013; Chow et al., 2008). Data revealed topological similarities in the coordination patterns for both conditions (i.e., aquatic and dry-land) for all participants (Barris et al., 2013). Barris and colleagues' study developed a method based on the topological analysis of diagrams of joint kinematics, suggesting a measure for *action fidelity* and thus for a key principle of task representativeness.

A different approach to understanding the representativeness of practice designs was made by Travassos and colleagues (2012), who developed a study in futsal manipulating the affordances (i.e., possibilities of action) to pass the ball. The method consisted of increasing the uncertainty for the ball carrier regarding where the pass should be performed (i.e., passing direction). The rationale was that increasing the uncertainty of the passing direction increases the similarity of affordances to those of the competitive matches. The ball speed regularity and passing accuracy were the variables used to compare players' performances in practice and competitive match conditions (Travassos et al., 2012). Results revealed that increasing the uncertainty as it happens in a match made the practice more representative of the competitive setting.

Representativeness of a task can be expressed with the frequency (i.e., number of actions performed on time) and location (i.e., where those actions occur) of actions (e.g., passes; shots to goal; players' running line trajectories; players' interpersonal distances) that occur during practice. Thus we may suggest that a relevant contribution of performance analysis could be in developing tools to quantify the representativeness of a practice design. However, we must consider that in training, players need to take breaks in order to recover or to provide feedback and instructions to other players in a way that is not possible to achieve in competition. This causes that rightfully a training session deviates from the representativeness of a match. Notwithstanding, we should consider the aim of the training session. If the aim is focus on technical and tactical issues then representativeness should be considered only in the periods in which players are in practice; but if the aim is focus on physiological issues then the ratio between practice and rest periods should be considered to measure the representativeness of the training session.

How to improve tactical creativity?

Beyond the individual creativity that is prominent in expert players of different team sports, collective creativity is relevant for performance analysis. But how to measure this sort of on-field collective creativity? We will present some suggestions aiming to answer this question. Notwithstanding, individual skills are a crucial issue on team sports, especially those skills that go beyond the obvious (i.e., that deviates from the 'ideal' technical models) but which are highly functional.

The support for tactical creativity has been developed based on the concepts of *divergent thinking* and *convergent thinking* (Guilford, 1956, 1967). Convergent thinking sustained players' behaviour aiming for 'ideal' pre-defined solutions for problems. In contrast, divergent thinking leads the players to search for other functional solutions beyond those that are the most commonly used. For example, *tactical game intelligence* is supported by the convergent thinking process, whereas *tactical creativity* is supported by the divergent thinking process. In the latter, what is emphasised is the variety of solutions for the same end (Memmert, 2013; Memmert et al., 2013).

The aim of practice in sports is to push performance to a higher level. Such improvement occurs, not simply by optimising an existing well-learned technique or tactics, but by the invention of a 'new' movement pattern (Hristovski et al., 2011). On one side, tactical creativity implies to perform unexpected actions which block any anticipative action

56

from the opponents, such as the interception of a pass. On the other side, it promotes defender disorganisation, such as the emergence of a gap between defenders that affords a shooting opportunity or opening a passing line to a support player. Notwithstanding, creativity is not a common ability to all the players; the differences can be grounded in players' past experiences, which has influence in the way that each explores the relevant information available in a competitive context. The nature of the learning contexts from where players evolve determine how they will explore tasks and environmental constraints in a near future.

The relevance of tactical creativity in team sports increases due to the ability of the teams' technical staff to collect information about the opponent's technical and tactical actions (Memmert, 2013; Memmert et al., 2013). The improvements in the technology over the last years led to an increase in the information provided by performance analysis; consequently it is possible to anticipate (with a considerable level of accuracy) how the opponent team will play in the next match. However, these gains due to technological advances can be balanced with original and unexpected collective performance solutions. Thus tactical creativity is a tool that teams should develop to enhance the degree of uncertainty of teams' collective actions.

Measuring creativity in sports

Concerning performance analysis, tactical creativity in team sports is a difficult skill to measure (Memmert, 2013; Memmert et al., 2013). Notwithstanding, three major tools to measure and explain tactical creativity have been developed: the *game test situation* (Memmert & Roth, 2007), the *video test* (Johnson & Raab, 2003) and the *solving problem under constraints* approach (Hristovski et al., 2011). In the first two approaches tactical creativity was assessed with expert validation, whereas the last used the dynamical structure of collective variables to quantify issues such as originality in sports performance.

In common to these approaches are three features used to characterise tactical creativity: the *fluency*, the *flexibility* and the *originality* of the solutions performed (Guilford, 1967; Torrance, 1966). The fluency is the frequency of tactical actions performed during a match; the flexibility is related with variety of the tactical solutions performed, and the originality is related with the novelty of tactical solutions performed during a match. However, to be considered as a creative behaviour (despite being technical or tactical) two key dimensions must be included: (i) the *novelty* (i.e., uniqueness, originality); and (ii) the *functionality* (i.e., effectiveness, usefulness, success, appropriateness). This means that to be characterised as creative the consequences of performing a 'unique' movement must always be related to the outcome (Hristovski et al., 2011; Runco, 2004). This linkage between uniqueness and functionality excludes any bizarre movement to be considered within the scope of creative behaviours.

For the analysis of creative behaviours, two frames of reference must be considered. The first refers to the player's own performance and the second frame of reference is related to the social context where the behaviour is performed. These two frames of reference were previously characterised as two types of creativity named in the literature as 'mini-c' and 'Big-C' types of creativity (Beghetto & Kaufman, 2007). In the sports performance context, a 'mini-c' creative behaviour occurs when an athlete 'discovers' a functional behaviour that was not a part of his/her own motor repertoire, regardless of the fact that such an action may already have been performed by other athletes. Whereas the 'Big-C' type of creativity is much more unique; the most well-known example was the Fosbury Flop used in the track and field high jump competition (Beghetto & Kaufman, 2007). Within the 'Big-C' type of creativity fit the movement forms that did not exist in a specific sports movement culture prior to their creation; gymnastics, figure skating and snowboarding are just a few examples of sports in which there are plenty of examples of this. It's an innovative action mode that was not previously a part of the social-cultural landscape where it was performed. It is important to note the delicate relationships between these two types of creativity. Also it is worth noting that creativity should not be interpreted in the same way in the different stages of learning (i.e., from novices to expert players). In the early stages of learning, it is more likely that there will be 'mini-c' creative actions, whereas 'Big-C' creativity is more likely to occur with expert players (Simonton, 1999). Additionally, stimulating 'mini-c' creativity during the earlier stages of learning may enhance the odds for the occurrence of 'Big-C' creative actions later in skilled and expert performances (Beghetto & Kaufman, 2007).

For that to happen, the learning environments must promote the occurrence of those creative behaviours. Therefore the performance of multiple

58

possible solutions is always needed for the emergence (i.e., not imposed from an external source – for instance, a coach's instructions) of innovative behaviours in a system under changing task constraints (Hristovski et al., 2011). This could mean that the variability of players performance mirror the players exploratory behaviour aiming to find different solutions for the same task goal, a crucial issue for creative behaviours. Moreover players' exploratory activity is strongly dependent on the set of task constraints imposed on the learning settings. For instance field boundaries, goal location and rules of the game are task constraints that influence players' behaviour. Additionally the relative positioning of teammates and opponents are also game constraints which influence players' performances – for instance, decreasing attacker–defender interpersonal distances will influence both players' behaviour due to less time available for decision-making. However, while field boundaries and rules remain unchanged during competitive performance, players' relative positioning is a task constraint that continuously alters due to the location and proximity of others. For example, attackers change their positions due to changes in defenders' locations. Defending players in turn adapt their positions in response to the positional changes of attackers and support players (Passos & Davids, 2015).This observation implies that, during practice, no explicitly prescriptive list of possible actions needs to be provided beforehand to the performer so that he/she might realise them (Hristovski et al., 2011).

The role of enhanced exploratory breadth consists of forming an ever-growing set of task dependent predispositions of couplings among players. In other words, the mutual and reciprocal influence among a set of players work as game constraints which bind the perceptual-motor workspace and call for the emergence of creative behaviours (Hristovski et al., 2011). The dynamics of play with others and for others (i.e., teammates and opponents) create conditions for creativity that never occur when someone plays alone.

Methods and tools to measure creativity

The *game test situation* is a context-dependent setting which aims to represent the same task and environmental constraints that players face in a competitive match. Players' tactical performance is video recorded and then assessed by a panel of experts who used the previously mentioned criteria of originality, flexibility and fluency (Memmert, 2010;

Memmert & Furley, 2007; Memmert & Roth, 2007). The *video test* is a decision task, where the players watch match-specific videos, then the image is paused after one minute and the player needs to describe an entire set of possible actions which move him/her to the goal. Similar to the *game test situation* the players' responses were assessed by an expert panel using the same criteria (Johnson & Raab, 2003). The major issue with the *video test* is the separation between players' technical skills and tactical decisions. This separation limits the relevance of this sort of analysis.

Notable, tactical decisions are strongly supported by coupled perception and action (Araújo et al., 2006; Fajen et al., 2009; Passos & Davids, 2015). In other words the way that each player moves is crucial for his/her perception of others' movements and consequently for tactical decisions. It is the information that is created due to players' movements that will support decisions and actions on the pitch (Fajen et al., 2009). Also, a player moves differently on the pitch due to his/her technical skills, which consequently influence tactical decisions. For instance players who have the ability to perform accurate passes over long distances will explore different tactical solutions than those who only have the ability to pass the ball short distances. Therefore as sports analysts we should be aware that verbal reports of tactical decisions based on frozen images are quite different from tactical decisions that a player has to make in competition.

Thus how to measure tactical creative behaviours? To answer this question Robert Hristovski and colleagues suggested that collective variables are useful to measure the novelty of a technical or tactical action (Hristovski et al., 2011). Collective variables (also known in the literature as coordinative variables or order parameters) are relational quantities that are created by the cooperation among players (Kelso, 2009). In other words collective variables describe the interactive behaviour among players.[4] Figure 4.1 displays the defender–ball carrier angle as a collective behaviour of the same dyad on several trials in rugby union (Hristovski et al., 2011).

These collective variables (e.g., ball carrier interpersonal angles with defenders) are strongly influenced by small changes in system parameters (e.g., ball carrier–defender interpersonal distance; players' relative velocities) (Passos et al., 2008). For instance a decrease in the ball carrier–defender interpersonal distance (as a system parameter) can drive the

60

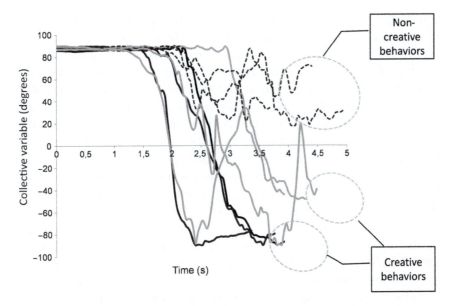

Figure 4.1 The defender–ball carrier angle as a collective variable (reprinted with permission of *Nonlinear Dynamics Psychology and Life Sciences*).

ball carrier to change position; consequently the player's interpersonal angle (as a collective variable) will change. These changes (i.e., variabilities) over can be used to classify each player's performance as unique. However, players' behaviour can't be classified as creative only for its uniqueness. As previously stated it is the functional efficiency (in satisfying a task goal) of the performance that helps us to define a behaviour as creative. For instance, a ball carrier in rugby union performs unique running line trajectories every time he/she faces an opponent. However, his/her performance can only be classified as creative if it was functional – that is, if he/she successfully overtakes the defender and runs free towards the goal line (Figure 4.1 black filled line).

It should be noted that creativity is not a predictor of success (Hristovski et al., 2011). Therefore another relevant issue for performance analysis is related to the criteria used to define functionality. If these criteria are only based on the ultimate performance goals of the game (e.g., to score a try in rugby union or a goal in football), performance situations that featured plenty of creativity in reaching performance sub-goals were not classified as creative due to individual performance errors (e.g., a support player in rugby union fails to catch the ball). To classify any player behaviour as creative only based on the ultimate performance goal of scoring is a highly reductionist criterion. Therefore players' behaviour should be classified as creative according to the achievement of identified performance task sub-goals (Hristovski et al., 2011). Moreover creativity must be considered at different time scales. At a short time scale, displayed with immediate movement adaptations due to current changes in the task constraints (e.g., to perform a pass behind the back to assist a teammate in basketball or in rugby union because it is the technical action with more chances to succeed on a specific moment); and a long time scale where a 'new' creative solution may take months or years to become accurate (e.g., dribbling skills in basketball or puck handling skills in hockey) (Hristovski et al., 2012). Another example of creativity at a short time scale is players' improvisation skills. More specifically, for those players who break the set patterns of action because they identify other (more) functional actions. This requires that all the players within a team should be aware of the possibility of improvisation of a teammate and promptly adapt. A team with these creative and adaptive skills will be able to create several solutions for the same goal, a required feature to success in team sports.

Technical effectiveness

This section is dedicated to performance beyond 'ideal' models. In the last few decades team sports have evolved towards a perspective where technical skills are viewed as a tool used to solve tactical issues. Thus the effectiveness of technical skills can only be assessed within practices that require solving tactical problems. This perspective has lead coaching methods to a stage where it does not make much sense to separate technical from tactical behaviour. Here we will discuss the implications of the complementary nature between technical and tactical behaviours.

Effectiveness means achieving a performance goal (e.g., to score points; to tackle the ball carrier; to intercept a pass; to manage the energetic resources to have strength all the way through the end of the match). There are several factors that might constrain technical effectiveness; these are as follows: the rules of the game, resources for maintaining high energy, the movement goals and sub-goals, the existence of a reference model and the adaptation demands to external constraints (Palao & Morante, 2013).

62

These factors imply that the movements required to perform an effective technique are unique not only to each sport (e.g., the dribbling actions in football are quite different from the dribbling actions in rugby union) but also within a sport (e.g., the required kicking accuracy in rugby union is different when a player kicks to score from when he/she kicks to place the ball behind the defenders; the first kick is effective if it scores and the second is effective if the ball carrier or a teammate regains ball possession). Thus technical effectiveness should always be regarded with achieving a performance goal.

Whether the goal is a team scoring a point or an individual movement organisation to kick, catch or pass a ball, there are usually many ways to complete these tasks. When performing a motor task (e.g., kick, catch or pass) individuals (e.g., players) can display several solutions to achieve the same goal (e.g., to score); this is called equifinality and is what affords exploratory behaviour beyond 'ideal' models of performance (Bernstein, 1967). Due the huge amount of variables (e.g., physical, technical, tactical, psychological) that constrain each player's behaviour, players interactions within team sports are characterised as non-linear (meaning it is not possible to predict with total accuracy what is going to happen in the next moment) (Strogatz, 2004). Therefore competitive performance settings are very uncertain and unpredictable environments, which are characterised by sudden, unexpected and quick changes in the vast amount of movements of the ball, teammates and opponents (Passos et al., 2008). Thus there is always more than one possible effective solution to achieve a goal (Warren, 2006), and the effectiveness of solutions can't be previously set due to this interactive non-linear nature among individuals with different performance goals (Hristovski et al., 2012). Moreover, the divergent performance goals among opponent players lead to the fact that players often intentionally act in such a way as to change the opponent's behaviours, to create a situation that affords an efficient action corresponding to achieving some sub-goal (e.g., a ball carrier to dribble past a defender) or the main goal of the game (e.g., an open gap which affords a shot at the goal) (Esteves et al., 2011). Consequently players can't perform according to a single predetermined supposedly 'correct' solution, but to the contrary, a performance goal can usually be achieved through a variety of effective solutions afforded by an ever-changing (i.e., dynamic) competitive setting. However, multiple solutions must be in the skill set of the player in order for him/her to be effective.

Whether a player is performing in practice or in a competitive match, he/she attempts to satisfy specific task constraints (e.g., location of the ball, teammate's relative position, distance to the goal, interpersonal distance to a marked defender), which are continuously changing during performance. This might be the major reason to (Handford, 2006) criticise the 'one size fits all' method regarding the learning process of technical elements in a generic way across all players in team sports. Hence, it is futile to try and identify a common, idealised movement pattern towards which all learners should aspire (e.g., learning a classical passing technique in volleyball) (Hristovski et al., 2011; Phillips et al., 2011). Due to different individual constraints (e.g., different heights, different arm lengths, different cognitive and emotional skills, different levels of individual technique) it is dysfunctional to seek to establish universal optimal learning development pathways based on 'ideal' (i.e., mechanical) models of performance to which all learners should adhere. Differences in anthropometric, cognitive, technical and tactical skills clearly emphasise the relevance of creating individualised solutions to the learning of movement techniques (Hristovski et al., 2011). Thus performance analysis should seek for quantifying the *effectiveness* of movement technique and not the movement by itself, especially if based on supposed 'ideal' models of execution, which are useful references but should be analysed considering acceptable ranges of movement variability.

In team sports the criteria to assess technical effectiveness should be related to achieving tactical goals and sub-goals (Palao & Morante, 2013) – for instance, acquire a constant relative position to the defenders avoiding the attacking team to get closer to the goal (a criterion that could be used in football, rugby union or basketball); or how the frequency of the ball carrier dribbling skills opens a gap in the defensive line affording an attempt to score (in football, in basketball or in handball). After setting the criteria the next stage is to define the parameters to assess technical effectiveness, which can be *quantitative* or *qualitative* parameters. Examples of quantitative parameters of effectiveness are points scored, tackles performed, ball interceptions, the angle between ball carrier and defender closing the gap to the goal, the opponent players' interpersonal distance, etc.; this involves a numerical description of movement on a chosen scale (e.g., number of occurrences in the same match or in different matches). On the other side, qualitative parameters involve the description of movement using category systems which usually assess effectiveness with nominal scales (it refers to the technique that was used to achieve a goal)

64

or ordinal scales (which place the effectiveness of a technique on a range such as first, second, third; or poor, average, excellent). Qualitative data can be later 'transformed' into quantitative data using a process called normalisation, which relates qualitative data with references values.

The complementary nature between technical and tactical behaviour

From a performance analysis perspective it is possible to analyse separately players' technical skills and players' tactical skills, but the separation of these cornerstones of players' behaviours in team sports doesn't make much sense. The main reason to avoid this separation is that team games can be conceptualised as complex dynamical systems whose patterns of behaviour are created by continuous changes in the players' behaviours due to the changes of the others (i.e., teammates, opponent players) in the area (Passos et al., 2011; Passos et al., 2013). Technical skills are what players use to solve tactical issues during a match. In turn, tactical issues are task constraints which demand players' adaptive behaviour (due to changes in the other player's behaviour) achieved through the use of individual technique. It is from this mutual and reciprocal dependency between players' individual techniques and team/match tactical constraints that emerges its complementary nature.

Moreover a player's individual technique evolves through the practice under tactical constraints, and in turn an improved technique leads the player to explore 'new' tactical solutions that were not available before (Passos & Davids, 2015) (Figure 4.2).

Although during a match the players can display similar patterns of movement on different occasions, those movements are never repeated identically (e.g., the players never score from the same location; the technique used to score or to pass the ball always has slight differences). It is the many components of the human movement system that provides the players with the means to adjust their behaviour in order to maintain goal-directed activity (e.g., adapt their dribbling action to avoid an approaching defender; to perform a pass behind the legs because it is the most accurate solution to perform a fast pass to the support player) (Passos et al., 2008). Since the constraints imposed by neighbouring players always exhibit different characteristics (e.g., different relative positions; different interpersonal distances; different relative positions to the goal)

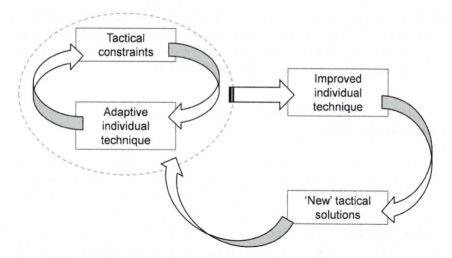

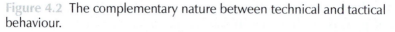

Figure 4.2 The complementary nature between technical and tactical behaviour.

due to the use of different tactical systems (e.g., in basketball a full court man-to-man pressure defence is different from a zone press defence; in football use of a defence in the opposition's midfield is different from using a defence in one's own midfield with less space between defensive lines). It follows that each player's specific technique must satisfy those tactical constraints; see, for instance, the different solutions that basketball players must have to score close to the basket, due to the opponent player's proximity and relative position to the basket. This type of fast and refined behavioural adaptation to tactical task constraints is only possible due to the variability of each player's individual technique.

Self-organisation in team sports – implications for performance analysis

Contrary to performance indicators which are product-oriented, self-organisation is a process-oriented concept. Consequently a major benefit for sports analysts to use the self-organisation concept is that it has the potential to link behaviour with performance outcomes. The other benefit is that it can be used to analyse coordination and control at different levels of sports performance, from dyadic interactions to collective (e.g., inter-team) behaviours (Glazier, 2010; Glazier & Robins, 2013).

66

Over the last decade research trends in team sports collective behaviours had proposed self-organisation as a mechanism to explain the tendencies for players to interact with each other, displaying functional co-adaptive behaviours without the need for external control (Passos et al., 2013). This means that beyond coaches' instructions or pre-planned strategies, players within the playing field can organise to interact with others according to rules such as keeping an optimal distance from a teammate (please see Camazine et al. for a detailed definition of self-organisation) (Camazine et al., 2001). It is the perceptual information of the interpersonal distance to teammates that keeps the players of the same team within 'optimal' distances. Thus the players of a team organise themselves within the playing field grounded on information that is created by their own behaviour, and this is why it is truthful to say that they self-organise. Therefore inherent self-organising coordination tendencies can be exploited to underpin interpersonal interactions among players.

However, it is worth noting the role of pre-planned actions or coaches' instructions. The suggestion is that effective interactions between players in team games (both intra- and inter-teams) can emerge through spontaneous self-organisation processes, under the influence of advanced, prescriptive planning of collective actions that operate as umbrella task constraints (Passos et al., 2013). In other words coaches' instructions and previous planned movements work as boundaries (i.e., constraints) which set the path to achieve a goal, how the players explore and use that path is ruled by local information grounded on the movements of the players in the neighbourhood. For instance the previous planned movements of a set of attackers in rugby union aim to create a gap in the defence line in a particular spot of the play field, but due to an excellent performance of the opposition team that gap never occurs. As a consequence the attackers need to explore a different solution to decrease the distance to the score line. That solution will emerge from players, interactive behaviour, supported on information locally created, and it is thus self-organised.

Self-organised systems possess a general feature called context dependency. Within team games, sports performance requires that players continuously co-adapt to the behaviours of other players in close proximity on the field of play, which sets the context dependency where the local interaction rules gain influence on the players' interactive behaviours. This perspective identifies attackers and defenders as components of a self-organising system (i.e., whose behaviour is guided without an external controller) that are linked by visual and other perceptual informational fields (e.g., tactile; acoustic) (Schmidt & O'Brien, 1997). It is the players' contextual dependency that created the so-called *critical regions* of performance, typically characterised by low values of interpersonal distances between attackers and defenders (Passos et al., 2008). Within these critical regions the movements of each player constrains and is constrained by the movements of the others, consequently actions should not be prescribed by pre-planned rules through a coach's instructions but rather emerge from the continuous interactions between players as a game evolves (Passos et al., 2013). The contextual dependency that characterises the critical regions leads to non-linearity of players' interactive behaviour. This means that it is not possible to accurately predict what is going to happen in the next moment of the match. Every competitive match evolves alternating relatively stable moments (where nothing significantly occurs) with moments of plenty of variability (e.g., with turnovers; or a sudden decrease of the attackers distance to the goal; or when the ball carrier breaks the defensive line) with stable moments again.

Challenges for performance analysis – the time component, the critical fluctuations and the successful thresholds

Due to its explanatory power the insights from concepts as self-organisation, critical regions and contextual dependency bring interesting questions for performance analysis related to the following: (i) variables that relate the *spatial* dimension with the *temporal* dimension of collective behaviours, mainly related to players' relative positions (the spatial dimension) but also 'how fast' these relative positions change over time (the temporal dimension); (ii) the magnitude of the variability (i.e., critical fluctuations) of the collective variables; and (iii) identifying thresholds which allow for successful conditions for teams and players.

Regarding the spatio-temporal dimension of the collective variables it is possible to characterise the rate of change of players' relative positions. For instance, after a volatile period where attackers attempted to break the defensive lines, how long did it take the defenders to restore the stability of the defensive system closing the gaps to the goal? After regaining ball possession, how long did it take a team to stretch an attacking line? How can we identify/measure when the ball carrier has an 'open' line

68

to shoot at the goal? And for how long is that shooting line 'available? This exemplar set of questions can be answered by assessing players' relative positions; this provides metrics from such collective variables as players' interpersonal distances, players' relative velocities or players' interpersonal angles.[5]

Measuring the *magnitude of the variability* (i.e., critical fluctuations) and identifying successful *thresholds* highlight the possibility to set predictions grounded in the dynamics of the collective variables (e.g., interpersonal distances, relative velocity, interpersonal angles). For instance, what is going to occur due to the changes in time (i.e., variability) of attacker–defender interpersonal angles? A significant part of the variability in the opposition player's relative positions is due to deceptive movements performed by the attackers. Any fake movement performed by the ball carrier aims to deceive the defender, make him/her change his/her relative position and consequently open a gap which affords the ball carrier to go forward towards the goal (e.g., basket, try line). However, this deceptive movement must be performed at a close interpersonal distance to the defender; otherwise the defender is able to recover the initial position. Also, it is expected that if properly executed, this causes uncertainty and consequently decreases the defender's velocity. This prediction highlights the need to test the relative angle between ball carrier and defender as a relevant parameter that might be responsible for the 'new' configuration in the attacker–defender system – for instance, the attacker breaks the defensive line and is now closer to the goal (Diniz et al., 2014). It is predictable that a deceptive movement, (e.g., dummy pass in rugby, basketball or football) changes the angle and the relative velocity values between ball carrier and defender, which under certain (unknown) variability values, affords the ball carrier and opportunity to go forward and attempt to score. Another example of how the variability of players' interactive behaviour may have a predictive effect was a study with a 2vs1 situation in rugby union, which revealed that the variability of the ball carrier and marked defender distances to the nearest sideline influenced the ball carrier's decision to pass the ball to the support player or move forward towards the try line. High variability of defender position to the closest sideline affords the ball carrier the opportunity to go forward to the score line (Passos et al., 2012).

Finally players' decision making is partially influenced by contextual information that is created due to players' interactive behaviour. As previously stated this contextual information can be described through collective variables as changes on player's interpersonal distances in time. It is possible to identify the threshold between successful and unsuccessful decisions. For instance, when in rugby union the ball carrier decides to perform a grubber kick, the interpersonal distance to which the grubber kick is performed has a critical threshold. If the grubber kick is performed above the threshold, it affords both players to run and grab the ball from the ground; if performed below the threshold, the players' relative velocity assumes a crucial role in the outcome. Usually after the kick the defender has to turn and start running from an 'almost' stopped position, which creates an advantage for the attacker. After the kick, both players will run towards the ball. Thus, the interpersonal distance threshold can be defined based on the players' acceleration profile, which defines how long each one takes to run a certain distance (Diniz et al., 2014).

Thus, adding time to spatial variables, analysing the magnitude of the variability of the collective variables, and identifying successful threshold values for decision making support the explanatory and predictive features of these sorts of variables, which will provide performance analysts with appropriate tools to answer challenging questions in the near future.

REFERENCES

Araújo, D., & Davids, K. (2015). Towards a theoretically-driven model of correspondence between behaviours in one context to another: Implications for studying sport performance. *International Journal of Sport Psychology, 46*(6), 745-757. doi: 10.7352/Ijsp.2015.46.745

Araújo, D., Davids, K., Bennett, S., Button, C., & Chapman, J. (2004). Emergence of sport skilld under constraints. In A. M. Williams & N. J. Hodges (Eds.), *Skill Acquisition in Sport Research, Theory and Practice* (pp. 409–433). London: Routledge.

Araújo, D., Davids, K., & Hristovski, R. (2006). The ecological dynamics of decision making in sport. *Psychology of Sport and Exercise, 7*(6), 653–676.

Araújo, D., Davids, K., & Passos, P. (2007). Ecological validity, representative design, and correspondence between experimental task constraints and behavioral setting: Comment on Rogers, Kadar, and Costall (2005). *Ecological Psychology, 19*(1), 69–78.

Araújo, D., Davids, K., & Serpa, S. (2005). An ecological approach to expertise effects in decision-making in a simulated sailing regatta. *Psychology of Sport and Exercise, 6*(6), 671–692.

Barris, S., Davids, K., & Farrow, D. (2013). Representative learning design in springboard diving: Is dry-land training representative of a pool dive? *European Journal of Sport Science, 13*(6), 638–645.

Beghetto, R. A., & Kaufman, J. C. (2007). The genesis of creative greatness: Mini-c and the expert performance approach. *High Ability Studies, 18*(1), 59–61.

Bernstein, N. A. (1967). *The Co-ordination and Regulation of Movements.* Oxford: Pergamon Press.

Brunswik, E. (1956). *Perception and the Representative Design of Psychological Experiments* (2nd ed.). Berkeley, CA: University of California Press.

Camazine, S., Deneubourg, J. L., Franks, N. R., Sneyd, J., Theraulaz, G., & Bonabeau, E. (2001). *Self-organization in biological systems.* New Jersey: Princeton Studies in Complexity.

Chow, J. Y., Davids, K., Button, C., & Koh, M. (2008). Coordination changes in a discrete multi-articular action as a function of practice. *Acta Psychologica (Amst), 127*(1), 163–176.

Davids, K., Button, C., & Bennett, S. (2008). *Dynamics of skill acquisition. A constraints-led approach.* Champaign, IL: Human Kinetics.

Dicks, M., Davids, K., & Araújo, D. (2008). Ecological psychology and task representativeness: Implications for the design of perceptual-motor training programmes in sport. In Y. Hong & R. Bartlett (Eds.), *The Routledge Handbook of Biomechanics and Human Movement Science* (pp. 129–139). London: Routledge.

Diniz, A., Barreiros, J., & Passos, P. (2014). To pass or not to pass: A mathematical model for competitive interactions in Rugby union. *Journal of Motor Behavior, 46*(5), 293–302.

Esteves, P. T., de Oliveira, R. F., & Araújo, D. (2011). Posture-related affordances guide attacks in basketball. *Psychology of Sport and Exercise, 12*(6), 639–644.

Fajen, B. R., Riley, M. A., & Turvey, M. T. (2009). Information, affordances, and the control of action in sport. *International Journal of Sport Psychology, 40*(1), 79–107.

Glazier, P., & Robins, M. (2013). Self-organisation and constraints in sports performance. In T. McGarry, P. O'Donoghue, & J. Sampaio (Eds.), *Routledge Handbook of Sports Performance Analysis* (pp. 42–51). London: Routledge.

Glazier, P. S. (2010). Game, set and match? Substantive issues and future directions in performance analysis. *Sports Medicine, 40*(8), 625–634.

Guilford, J. P. (1956). The structure of intellect. *Psychological Bulletin, 53*(4), 267–293.

Guilford, J. P. (1967). *The Nature of Human Intelligence.* New York: McGraw-Hill.

Handford, C. (2006). Serving up variability and stability. In K. Davids, S. Bennett, & N. K. (Eds.), *Movement System Variability* (pp. 73–83). Champaign, IL: Human Kinetics.

Hristovski, R., Davids, K., Araújo, D., & Passos, P. (2011). Constraints-induced emergence of functional novelty in complex neurobiological systems: A basis for creativity in sport. *Nonlinear Dynamics, Psychology, and Life Sciences, 15*(2), 175–206.

Hristovski R., Davids K., Passos P., Araújo D. (2012). Sport performance as a domain of creative problem solving for self organizing performer-environment systems. Open Sports Sci. J. 5(Suppl. 1–M4), 26–35. 10.2174/1875399X012050 10026

Johnson, J. G., & Raab, M. (2003). Take the first: Option-generation and resulting choices. *Organizational Behavior and Human Decision Processes, 91*(2), 215–229.

Kelso, S. (2009). Coordination dynamics. In R. A. Meyers (Ed.), *Encyclopedia of Complexity and System Science* (pp. 1537–1564). Heidelberg: Springer.

Memmert, D. (2010). Testing of tactical performance in youth elite soccer. *Journal of Sports Science and Medicine, 9*(2), 199–205.

Memmert, D. (2013). Tactical creativity. In T. McGarry, P. O'Donoghue, & J. Sampaio (Eds.), *Routledge Handbook of Sports Performance Analysis* (pp. 297–308). London: Routledge.

Memmert, D., & Furley, P. (2007). 'I spy with my little eye!': Breadth of attention, inattentional blindness, and tactical decision making in team sports. *Journal of Sport and Exercise Psychology, 29*(3), 365–381.

Memmert, D., Huttermann, S., & Orliczek, J. (2013). Decide like Lionel Messi! The impact of regulatory focus on divergent thinking in sports. *Journal of Applied Social Psychology, 43*(10), 2163–2167.

Memmert, D., & Roth, K. (2007). The effects of non-specific and specific concepts on tactical creativity in team ball sports. *Journal of Sports Sciences, 25*(12), 1423–1432.

Palao, J. M., & Morante, J. C. (2013). Technical effectiveness. In T. McGarry, P. O'Donoghue, & J. Sampaio (Eds.), *Routledge Handbook of Sports Performance Analysis* (pp. 213–224). London & New York: Routldege.

Passos, P., Araújo, D., & Davids, K. (2013). Self-organization processes in field-invasion team sports: Implications for leadership. *Sports Medicine, 43*(1), 1–7.

Passos, P., Araújo, D., Davids, K., Gouveia, L., Milho, J., & Serpa, S. (2008). Information-governing dynamics of attacker-defender interactions in youth rugby union. *Journal of Sports Sciences, 26*(13), 1421–1429.

Passos, P., Araújo, D., Davids, K., & Shuttleworth, R. (2008). Manipulating constraints to train decision making in rugby union. *International Journal of Sports Science & Coaching, 3*(1), 125–140.

Passos, P., Cordovil, R., Fernandes, O., & Barreiros, J. (2012). Perceiving affordances in rugby union. *Journal of Sports Science, 30*(11), 1175–1182.

Passos, P., & Davids, K. (2015). Learning design to facilitate interactive behaviours in team sports. *Revista Internacional de Ciencias del Deporte, 11*(39), 18–32.

Passos, P., Milho, J., Fonseca, S., Borges, J., Araújo, D., & Davids, K. (2011). Interpersonal distance regulates functional grouping tendencies of agents in team sports. *Journal of Motor Behavior, 43*(2), 155–163.

Phillips, E., Davids, K., Araújo, D., Renshaw, I., & Portus, M. (2011). Comments on 'expert performance in sport and the dynamics of talent development' reply. *Sports Medicine, 41*(7), 610–611.

Pinder, R. A., Davids, K., Renshaw, I., & Araújo, D. (2011). Representative learning design and functionality of research and practice in sport. *Journal of Sport & Exercise Psychology, 33*(1), 146–155.

Runco, M. A. (2004). Creativity. *Annual Review of Psychology, 55*, 657–687.

Schmidt, R. C., & O'Brien, B. (1997). Evaluating the dynamics of unintended interpersonal coordination. *Ecological Psychology, 9*(3), 189–206.

72

Simonton, D. K. (1999). Creativity as blind variation and selective retention: Is the creative process darwinian? *Psychological Inquiry,10*(4), 309–328.

Stoffregen, T. A., Bardy, B. G., Smart, L. J., & Pagulayan, R. J. (2003). On the nature and evaluation of fidelity in virtual environments. In L. J. Hettinger & M. W. Haas (Eds.), *Virtual and Adaptive Environments: Applications, Implications, and Human Performance Issues* (pp. 111–128). Mahwah, NJ: Lawrence Erlbaum Associates, Inc.

Strogatz, S. (2004). *Sync: The Emerging Science of Spontaneous Order.* London: Penguin Press Science.

Torrance, E. P. (1966). *The Torrance Tests of Creative Thinking-Norms-Technical Manual Research Edition-Verbal Tests, Forms A and B-Figural Tests, Forms A and B.* Princenton: NJ: Personnel Press.

Travassos, B., Duarte, R., Vilar, L., Davids, K., & Araújo, D. (2012). Practice task design in team sports: Representativeness enhanced by increasing opportunities for action. *Journal of Sports Science, 30*(13), 1447–1454.

Warren, W. H. (2006). The dynamics of perception and action. *Psychological Review, 113*(2), 358–389.

CHAPTER 5

TEAM MEMBER INTERACTION ANALYSIS

Leading author: Pedro Passos

INTRODUCTION

This chapter aims to cover the variables used to describe and explain players' interactive behaviour in team sports. The main question for this chapter is: How can team member interactions be measured? For this purpose two different approaches have been used: (i) notational analysis–based approach; (ii) dynamical analysis-based approach.

The first part of the chapter presents a survey of notational analysis research focused on players' interactions in team sports. This part aims to explain to the reader the differences between a notational analysis, based on discrete variables, and dynamical analysis of performance in team sports. The first topic of this part discusses the pros and cons of performance indicators through the prism of internal versus external validity concerns. The second part focuses on the coordination variables that have been used to describe and measure the dynamics of players' interactions – namely, interpersonal distances, angles between players and angles between the ball carrier and the goal, centroids' positions over time, angles between team centroids, the stretch index, team width and length, as well as the use of the relative phase to measure interpersonal coordination. From an applied perspective a brief summary on how to create a coordination/interaction variable is presented.

The third part of chapter is focused on how social networks–based methodologies can be used to enhance knowledge on individual and team performances.

74

PART I – MEASURING INTERACTIONS

Notational analysis-based approach

Notational analysis is the process of labelling and recording previously identified action variables that describe players' behaviour during practice (McGarry et al., 2013). The essence of notational analysis is to capture the frequency of events captured by a set of discrete variables which occur in a specific context (e.g., number of shots to goal; number of turnovers; number of successful passes). Usually these variables describe technical and physical individual actions, but they can also describe tactical actions performed by a set of players. For that purpose the frequency of actions is related to time and space – for instance, the frequency of a counter-attack during the first quarter of a basketball match or the frequency of technical actions according to pitch location, such as the number of passes in the last third of the pitch. Therefore, the general issues to perform a notational analysis are as follows: (i) select the set of action variables; (ii) select the set of players under analysis, which can be done according to players' positions (e.g., attackers; defenders); (iii) select the space, which means to split the performance field into different areas – here you have several options, which go from defence, midfield and attacking areas of play, or sideline (left and right) and midfield corridors; (iv) select the time scale, which can go from a minute-to-minute record to a full match analysis, or even across a set of matches. The importance of the time scale is related to the possibility to perform a longitudinal analysis or a transverse analysis. The advantage of a longitudinal analysis is that by capturing the variability of players' performances it is possible to analyse the fluctuations of the quality of performance over time. The disadvantage is that the approach is more time consuming and usually requires more human resources. However, with a transverse analysis there is a loss of information regarding how the performance runs over time, but there is a gain of objective data regarding absolute and/or relative frequency of the variables selected for an entire match. The advantage is that usually transverse analysis is less time consuming.

Less common variables used in notational analysis systems are those that describe players' interactive behaviour. The next section presents several studies, where notational analysis was grounded in variables that describe players' interactions in team sports.

Measuring the players interactions

As stated in the previous section, notational analysis is usually based on recordings of discrete action, which express players' technical and tactical performance or physiological task demands. Measuring players' interactive behaviour is not the main focus of notational analysis. However, it is possible to find a few examples of notational analysis research that used variables which describe players' interactive behaviour.

In soccer the overall success of the attacking team has been described by three variables related to team strategy and players' positions on the pitch: (i) the relative positions of the attacker and defenders; (ii) the attacker/defenders ratio on each attacking phase; (iii) the interpersonal distance of the defender and ball carrier (Harris & Reilly, 1988).

Aiming to determine the main features that constitute an effective tackle in rugby union, the actions performed by the tackler during match play have been analysed using variables that describe the 'direction' of the tackler regarding the ball carrier position, which clearly expresses players' interactive behaviour. The set of interactive variables include the following: (i) *side-on* if the tackler tackled the ball carrier laterally; (ii) *front-on* when both players face each other; (iii) *behind* when the tackler tackled the ball carrier from behind; (iv) *oblique* when the tackler–ball carrier angle was somewhere between front-on and side-on (van Rooyen et al., 2014).

In order to analyse the effectiveness of the offensive ball carrier in rugby union a set of variables that express (yet with some subjectivity) the ball carrier–tackler interactive behaviour has been suggested by Sayers and Washington-King (2005). The authors set two types of descriptors that characterised the ball carrier's movements: (i) the running patterns; and (ii) the evasive manoeuvres. Both descriptors were defined by the ball carrier's direction regarding the defender's position, which means that in a certain way the ball carrier needs to adapt to defender's position, as the authors stated: 'Subtle shifts in running line result in marked increases in ball carry effectiveness' (Sayers & Washington-King, 2005, p. 101). The ball carrier's running patterns were 'to the defender' (directly towards the defender); 'oblique' (towards the defensive line to a temporarily space between defenders); and 'angled running pattern' (fast around the defence). The evasive manoeuvres descriptors were supported on the 'swerve' (evasion technique started from the inside leg); on the 'forward step' (evasive technique involving stepping motions in a forward motion); and also on the 'lateral step' (predominately performed

76

with sideways stepping motion) (Sayers & Washington-King, 2005). Although it is not mentioned in the study these evasive manoeuvres only gain a 'functional meaning' within specific values of interpersonal distance between the ball carrier and defender (please see Passos et al., 2008). Wheeler and colleagues add some metrics to the analysis of ball carrier–defender interactive behaviour in rugby union. The authors took into account the opponent players' interpersonal distance in the analysis of the ball carrier success (i.e., tackle-break). The ball carrier–defender interpersonal distance was measured using body length as a benchmark. For instance, when the ball carrier received the ball while running at a distance of two body lengths, it was considered that the conditions for a tackle-break were created (Wheeler et al., 2010). In the analysis of the evasive manoeuvres (e.g., side step) the suggestion of Sayers and Washington (2005) was upgraded by introduction of the change in the ball carrier's running direction angle (i.e., between 20° and 60°) when the side step was performed. Moreover, the analysis of the side step (sustained on change of the direction angle) was only taken into account within a 'short' interpersonal distance (i.e., one to two body lengths) between the ball carrier and defender (Wheeler et al., 2010).

Network analysis in team sports

The most recent tool to analyse players' interpersonal behaviour is supported by the number of times an event has happened. In the last years the scientific research regarding the use of social networks to describe the players' interactive behaviour increased considerably (Duch et al., 2010; Fewell et al., 2012; Gama et al., 2014; Grund, 2012; Passos et al., 2011; Yamamoto & Yokoyama, 2011).

Networks can be particularly useful in the low scoring team sports (e.g., soccer, hockey, field hockey), where the players' scoring opportunities could not be considered as a reliable measure of individual performance. The performance of each single player in team sports is always related to the plays of a team and could be measured by the frequency and distribution of passes to the teammates. This analysis allows one to depict the structure of players' interactive behaviour networks and reveal the impact of each player within the team performance (Duch et al., 2010). Thus, the main goal of networks is to capture and depict in a graph the interactive behaviour among subjects (e.g., players) within a group (e.g., team sports) (Duch et al., 2010; Fewell et al., 2012; Grund, 2012). The first step in network analysis is to define the nodes (i.e., vertices) and the edges that link the nodes. From the few studies that applied networks to team sports so far the players were the most common entities used as nodes. Players as nodes were linked with ball movements (i.e., passes between players); these linkages are usually known in the specific literature as edges (or arcs). The edges are weighted accordingly with the frequency of passes successfully performed between two players (Duch et al, 2010; Fewell et al, 2012; Gama et al., 2014; Grund, 2012; Passos et al., 2011). Edges can be outgoing (i.e., passes made by a player) or incoming (i.e., passes received by a player) (Gama et al., 2014; Grund, 2012). The most commonly used edges represent passes between players, but other edges are also available. For instance, Passos and colleagues in a study in water polo used passes between players as edges, but also considered as edges the players positional changes (Passos et al., 2011). A similar approach is suitable for nodes selection. Nodes may represent players (Passos et al., 2011), but also inbounds and outcomes (Fewell, et al., 2012), shots to goal and shots wide (Duch et al., 2010). The number of interactions and the identities of the players involved define the pattern that characterises how players interact within a team. This pattern can be represented in a graph and quantified with the network metrics (Figure 5.1).

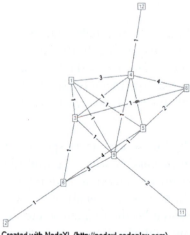
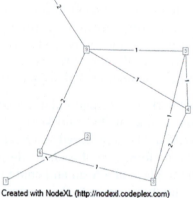

Created with NodeXL (http://nodexl.codeplex.com)

Created with NodeXL (http://nodexl.codeplex.com)

1.a Portugal vs Canada
26-7

1.b Portugal vs South Africa
0-36

Figure 5.1 Network of the Portuguese 7's Rugby National Team on the Dubai 7's 2014. 1.a Portugal vs Canada; final result 26–7; 1.b Portugal vs South Africa; final result 0–36.

78

Capturing this sort of data, researchers quantify features that define a network structure supported on such metrics as degree of centrality, network density and intensity, clustering coefficient and also ball movement rate. Ball movement rate is measured as path length (i.e., absolute frequency of passes between players) and path flow rate (i.e., the frequency of passes per unit of time); both can capture differences in ball movements according to players' physical, technical and tactical skills (Fewell et al., 2012).

These metrics are revealed to be very useful to compare the effect of different team strategies on players' interactive behaviour. For instance, it may be revealed if a strategy affords movement of the ball evenly among team members (i.e., decentralised distribution), or if the higher number of passes is centralised only on a few key players (i.e., centralised distribution), which quantifies relative involvement of each player in team strategy. As a feature that describes players' positional distribution and roles centralisation is defined as 'the degree to which network positions are unequally distributed in a team' (Grund, 2012, p. 684). Previous researches support the hypothesis of a negative relationship between team centralisation and team performance (Duch et al., 2010; Fewell et al., 2012; Grund, 2012). There are a few types of centrality: in a network a player is 'central' when he/she is on the shortest path between two other players, which quantifies a structural property of a network called *betweeness centrality* (Freeman, 1977). Based on this structural property it was possible to measure the utility of an individual player to team success using a metric called *individual flow centrality*, which is calculated by the frequency of passing sequences of all plays that resulted in a shot (i.e., attempt to score), where the player was one of the nodes, normalised with the absolute frequency of plays which finished with an attempt to score (Duch et al., 2010; Fewell et al., 2012).

A feature to measure the level of interaction among players within a team is the *network density*, which is related to the amount of 'strong' linkages among all players in a team. This feature is revealing of an increase of the mutual interdependency among team members due to cooperation and interpersonal coordination (Grund, 2012). Thus, networks are dense due to mobilisation of the network resources, such as the players' availability to create passing lanes, which affords the team to retain ball possession and increase the shooting opportunities. Network density can thus be calculated by the number of edges in a network (e.g., number of passes performed between different players during a match) divided by the number of potential edges available in that match (Grund, 2012). This means that the higher number of passes between different players creates greater network density. High network density increases the odds of a successful performance (Grund, 2012). Another relevant measure for the level of interaction between players is the *network intensity*, which is the passing rate within network nodes (e.g., players). To calculate the network intensity it is necessary to notate the number of passes made by each player (i.e., outgoing passes) and the number of passes received by each player (i.e., ingoing passes), which are normalised by the time that each team has ball possession during a match (for further details please, see Grund, 2012). The network intensity displays a positive relationship with team performance. Another metric used to capture players' interactions within a network, but at a more local level, is the *clustering coefficient*, which describes the relative intra-team connectedness among sets of players (Fewell et al., 2012). Teams with higher connectedness have more situations (e.g., offensive plays) where sets of players link to each other; the clustering coefficient measures the number of groups of players (e.g., groups of three players in basketball or four players in rugby union) in a network as a percentage of all possible groups (Fewell et al., 2012). Therefore, a high coefficient of clustering reveals a high level of team connectedness. Usually the clustering coefficient has a negative relationship with the degree of centrality, but both metrics are relevant features of team strategy (Fewell et al., 2012). The clustering coefficient was a key feature to characterise the differences between the Portuguese 7's Rugby National Team when playing against Canada and also when playing against South Africa in the Dubai 7's 2014. Against Canada, the Portuguese team achieved a clustering coefficient of 0.377 and against South Africa the Portuguese only achieved a clustering coefficient of 0.229. This data revealed that against Canada, the Portuguese player's linked to each other (through passes) instead of making individual decisions, achieving a high level of connectedness, which created appropriate conditions to succeed.

However, as any other methods networks also have limitations. A first limitation is related to the causality issue, which means that it is not possible to conclude if it was team performance that influenced the network structure or if it is the network structure that influenced team performance.

This limitation can be largely eliminated with longitudinal data, which reveals players' interactions over several matches (Grund, 2012).

A second limitation is that the way the data was collected to build the networks (i.e., usually notational data with cross-sectional designs) makes it difficult to relate the occurrences with the outcome (Grund, 2012). It could be possible that at the moment of scoring the winning goal the team is playing its 'worst'. Unfortunately with a cross-sectional analysis it is not possible to capture this relationship. It is also important to connect the network's structure with spatial and temporal models (Fewell et al., 2012).

Another limitation is that in some cases the network structure is not related to the area of the pitch, where the nodes (e.g., players) are located. A suitable example of the importance of relating the network structure to the physical location of the nodes is found in the football study by Gama and colleagues, who identified the areas of the pitch where the key players usually play (Gama et al., 2014). Finally, cross-sectional analysis (based on a single match) has some limitations; future research should collect data over time (i.e., a single variable from several matches of the same team or a single variable from different moments along the match), which allows the dynamic structure of the networks within an event to be revealed (Gama et al., 2014; Grund, 2012). A suitable example is the study of Yamamoto and Yokoyama (2011) in football; they applied a networks approach at every five minutes of the match. This sort of analysis allows different structures of intra-team interactive behaviour to be identified.

In summary, the notational analysis is based on the record of the frequency of relevant and very useful individual (i.e., technical or tactical skills) and collective (i.e., positional) actions which lead to individual success. However, the relevance of this notational approach for team success is questionable. Often whithin the same skill level (e.g., when teams under analysis play in the same league or championship) teams display a similar frequency of individual and collective actions. Thus, it is not only the number of occurences that defines a team's success, but rather how a team 'used' those occurences (Sayers & Washington-King, 2005). The term 'used' is higly relevant here because it is related to the 'time' and 'space' where the occurences happen; a notational analysis has some problems in addressing this issue. A dynamic systems–based approach seems to be more suitable to fill this 'time and space' gap.

Dynamic systems–based approach

A dynamic analysis in team sports implies that performance data expresses the players' behaviour over time. One significant issue for this dynamic analysis is the temporal scale of analysis because different things are highly related with the temporal scale of analysis that we are using. If we choose to analyse a phenomenon with a very short time scale – for instance, players' behaviour at 25 images per second (i.e., 25 Hz) – the level of detail and consequently the type of information that is captured is quite different from choosing to analyse the same players over a longer time scale – for example, from match to match over a season. Time scales define the level of analysis.

Previous studies on individual sports, such as badminton, squash or tennis (McGarry et al., 1999; Palut & Zanone, 2005), provide suitable methods that were later used to analyse and describe subjects' inter-actions with teammates or opposing players in team sports. Based on players' positions over time, previous research on squash used relative phase analysis to describe interpersonal coordination patterns between opposing players during squash rallies (McGarry et al., 1999). There-fore, when applying these concepts to team sports the main issue for the dynamic systems approach (DST) is to create or identify coordinative variables, which describe players' interactive behaviour. By definition coordinative variables are 'relational quantities that are created by the cooperation among the individual parts of a system. Yet they, in turn, govern the behaviour of the individual parts' (Kelso, 2009). There are two main features of team sports which should be considered for per-formance analysis – cooperation (among players of the same team) and competition (among opponents) – which set two levels of interactive behaviour among players: the intra-team level and the inter-team level. Part II of this chapter presents several suggestions of coordinative vari-ables for intra-team and inter-team levels of analysis.

PART II – MEASURING THE DYNAMICS OF PLAYERS' INTERACTIVE BEHAVIOUR

For the purpose of describing players' interactive behaviour several vari-ables were created, but one starting point was common to all of them: they are all based on players' positions (x, y) over time. The methods which are used to capture players' positions vary from GPS to video-grammetry, and both have frequencies of data collection.

Centroids

By definition 'a team centroid is a geometrical configuration that represents the mean position of a group of points' (Frencken et al., 2012, p. 1209). Centroids can be used as a collective variable to describe the interactive behaviour of a set of players (Frencken et al., 2011; Frencken et al., 2012; Folgado et al., 2014; Sampaio & Macas, 2012; Silva et al., 2014; Travassos et al., 2014). The advantage of this variable is that it reduces data overflow, concentrating the necessary information on a single value. For instance, when the aim is to analyse the running path of a set of players, instead of analysing each individual player path, it is more simple to use a measure like a centroid, which concentrates the most relevant information regarding the collective behaviour of that set of players (Figure 5.2).

Thus, as an intra-team collective variable, a centroid is useful to simplify the analysis of sets of players (i.e., from groups to small-sided, to full-sized teams). However, as any other variable, centroids also has some limitations. If players of a team diverge or converge to the same extent,

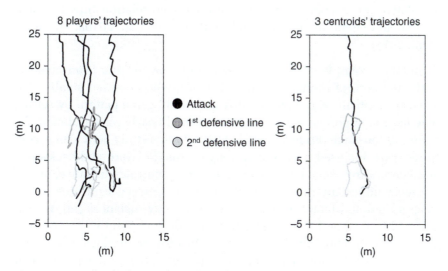

Figure 5.2 Individual running path and corresponding centroids.

the position of the centroid remains exactly the same. For instance, if the players on opposite sides run in opposite directions at an identical speed, the centroid position does not change. Also if one of the players of the set exhibits random behaviour (e.g., stay still due to fatigue or injury; or delay to support the teammates), this will affect the centroid position.

Besides intra-team centroids, which can describe the interactive behaviour of players of the same team – analysing, for instance, the centroid distance to the goal (Silva et al., 2015) – centroids have also been used for inter-team analysis. In sports sciences literature there can be found a few examples of research which used centroids to concentrate the most relevant information regarding the behaviour of a set of players who belong to the same group on a single (collective) variable.

After calculating the centroid the next step for an inter-team analysis is to apply tools which are related to centroid displacements. Some studies conducted in football used for --this purpose the Pearson correlation (Frencken et al., 2011), cross-correlation analysis (Frencken et al 2012) and running correlations (Frencken et al., 2013). Kinematic variables, such as the centroid's distance to a goal or the distances between centroids, have also been used to relate opponent (e.g., attacker–defender) centroid displacements (Frencken et al., 2011). Studies in basketball and futsal (five-a-side indoor football) used other collective variables, such as relative phase analysis, to capture inter-team relationships in longitudinal and lateral displacements (Bourbousson et al., 2010a; Travassos et al., 2014).

A suitable example of the use of centroids for an inter-team analysis is the research of Frencken and colleagues, who analysed small-sided games in football, aiming to identify an overall game pattern by setting whether the opponent team's centroids were linearly related during the course of the game (Frencken et al., 2011). In this study both teams' centroids were analysed over time in longitudinal (forward and backward) and lateral directions. Besides the inter-team centroids distance, one of the most important variables is the relation between centroids in the longitudinal and lateral directions (measured by distances [m] of each centroid to the goal). The Frencken and colleagues' study (Frencken et al., 2011) highlighted the importance of the forward–backward (i.e., longitudinal) oscillations. This variable displayed that in 53 per cent of attacking situations prior to a goal the attacking centroid overtook the

84

defending centroid (i.e., the attacking centroid gets closer to the goal). These results reveal the predictive character of the relationship among collective variables, which means that every time the centroid of the attacking team overtakes the centroid of the defending team (at least in small-sided games), the probability to score increases. However, goal scoring is highly dependent on players' technical skills. In order to avoid a bias because of individual skills we suggest analysing inter-team centroid positions prior to attempts to score. The results of this first study created the background for a second study, which analysed the variability (instability) of both teams before such critical match events as goal attempts (Frencken et al., 2012).

How are centroids calculated? Centroids can be calculated as the average position (x, y) of N outfield players (x_n, y_n) of one team (Frencken et al., 2011). In other words centroids can be calculated from the mean distance of the group members to the spatial centre (Bourbousson et al., 2010). As we usually work in a Cartesian space, the first step is to define the origin, which can be the centre of the pitch or one of the corners (e.g., the lower left corner). Then from the centroid position of both teams it is possible to extract three measures; these are added to characterise the dynamics of the flow of movement of a set of players. Changes in the x-axis represent forward–backward displacement, which is usually displayed as a centroid distance (m) to the origin, whereas changes in the y-axis represent lateral displacement (also displayed as a centroid distance [m] to the origin). It is also possible to calculate radial distance (m), comprising both forward–backward and lateral displacements (Frencken et al., 2011).

Interpersonal angles

Another suitable variable to describe players' relative positions is the interpersonal angle. This variable was used in a research conducted in rugby union; it aimed to describe the behavioural dynamics of attacker–defender dyads (Passos et al., 2009). This angle was calculated with a vector from the defender to the ball carrier with an imaginary horizontal line parallel to the score line. This means that when the ball carrier is running in a straight line with the defender, the angle assumes a value close to 90°, but with the decreasing of the attacker–defender interpersonal distance the ball carrier performs evasive manoeuvres to avoid being tackled. These will provoke fluctuations on the interpersonal angle values, which indicates that the dyad is entering a critical region, where one of two things might happen: the defender tackles the ball carrier or the ball carrier avoids the tackle and runs free towards the goal line. The interpersonal angle as a collective variable was successfully applied on 1v1 dyads in rugby union, basketball and also in football (Passos et al., 2013) (Figure 5.3).

The grey dashed line (Figure 5.3) indicates where the ball carrier overtakes the defender, and the negative interpersonal angle value means that the ball carrier is now the player closer to the goal (Passos et al., 2009; Passos et al., 2013).

Opponent players' angular relations were extended to studies in other team sports. Team sports has different task constraints to be considered – for instance whereas in rugby union the area to score is the width of the field (i.e., the try area), in basketball the goal (i.e., basket) is in the middle of the bottom line of the pitch; as a consequence any behavioural analysis which involves players' positions and displacements should

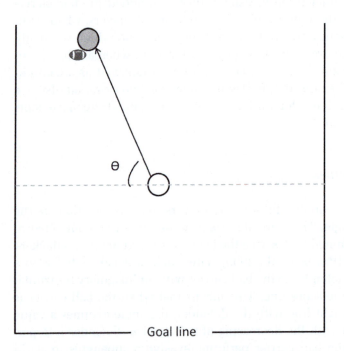

Figure 5.3 Interpersonal angle as a collective variable.

consider the location of the goal. Previous research in basketball also used the interpersonal angle to describe the attacker–defender dyadic behaviour in nine different areas of the field using the basket location as a reference (Esteves et al., 2015). Esteves and colleagues hypothesised that attacker–defender relative positions captured by the interpersonal angle allowed for the description of how the ball carrier dribbled past the defender (Esteves et al., 2015). Thus, the angle between the ball carrier and defender as related to the basket requires four steps: (i) the first step is to calculate a vector orthogonal to the side lines; (ii) then a vector orthogonal to the end line should be computed; (iii) the third step is to calculate a vector from the defender to the attacker; (iv) finally, the attacker–defender–basket (ADB) angle is computed using the defender–attacker vector with the vector orthogonal to the side lines (Figure 5.4).

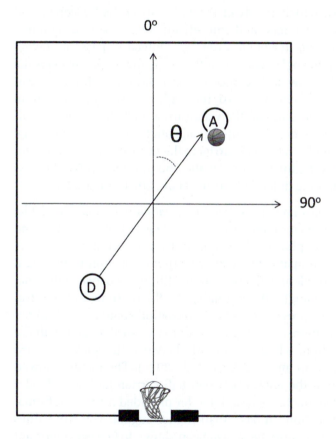

Figure 5.4 The attacker–defender–basket (ADB) angle.

For that purpose a rotation of -90° clockwise was required (for further details, please see Esteves et al., 2015).

Esteves and colleagues also suggested the need to explore other variables, such as angular velocity and angular variability, to describe and explain ball carrier advantages. Results revealed the existence of more functional areas (e.g., the centre of the court; the left side of the dyad) explored by the ball carrier to avoid the defender and shoot to the basket. Additionally, successful trials revealed higher values of angular velocity and lower values of angular variability (Esteves et al., 2015).

Other research that used interpersonal angles as a collective variable was the study by Correa and colleagues (Correa et al., 2014) in futsal. Aiming to describe the coordination tendencies which afford a pass to the ball receiver, Correa and colleagues calculated two types of angles: intra-dyads angles, which involved the ball carrier, ball receiver and respective nearest defenders, and inter-dyads angles, which included other attacker–defender dyads not directly involved in pass and reception. The intra-dyads angles were as follows: (i) the angle between the vector from a ball carrier to ball receiver and the vector from the ball carrier to the nearest defender; and (ii) the angle between the vector from a ball carrier to ball receiver and the vector from the ball carrier to a ball receiver's nearest defender. The inter-dyads angles were the following: (i) between the vector from the ball carrier to the nearest marking defender and the vector from the furthest teammate who did not receive the pass and the nearest marking defender (Correa et al., 2014) (Figure 5.5).

The intra-dyads angles have been used to create a compound variable, which provided information about which angle acted as a constraint on the pass direction. As players' decisions and actions in team sports are not only influenced by spatial but also by temporal constraints, the angular velocity was also calculated based on the difference between the final angle and the initial angle. Additionally the fluctuations in the intra-dyads angles can also provide suitable information about the stability of players' relative positions. The angle variability was calculated with the coefficient of variation, which is the ratio between the angle standard deviation and the mean angle (Correa et al., 2014). The results showed that the dynamics of the angles between ball carrier–nearest defender and ball carrier's teammate–closest defender provided relevant information for passing direction. In basketball higher angular velocity values and lower angular variability have also been shown to be very important for the attacker to succeed (Correa et al., 2014; Esteves et al., 2015).

88

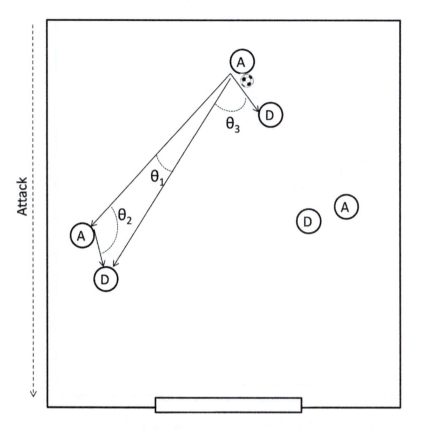

Figure 5.5 Inter-dyads angles.

The dynamics of opponent players' relative positions has been demonstrated to constrain scoring opportunities in futsal. These dynamics create spatio-temporal gaps between attacker and marking defender, which afford the attacker the opportunity to score. Vilar and colleagues analysed the displacement trajectories of the attacker and marking defender during 10 futsal matches. It was hypothesised that the players' relative positions before the attacker receives the ball is an essential constraint, and it drives the attacker–defender dyad to one of three different outcomes: (i) play ends in a goal, (ii) goalkeeper keeps the ball from scoring or (iii) defender intercepts the ball. To describe players' relative positions related to goal location the interpersonal angle was calculated as that between the defender vector to the centre of the goal and the defender vector to the attacker (Vilar et al., 2012) (Figure 5.6).

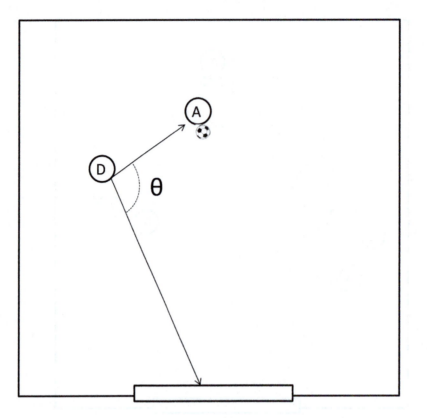

Figure 5.6 Attacker–defender angle related to the goal.

Results revealed that an attacker–defender misalignment related to the goal is paramount to create opportunities to score. The angle between attacker and defender and centre of the goal can capture this misalignment. If the angle was too wide, this afforded a goalkeeper to save, and if it was too narrow it afforded a shot to the goal. This attacker–defender misalignment (particularly for narrow angles) was revealed to be crucial if it was achieved before the attacker received the ball (Vilar et al., 2012).

In sum, interpersonal angles describe players' relative positions, which were used in previous analysis of team sports to characterise key issues for success, as passing or shooting opportunities. The dynamics of interpersonal angles (calculated from time series data) provide useful information regarding players' interactive behaviour. For instance, fluctuations in the angle values identify critical regions of interpersonal distance between attacker and defenders. Additionally the temporal component,

90

which is usually expressed with angular velocity and angular variability, allows the quantification of when the interactive behaviour between two or more players affords an opportunity to score, to pass or to overtake a defender.

Interpersonal distances

Interpersonal distances provide information regarding the space that is available between players. These variables are used in intra-team or inter-team analysis.

In team sports some collective behaviours (e.g., attacking phases in rugby union) require from players interactive behaviour, which is constrained by a set of rules. For instance, it is necessary to keep an interpersonal distance from teammates (e.g., attackers come close to create 'functional' interpersonal distances, but not closer that there are collisions), and to run at the same pace and in a similar direction (e.g., to support the ball carrier some variability in the speed and running line directions are crucial).

This adjustable behaviour among players allows for the formation of a sub-unit with a specific collective structure, which allows facing the opponents. However, because of the proximity of the opponents, the stability of this collective structure is disturbed and players should adjust positions to maintain functional collective behaviour. Research on rugby union aimed to describe how a set of players within an attacking sub-unit (forming a diamond-shapes structure) adjusted relative positions with the decreasing of interpersonal distances to defenders (Passos et al., 2011). To describe the players' interactive behaviour the players' interpersonal distances were calculated based on each player's displacement trajectories and with a vector from each player to another within the attacking sub-unit. A MatLab routine has been created for that purpose. After that the mean of the interpersonal distances between the four attackers were calculated and plotted for two different task constraints: (i) before the first defensive line; and (ii) between the first and second defensive lines. Results displayed an increase in the mean of interpersonal distances between the players of the attacking sub-unit after overtaking the first defensive line. This means that players' interpersonal distances are sensitive to such task constraints as the proximity to the opponent players (Passos et al., 2011). Despite the relevance of interpersonal distances, other studies used different distances to describe players' interactive behaviours (Headrick et al., 2012; Passos et al., 2012). Headrick and colleagues demonstrated how other distances such as the players' distances to the ball in football were also sensitive to such task constraints as the proximity to the goal (Headrick et al., 2012). Passos et al. (2012) displayed how the ball carrier's decisions and actions in rugby union were influenced by the defenders' distance to the sideline (Passos et al., 2012).

The study conducted by Headrick and colleagues on football aimed to analyse if the attacker's distance to the ball and the defender's distance to the ball were influenced by the location of the pitch, where the 1v1 occurred. For that purpose an experimental design with three different performance locations was created. From the defender perspective the scenarios were as follows: (i) close to one's own goal; (ii) the midfield; and (iii) close to the opposing goal. It was hypothesised that due to the proximity to the goal the defenders could manage their interactions with the ball differently. Based on players' displacement trajectories during 1v1 situations the attacker-to-ball distances and the defender-to-ball distances were calculated based on a vector from each player to the ball using a MatLab routine created for that purpose. Results displayed significant differences in defenders' distances to the ball as regarded pitch location. Being close to one's own goal the defender maintained more space between him and the ball then when he was close to the opposing goal. In the latter case the defender rapidly decreased the distance to the ball; probably close to one's own goal the major concern was to close the ball carrier's shooting and passing lines (Headrick et al., 2012).

In a study that used a 2v1 situation in rugby union the ball carrier distance to the closest sideline and the tackler distance to the same sideline were used to capture both players' relative positions; this information provides insight regarding ball carrier decisions and actions (Passos et al., 2012). Players' distances to the sidelines were only considered when players were within 2m of each other, which authors assumed as a critical region because it was only within that distance that a ball carrier's decision to pass to the support player occurred, or to perform a deceptive action and go forward to the goal line. The data were as usual supported by players' trajectories (x, y), but contrary to the previous studies the players' distances to the sidelines were measured using the values of each player on the x-axis. Additionally, the players' distances to the sidelines were measured not only in absolute values at the moment of the

92

pass or when players went forward, but also it was analysed how these distances changed over time until those moments. Results revealed that the ball carrier tended to perform a pass when the tackler was farthest from the sideline. The moment when the ball carrier decided not to pass the ball but to go forward towards the goal line was influenced by the fluctuations in the tackler's relative position, which was captured by the rate of change of the tackler's distance from the sideline. This rate of change was calculated with the first derivative of the tackler's position in each frame (Passos et al., 2012).

There are two studies in futsal which are worth noting. The first aims to analyse how pitch dimensions might influence ball carrier opportunities to pass the ball, shoot for a goal or keep ball possession in small-sided games in football (Vilar et al., 2014). The second study aims to analyse how the numerical advantage may influence attacker–defender interactions (Vilar et al., 2014). In both studies the players' interpersonal distance and the defender's relative distance to intercept a pass or a shot were used as dependent variables. To define the attacker's role at each moment, every attacker's distance to the ball was calculated. Then interpersonal distances between attackers and defenders were computed assuming that the lower attacker–defender interpersonal distances increased the difficulties for the ball carrier to keep ball possession. Finally, aiming to identify ball carrier shooting and passing opportunities, the distance from each defender to the point of ball interception was calculated. To determine the relative distance to intercept a shot computing the following variables is required: (i) a vector from the ball carrier to the centre of the goal (which represents an imaginary shooting line); (ii) the *shooting interception point*, by calculating a vector, which quantifies the shortest distance between the defender and the imaginary line between the ball carrier and the centre of the goal; (iii) the ball carrier distance to the shooting interception point; and (iv) the ratio between the shortest defender distance to the interception point and the ball carrier distance to the interception point (Figure 5.7) (for further details, please see Vilar et al., 2014).

The *passing interception point* has similar procedures, but the reference to calculate the interception point in this case was not the goal but any of the other attackers.

Several studies used the methods presented in this chapter. To collect data the players' performance was video recorded using one or two video

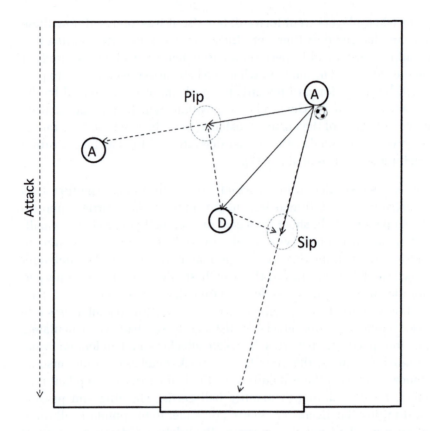

Figure 5.7 Pip – passing interception point; Sip – shooting interception point (adapted from Vilar et al., 2014).

cameras. The cameras were fixed on tripods and placed up high so that all players could be seen at all times. After storing the files on a personal computer the images were digitised using the software TACTO 8.0 at a frequency of 25 Hz (Fernandes & Malta, 2007). There are other softwares for digitising which are freeware – for instance, Kinovea (www.kinovea. org). To track the players' trajectories a point at ground level and located between the feet of each player was used; this allowed the researches to capture the coordinates of players or ball displacements in a bidimensional plane (*x* and *y*) over time. After that there was the need to convert the *x* and *y* 'virtual coordinates' (which are in pixels) into 'real world' coordinates (e.g., meters). For that purpose a minimum of four calibration points were needed, and to convert the coordinates Direct Linear

Transformations was used (Abdel-Aziz & Karara, 1971); that was applied with a routine that runs on MATLAB® software.

Regarding data analysis, two methods were used by the researchers to calculate all distances. The first was computing a vector from point *a* to point *b*. These points can represent players (e.g., attackers, defenders), the ball, the mid-point of the goal or a point on the closest sideline (Passos et al., 2009, 2011, 2012). A second method to calculate the dyadic interpersonal distances was the Pythagorean Theorem, with *x* and *y* coordinates of each player of the dyad (Correa et al., 2014; Travassos et al., 2012).

The studies presented so far only focus on the spatial component of Euclidian distances. However, a temporal component should be added to this analysis. Interactive behaviours change in space and time and thus a spatial-temporal analysis may provide relevant insights which help to better describe players' interactive behaviours. Sustained on Euclidian distances it was possible to calculate velocities. For instance, a study by Travassos and colleagues goes beyond the spatial component provided by the Euclidian distances. Aiming to calculate ball carrier shooting and passing opportunities the velocity of each defender was calculated at each frame by the rate of change of the distance between a current position and the nearest point of the ball's projection trajectory (Travassos et al., 2012). The dynamics of such kinematic variables as interpersonal distances, distances to the ball or to the goal, or distances to the sidelines provided suitable information which support players' decisions and actions over the course of a match.

Team length, team width and the lpwratio

Other variables used to analyse collective tactical behaviour are team length, team width and the ratio that can be calculated with these variables – that is, the length per width ratio, or *lpwratio*. The team length represents the maximum length of a team, and is calculated as the difference between the maximum and minimum positions of players in the field's longitudinal dimension (i.e., *x*-axis) in each time frame (Figure 5.8). The team width represents the maximum width of a team, and is calculate as the difference between the maximum and minimum positions of players in the field's lateral dimension (i.e., *y*-axis) in each time frame (Duarte et al., 2013; Frencken et al., 2011; Folgado et al., 2014).

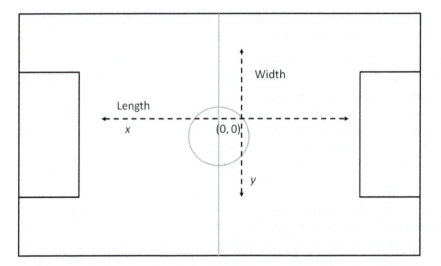

Figure 5.8 Team length and width (adapted from Frencken et al., 2011).

From these team length and team width values, the *lpwratio* was calculated for each time frame. The creation of a ratio was grounded in the idea that performance indicators (i.e., variables which characterise a player's level of performance), expressed as nondimensional ratios, are independent of any unit which may constitute an advantage of being tacitly independent of any variable (Hughes & Bartlett, 2002). The *lpwratio* is calculated as the relationship between team length and team width at any given moment. As a reference, if the *lpwratio* achieved a value of 1, this means that the team has exactly the same length and width.

Lpwratio = team length/team width

Previous research with youngsters (Folgado et al., 2014) and elite football players (Duarte et al., 2013) highlighted the relevance of using these collective variables (i.e., *team width, team length, lpwratio*). The study by Folgado and colleagues (2014) aimed to identify how tactical collective behaviour varied with age, analysing U9, U11 and U13 teams in small-sided football games. For the analysis of intra-team behaviours the authors adopted the *lpwratio*. Results reveal that *lpwratio* values were influenced by the age of the players. Younger teams tended to present higher values of *lpwratio* in their dispersion on the pitch. The older players displayed less variability of the *lpwratio*, which suggests higher

96

consistency in a team's behaviour, as it stretches and compresses accordingly with the different moments of game (Folgado et al., 2014).

The study with elite football players aimed to analyse whether changes in the patterns of collective behaviours of football teams could be related to key events such as goals scored, proximity to half-time break and the end of the game (Duarte et al., 2013). The team length and team width were analysed across six periods of 15 minutes during a match. Results revealed changes in team length and width values across the six periods, which suggest changes in the team collective behaviours accordingly with the period of the match. When these collective variables were related to goals scored, results display larger values of team length and width by the home team after scoring two goals (Duarte et al., 2013). These results suggest that team length and team width as collective variables, which describe the players' interactive behaviours, are sensitive (i.e., change accordingly) to task constraints, such as the game period and current goal difference.

Surface areas

The surface area in team sports describes the coordinated flow of attacking and defending phases during games at an intra-team level. To calculate this collective variable (i.e., surface area of the teams) three measures are needed: (i) team length (m); (ii) team width (m); and (iii) surface area (m2). Length and width variables were described in the previous section. The surface area (Figure 5.9) was defined as the space covered by a team, denoted as the area within the convex hull. The convex hull can be computed using a modified Graham algorithm (Graham, 1972). For that purpose a pivot point needs to be determined; this is usually the player with the lowest *y*-value. The next stage is to calculate the angle from the pivot point to each player within the performance field. This angle is used to sort players, and those who are not part of the convex hull should be removed. After that an arbitrary point within the convex hull (e.g., the centroid) is used to form a triangle with the pivot point and one of the remaining players. Then the surface area is calculated by adding the triangles of consecutive points of the convex hull and the centroid (for further details, please see Frencken et al., 2011).

Aiming to identify team collective patterns in the buildup of goals Frencken and colleagues analysed changes in the surface areas of two

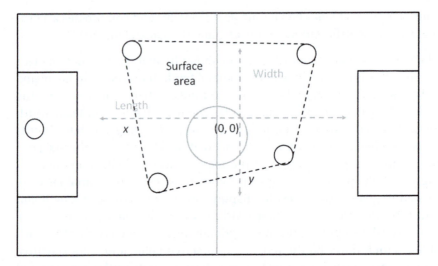

Figure 5.9 The team surface area. The white circles represent players of the same team (adapted from Frencken et al., 2011).

football teams during small-sided games (Frencken et al., 2011). Results revealed very low values of correlation between the surface areas of both teams under analysis and no specific patterns of the surface areas were identified prior to when a goal was scored. As with other variables the use and interpretation of surface areas requires same caution. The influence of each individual player to the surface area of his/her own team is large, especially if the teams under analysis have few players (e.g., basketball or small-sided games in football or rugby union); the consequence is that if one player makes a movement such as running in a random direction, this action immediately affects the surface area.

Voronoi diagrams

In the team sports context, spatial pattern analysis is associated with patterns of players' interacting behaviour. Recent works have tested Voronoi diagrams to analyse spatial patterns of collective behaviour that emerge during team sports matches (Fonseca et al., 2012; Fonseca et al., 2013).

The Voronoi diagram is a 2D spatial tessellation (i.e., decomposition) of a geometrical space (e.g., a team sports playing field). The play area is

98

divided by Voronoi cells, which define the dominant area of each player (Fujimura & Sugihara, 2005; Taki et al., 1996). Due to continuous adjustments of players' relative positions, each individual area (i.e., each Voronoi cell) changes continuously during a competitive team sports match; as a consequence there are continuous changes in the global spatial configurations of the play area.

To compute a Voronoi diagram first it needs a set of n points (e.g., players of a volleyball or basketball team) distributed in a plane (i.e., the performance field area, such as a volleyball court). After that a spatial construction divides the play area into n cells, where each cell must be associated only to one individual player; as a result each cell corresponds to the individual area of each player. The play area is mapped with a grid of width x height positions. The grid points that are closer to each player define the boundaries of his/her respective individual area. Each individual area can be used to describe how the size of the Voronoi cells changes over time for each team and/or for each player. To analyse the players' interactive behaviour the variability of the Voronoi cell sizes can be related to specific phases of the match (e.g., attack or defence) (Fonseca et al., 2012; Fonseca et al., 2013).

For an inter-team analysis Fonseca and colleagues suggest the *superimposition* of two Voronoi diagrams to provide a spatial analysis of individual and collective interaction behaviour (Fonseca et al., 2013). Beyond a qualitative analysis based on the visual inspection of the superimposed diagrams, from where it is possible to infer the similarity between the spatial distributions of two opponent teams, it is also possible to quantify the level of spatial similarity. For that purpose Fonseca and colleagues defined two variables: (i) the first is the Maximum percentage of Overlapped Area (Max%OA), which measures the degree of interpersonal coordination at the player level; and (ii) the second is the percentage of Free Area (%FA), which quantifies the interpersonal coordination at an inter-team level (Fonseca et al., 2012; Fonseca et al., 2013).

The Max%OA represents the maximum percentage of a Voronoi cell of each player that is covered by the cell of an opponent player or players. The smaller percentage of the Voronoi cell means the greater number of opponent players in his/her area. The %FA measures the degree of similarity between two overlapped Voronoi diagrams; it is calculated by extracting from the plane area the sum of the Max%OA of one of the teams. The %FA is inversely proportional to the degree of similarity between the spatial configurations of both teams and therefore can be used to analyse and characterise the interactive behaviour of two opposing teams (Fonseca et al., 2012; Fonseca et al., 2013).

Measuring synchronisation

Relative phase – *the dynamics of a rally or a trial*

Relative phase was initially used to measure synchronisation between two oscillating fingers, hands or legs as components of a dynamic system (Haken et al., 1985; Schmidt et al., 1990; Schmidt & O'Brien, 1997). The rationale to apply this tool to interpersonal coordination was as follows: when two components of a system are coupled not physically but informationally (e.g., visually), they can display similar patterns of synchronised behaviour, which could be captured by relative phase analysis (Kelso, 1995; Schmidt et al., 1999).

In the last decades relative phase analysis has been extended to research on interpersonal coordination in social systems and particularly in sports. Considering that most of the sports competitive situations tend to exhibit forward–backward and left–right *oscillating* movements on the field, McGarry and colleagues (2002) suggested that game dynamics is sustained in the coupling of players of the same team (i.e., intra-team interactions) and of players of opposite teams (i.e., inter-team interactions). Supported on this rationale they proposed that patterns of interpersonal coordination between players or teams could be captured using relative phase analysis (McGarry et al., 2002).

What is relative phase analysis?

Relative phase is a collective variable which captures the spatiotemporal relations between two oscillating agents by considering their amplitudes and frequencies (Haken et al., 1985; Oullier & Kelso, 2009). An oscillating agent can be considered as a player's cyclical behaviour that occurs in space and time, such as single player's backward and forward movements (Rosenblum et al., 2002). Two oscillating agents can be considered as coupled oscillators, with at least two different modes of interpersonal coordination. Imagine two players side by side on a pitch, when both are moving forward and backward at the same time; if there was no delay

100

in the synchronisation of the players, a 0° of relative phase angle (i.e., an in-phase mode of interpersonal coordination) may be observed. On the contrary, if one of the players is moving backwards while the other is moving forward exactly at the same time, the relative phase angle values display a delay of 180° (i.e., an anti-phase mode of interpersonal coordination). Therefore, in-phase and anti-phase are the two absolute modes of interpersonal coordination. Nevertheless interpersonal coordination usually is not supported by absolute modes of synchronisation, thus intermediate values of relative phase should also be considered; for instance -60° of relative phase indicates that the second player is leading the relationship by being one-sixth of a cycle ahead of the other player (Passos et al., 2013).

Advantages and limitations of relative phase analysis

One advantage of using relative phase to capture players' interactive behaviours in comparison with other linear measures (e.g., running correlations) is that relative phase measures the amplitude and the frequency of two signals (e.g., two players' trajectories) to calculate the phase relation, whilst linear measures just consider the frequency of the signals (Passos et al., 2013). By amplitude we mean the total range of values (e.g., distance) achieved, for instance, when two players are moving to the left and to the right on a performance field. Put simply, how far one player goes to the left and to the right is related to the other (e.g., teammate) and is what defines the amplitude of the oscillating movements between them. The frequency is related to the number of times that players change direction (e.g., between left and right) per unit of time. Thus, amplitude is related to space and frequency in time. Disregarding the amplitude of oscillation means not considering the space component of player's interactive behaviour, which may mask the dynamic coupling of players (Rosenblum et al., 2002).

A second advantage is related to the ability of relative phase to describe how the interaction among players influences the emergence of patterns of stability and also to characterise the variability among players' interactive behaviour. For instance, when a ball carrier and the marked defender move backward and forward in a synchronised movement this behaviour causes no changes on the relative phase values; when the ball carrier and the marked defender are no longer moving backward and forward in a synchronised fashion, with considerable changes on the relative phase values, it means that one of the players is gaining an advantage over the opponent and the ball carrier–defender system is poised for a transition (Vilar et al., 2012).

Identifying the stability and the variability patterns, which occur prior to transitions of the attacker–defender system, is a relevant issue that sport scientists and coaches need to pursue and understand in analyses of team sports performances (Araújo et al., 2006; Davids et al., 1994).

Relative phase analysis is based on the assumption that two oscillating components (e.g., fingers, legs, players) display a one-to-one frequency (i.e., isofrequency) ratio and exhibit a sinusoidal signal. A violation of these assumptions might be a limitation when aiming to use relative phase analysis to describe modes of coordination between system components. In other words, if the time series signal displays strong lack of harmony (i.e., not sinusoidal) and differences or a wide range of frequency components of the movement signals, these violations preclude reliable use of a coordinative measure, such as relative phase (Davids et al., 2006; Hamill et al., 2000).

Aiming to analyse inter-team dyadic couplings of players in basketball Bourbousson and colleagues (2010) used relative phase analysis to describe the different modes of coordination between all possible attacking–defending dyads. Results revealed a strong in-phase attraction in the longitudinal (basket-to-basket) displacements. In futsal Travassos and colleagues (2011) used relative phase to examine not only intra-team and inter-team players' interactions, but also the interaction that each player developed with ball trajectory. Results revealed a stronger in-phase attraction between players and ball than only between players. Moreover, a lag of 30° in the relative phase angle means that the ball led the spatiotemporal relationship with players (by 1/12 of a cycle), suggesting that players adjusted their positions just after the movement of the ball. From the Travassos and colleagues study it was possible to conclude that ball movement is an important task constraint on players' behaviour, and it needs to be further considered in performance analysis of team sports (Travassos et al., 2011).

However, for the analysis of intra-team and inter-team interactions other task constraints should also be considered. The different phases of the games, attack or defence, require different modes of coordination between players (Travassos et al., 2011). Task constraints that characterise different team sports also lead to different results. For example,

102

in futsal the stronger in-phase mode of coordination was achieved for the players' lateral displacements (sideline to sideline) (Travassos et al., 2011), whereas for basketball the stronger in-phase mode of coordination was observed in the players' longitudinal displacement (basket to basket) (Bourbousson et al., 2010).

Aiming to analyse interpersonal coordination between teams, Travassos and colleagues and Bourbousson and colleagues measured the phase relationships between the geometrical centres of each team in association with its location on the field of play with reference to goal position (Bourbousson et al., 2010b; Travassos, et al., 2014). Additionally Travassos and colleagues measured the variations in the angle between the geometrical centre of each team and the goal position, which allowed them to observe higher tendencies to specific modes of coordination as opposed to using only lateral and longitudinal displacements. These findings highlight the importance of considering in performance analysis the goal location as the relevant task constraint.

Running correlations

To describe the intra- and inter-team interpersonal coordination tendencies in team sports several studies used the running correlations. Running correlations is a statistical technique which captures continuous changes in coordination between system components over time (Corbetta & Thelen, 1996). Passos and colleagues used this technique to measure the 'strength' of coupling among players within an attacking sub-unit in rugby union (Passos et al., 2011). The variable used to run the running correlations was the distance of each attacker to the goal line (e.g., Attacker *A* Distance to try line correlated with Attacker *B* Distance to try line) for each entire trial using a 10 frames moving window size. A continuous correlation function that described ongoing interpersonal coordination tendencies of each possible dyad over time was obtained (Passos et al., 2011). Correlation values close to 1 indicated high levels of interpersonal coordination. Following the same procedures and aiming to analyse how interpersonal coordination tendencies may prevent the opponent from succeeding, another study conducted in rugby union also used running correlations to measure the interpersonal coordination tendencies within the defensive line and within attacking sub-units (i.e., ball carrier and the support player) (Rodrigues & Passos, 2013). Results revealed that when one team (e.g., attacking or defending) obtained higher correlation values and the opponent team lower correlation values the former succeeded (Rodrigues & Passos, 2013). Frencken and colleagues used running correlations with a three frames moving window size to measure the centroid longitudinal and lateral displacements of both teams in football. Results showed that opposing team centroids were more strongly correlated in the longitudinal plan of motion then in lateral plane (Frencken et al., 2013).

Correia and colleagues used running correlations to describe interpersonal coordination tendencies within attacker–defender dyads in rugby union. The variable used to run the running correlations was each player's distance to the closest sideline over time. Low attacker–defender correlation values may indicate that one player is running towards the sideline, whereas the other was momentarily running in the opposite direction. It means that a gap was opening and created an opportunity for the attacker to run towards the goal line (Correia et al., 2014).

CONCLUSIONS AND SUGGESTIONS

This chapter highlights the most recent tendencies, which pose further challenges for performance analysis in team sports in a near future. In sum, the most relevant information that drives a set of players to coordinate with each other are grounded in interpersonal distances, players' longitudinal displacements, players' lateral displacements, each player's distance to the ball, pitch location, relative velocity, players' acceleration/deceleration, players' distances to the sideline, ball location and speed. However, the relevance of each of these variables has been shown to be specific for each situation. These variables work as task constraints that influence players' behaviour, and consequently the outcome. Thus, the first challenge for coaches is to identify which variables produce information that is critical for players' behaviour in each moment of the match. These variables should be considered as performance indicators describing part or all aspects of sports performance, capturing complex, dynamic and non-linear features that characterise players' interactions in team sports (Hughes & Bartlett, 2002; Sampaio & Leite, 2013). Moreover, these variables help to describe how collective patterns of play in the effective play space (Gréhaigne & Godbout, 2013), positional variables in the length and width of the team, or any other configurations of play change over time. In sum, it should be highlighted that most

104

of these compound variables are built over 'simple' variables, such as players' positions on the pitch (based on x and y coordinates), players' interpersonal distances, and the rate of change of these interpersonal distances. It seems that the most relevant information emerges from players' interactions (within critical regions) and can be measured using the variables presented. The creation and development of coordinative variables which accurately describe players' interactive behaviour in competitive environments, together with the development of technology that allows one to capture data online, open a new era for performance analysis. Due to these improvements, in the next decades performance analysts may provide the team technical staff with more accurate and relevant data during the course of the match.

REFERENCES

Abdel-Aziz, Y. I., & Karara, H. M. (1971). *Direct linear transformation from comparator coordinates into object space coordinates in close-range photogrammetry.* Paper presented at the Symposium on Close-Range Photogrammetry.

Araújo, D., Davids, K., & Hristovski, R. (2006). The ecological dynamics of decision making in sport. *Psychology of Sport and Exercise, 7*(6), 653–676.

Bourbousson, J., Seve, C., & McGarry, T. (2010a). Space-time coordination dynamics in basketball: Part 1. Intra- and inter-couplings among player dyads. *Journal of Sports Science, 28*(3), 339–347.

Bourbousson, J., Seve, C., & McGarry, T. (2010b). Space-time coordination dynamics in basketball: Part 2. The interaction between the two teams. *Journal of Sports Science, 28*(3), 349–358.

Corbetta, D., & Thelen, E. (1996). The development origins of bimanual coordination: A dynamic perspective. *Journal of Experimental Psychology: Human Perception and Performance, 22*, 502–522.

Correa, U. C., Vilar, L., Davids, K., & Renshaw, I. (2014). Informational constraints on the emergence of passing direction in the team sport of futsal. *European Journal of Sport Science, 14*(2), 169–176.

Correia, V., Passos, P., Araújo, D., Davids, K., Diniz, A., & Kelso, J. A. (2014). Coupling tendencies during exploratory behaviours of competing players in rugby union dyads. *European Journal of Sport* Science, *16*(1), 1–9.

Davids, K., Bennett, S., & Newell, K. M. (2006). *Movement system variability.* Champaign, IL: Human Kinetics.

Davids, K., Handforf, C., & Williams, A. M. (1994). The natural physical alternative to cognitive theories of motor behaviour: An invitation for interdisciplinary research in sports science? *Journal of Sport Sciences, 12*(6), 495–528.

Duarte, R., Araújo, D., Folgado, H., Esteves, P., Marques, P., & Davids, K. (2013). Capturing complex, non-linear team behaviours during competitive football performance. *Journal of Systems Science & Complexity, 26*(1), 62–72.

Duch, J., Waitzman, J. S., & Amaral, L. A. (2010). Quantifying the performance of individual players in a team activity. *PLoS One, 5*(6), e10937.

Esteves, P. T., Araújo, D., Vilar, L., Travassos, B., Davids, K., & Esteves, C. (2015). Angular relationships regulate coordination tendencies of performers in attacker-defender dyads in team sports. *Human Movement Science, 40*, 264–272.

Fernandes, O., & Malta, P. (2007). Techno-tactics and running distance analysis using one camera. *Journal of Sports Sciences and Medicine, 6* (Suppl. 10), 204–205.

Fewell, J. H., Armbruster, D., Ingraham, J., Petersen, A., & Waters, J. S. (2012). Basketball teams as strategic networks. *PLoS One, 7*(11), e47445.

Folgado, H., Lemmink, K. A., Frencken, W., & Sampaio, J. (2014). Length, width and centroid distance as measures of teams tactical performance in youth football. *European Journal of Sport Science, 14 Suppl 1*, S487–492.

Fonseca, S., Diniz, A., & Araújo, D. (2013). The measurement of space and time in evolving sport phenomena. In K. Davids, R. Hristovski, D. Araújo, N. Balague Serre, C. Button, & P. Passos (Eds.), *Complex Systems in Sport*. London & New York: Routledge.

Fonseca, S., Milho, J., Travassos, B., & Araújo, D. (2012). Spatial dynamics of team sports exposed by Voronoi diagrams. *Human Movement Science, 31*(6), 1652–1659.

Freeman, L. C. (1977). Set of measures of centrality based on betweenness. *Sociometry, 40*(1), 35–41.

Frencken, W., De Poel, H., Visscher, C., & Lemmink, K. (2012). Variability of inter-team distances associated with match events in elite-standard soccer. *Journal of Sports Sciences, 30*(12), 1207–1213.

Frencken, W., Lemmink, K., Delleman, N., & Visscher, C. (2011). Oscillations of centroid position and surface area of soccer teams in small-sided games. *European Journal of Sport Science, 11*, 215–223.

Frencken, W., Van der Plaats, J., Visscher, C., & Lemmink, K. (2013). Size matters: Pitch dimensions constrain interactive team behaviour in soccer. *Journal of Systems Science & Complexity, 26*(1), 85–93.

Fujimura, A., & Sugihara, K. (2005). Geometric analysis and quantitative evaluation of sport teamwork. *Systems and Computers in Japan, 36*(6), 49–58.

Gama, J., Passos, P., Davids, K., Relvas, H., Ribeiro, J., Vaz, V., & Dias, G. (2014). Network analysis and intra-team activity in attacking phases of professional football. *International Journal of Performance Analysis in Sport, 14*(3), 692–708.

Graham, R. L. (1972). An efficient algorithm for determining the convex hull of a finite planar set. *Information Processing Letters, 1*, 132–133.

Gréhaigne, J. F., & Godbout, P. (2013). Collective variables for analyzing performance in team sports. In T. McGarry, P. O'Donoghue & J. Sampaio (Eds.), *Routledge Handbook of Sports Performance Analysis*, 101–115). London & New York: Routledge.

Grund, T. U. (2012). Network structure and team performance: The case of English premier league soccer teams. *Social Networks, 34*(4), 682–690.

Haken, H., Kelso, J. A., & Bunz, H. (1985). A theoretical model of phase transitions in human hand movements. *Biological Cybernetics, 51*(5), 347–356.

Hamill, J., Haddad, J. M., & McDermott, W. J. (2000). Issues in quantifying variability from a dynamical systems perspective. *Journal of Applied Biomechanics, 16*(4), 407–418.

Harris, S., & Reilly, T. (1988). Space, teamwork and attacking success in soccer. In T. Reilly, A. Lees, K. Davids, & W. Murphy (Eds.), *Science and Football* (pp. 322–328). London: E&F Spon.

Headrick, J., Davids, K., Renshaw, I., Araújo, D., Passos, P., & Fernandes, O. (2012). Proximity-to-goal as a constraint on patterns of behaviour in attacker-defender dyads in team games. *Journal of Sport Sciences, 30*(3), 247–253.

Hughes, M. D., & Bartlett, R. M. (2002). The use of performance indicators in performance analysis. *J Sports Sci, 20*(10), 739–754. doi:10.1080/026404102320675602

Kelso, S. (1995). *Dynamic Patterns. The Self-organization of Brain and Behavior (Complex Adaptive Systems)*. Cambridge, MA: MIT Press.

Kelso, S. (2009). Coordination dynamics. In R. A. Meyers (Ed.), *Encyclopedia of Complexity and System Science* (pp. 1537–1564). Heidelberg: Springer.

McGarry, T., Anderson, D. I., Wallace, S. A., Hughes, M. D., & Franks, I. M. (2002). Sport competition as a dynamical self-organizing system. *Journal of Sport Sciences, 20*(10), 771–781.

McGarry, T., Khan, M. A., & Franks, I. M. (1999). On the presence and absence of behavioural traits in sport: An example from championship squash match-play. *Journal of Sport Sciences, 17*(4), 297–311.

McGarry, T., O'Donoghue, P., & Sampaio, J. (2013). *The Routledge handbook of sports performance analysis*. London & New York: Routledge.

Oullier, O., & Kelso, J. A. S. (2009). Coordination from the perspective of social coordination dynamics. In R. A. Meyers (Ed.), *The Encyclopedia of Complexity and Systems Science* (pp. 8189–8212). Heidelberg: Springer.

Palut, Y., & Zanone, P. G. (2005). A dynamical analysis of tennis: Concepts and data. *Journal of Sport Sciences, 23*(10), 1021–1032.

Passos, P., Araújo, D., & Davids, K. (2013). Self-organization processes in field-invasion team sports: Implications for leadership. *Sports Medicine, 43*(1), 1–7.

Passos, P., Araújo, D., Davids, K., Gouveia, L., Serpa, S., Milho, J., & Fonseca, S. (2009). Interpersonal pattern dynamics and adaptive behavior in multiagent neurobiological systems: Conceptual model and data. *Journal of Motor Behavior, 41*(5), 445–459.

Passos, P., Araújo, D., Travassos, B., Vilar, L., & Duarte, R. (2013). Interpersonal coordination tendencies induce functional synergies through co-adaptation processes in team sports. In K. Davids, R. Hristovski, D. Araújo, N. Balague Serre, C. Button & P. Passos (Eds.), *Complex Systems in Sport*. London & New York: Routledge.

Passos, P., Cordovil, R., Fernandes, O., & Barreiros, J. (2012). Perceiving affordances in rugby union. *Journal of Sport Sciences, 30*(11), 1175–1182.

Passos, P., Davids, K., Araújo, D., Paz, N., Minguens, J., & Mendes, J. (2011). Networks as a novel tool for studying team ball sports as complex social systems. *The Journal of Science and Medicine, 14*(2), 170–176.

Passos, P., Milho, J., Fonseca, S., Borges, J., Araújo, D., & Davids, K. (2011). Interpersonal distance regulates functional grouping tendencies of agents in team sports. *Journal of Motor Behavior, 43*(2), 155–163.

Rodrigues, M., & Passos, P. (2013). Patterns of interpersonal coordination in rugby union: Analysis of collective behaviours in a match situation. *Advances in Physical Education, 3*(4), 209–214.

Rosenblum, M. G., Pikovsky, A. S., Kurths, J., Osipov, G. V., Kiss, I. Z., & Hudson, J. L. (2002). Locking-based frequency measurement and synchronization of chaotic oscillators with complex dynamics. *Physical Review Letters, 89*(26), 264102-1–264102-4.

Sampaio, J., & Leite, N. (2013). Performance indicators in game sports. In T. McGarry, P. O'Donoghue & J. Sampaio (Eds.), *Routledge Handbook of Sports Performance Analysis* (pp. 115–126). London & New York: Routledge.

Sampaio, J., & Macas, V. (2012). Measuring tactical behaviour in football. *International Journal of Sports Medicine, 33*(5), 395–401.

Sayers, M. G. L., & Washington-King, J. (2005). Characteristics of effective ball carries in super 12 rugby. *International Journal of Performance Analysis in Sport, 5*(3), 92–106.

Schmidt, R. C., Carello, C., & Turvey, M. T. (1990). Phase transitions and critical fluctuations in the visual coordination of rhythmic movements between people. *Journal of Experimental Psychology: Human Perception and Performance, 16*(2), 227–247.

Schmidt, R. C., & O'Brien, B. (1997). Evaluating the dynamics of unintended interpersonal coordination. *Ecological Psychology, 9*(3), 189–206.

Schmidt, R. C., O'Brien, B., & Sysko, R. (1999). Self-organization of between-persons cooperative tasks and possible applications to sport. *International Journal of Sport Psychology, 30*(4), 558–579.

Silva, P., Travassos, B., Vilar, L., Aguiar, P., Davids, K., Araújo, D., & Garganta, J. (2014). Numerical relations and skill level constrain co-adaptive behaviors of agents in sports teams. *PLoS One, 9*(9).

Silva, P., Esteves, P., Correia, V., Davids, K., Araújo, D., & Garganta, J. (2015). Effects of manipulations of player numbers vs. field dimensions on inter-individual coordination during small-sided games in youth football. *International Journal of Performance Analysis in Sport, 15* (2), 641–659.

Taki, T., Hasegawa, J., & Fukumura, T. (1996). *Development of motion analysis system for quantitative evaluation of teamwork in soccer games.* Paper presented at the International Conference on Image Processing, Proceedings – Vol 3.

Travassos, B., Araújo, D., Vilar, L., & McGarry, T. (2011). Interpersonal coordination and ball dynamics in futsal (indoor football). [Research Support, Non-U.S. Gov't]. *Hum Mov Sci, 30*(6), 1245–1259. doi: 10.1016/j.humov.2011.04.003.

Travassos, B., Araújo, D., Duarte, R., & McGarry, T. (2012). Spatiotemporal coordination behaviors in futsal (indoor football) are guided by informational game constraints. *Human Movement Science, 31*(4), 932–945.

Travassos, B., Goncalves, B., Marcelino, R., Monteiro, R., & Sampaio, J. (2014). How perceiving additional targets modifies teams' tactical behavior during football small-sided games. *Human Movement Science, 38*, 241–250.

van Rooyen, M., Yasin, N., & Viljoen, W. (2014). Characteristics of an 'effective' tackle outcome in six nations rugby. *European Journal of Sport Science, 14*(2), 123–129.

Vilar, L., Araújo, D., Davids, K., & Button, C. (2012). The role of ecological dynamics in analysing performance in team sports. *Sports Medicine, 42*(1), 1–10.

Vilar, L., Araújo, D., Davids, K., Travassos, B., Duarte, R., & Parreira, J. (2012). Interpersonal coordination tendencies supporting the creation/prevention of goal scoring opportunities in futsal. *European Journal of Sport Science, 14*(1), 28–35.

Vilar, L., Duarte, R., Silva, P., Chow, J. Y., & Davids, K. (2014). The influence of pitch dimensions on performance during small-sided and conditioned soccer games. *Journal of Sport Sciences, 32*(19), 1751–1759.

Vilar, L., Esteves, P. T., Travassos, B., Passos, P., Lago-Peñas, C., & Davids, K. (2014). Varying numbers of players in small-sided soccer games modifies action opportunities during training. *International Journal of Sports Science & Coaching, 9*(5), 1007–1018.

Wheeler, K. W., Askew, C. D., & Sayers, M. G. (2010). Effective attacking strategies in rugby union. *European Journal of Sport Science, 10*(4), 237–242.

Yamamoto, Y., & Yokoyama, K. (2011). Common and unique network dynamics in football games. *PLoS One, 6*(12), e29638.

PART II

CHAPTER 6

RESEARCH TOPICS IN SOCCER PERFORMANCE

Leading author: Duarte Araújo

INTRODUCTION

Soccer performance is influenced by several sources of constraint that exert their influence before, during and after a match (Davids et al., 2005). Soccer – officially called *association football* – is a game played on a field between two competing teams of 11 players each with the aim to propel a round ball into the opponent's goal by kicking or heading it. Applied sport scientists and coaches use performance analysis of soccer to make decisions about diagnostics and interventions.

The soccer game has evolved over the years, together with the development of technological and computerised systems that enable a more in-depth understanding of sports performance. However, recent reviews of performance analysis in soccer (Sarmento et al., 2014; Tenga, 2013) have shown that match analysis has predominantly used descriptions and associations among variables, thus investigating soccer without considering the dynamic, interactive and complex systems' properties that explain it (Davids et al., 2005). Aligned with this idea, Vilar et al. (2012) proposed that analysts need to move beyond merely documenting 'performance statistics' in order to study the emergent interactions among players in key areas of the field which underpin success in football. As follows, manipulation of task constraints (information) and motion analyses methods have been used to collect time series data on the displacement coordinates of players and ball (see Araújo et al., 2015, for a review in sport). By showing statistical relationships between the information of the performance environment and behavioural outcome measures, researchers have provided evidence on how players support successful performance through the use of that information (e.g., Travassos et al., 2012). Motion analysis methods help to identify players' performances on a continuum and transitions in their course of action during competitive performance. For example, Araújo and colleagues used motion analysis techniques to show that the time for the gap between the ball carrier and the defender to close (time to contact) constrained how players perform successful passes (Travassos et al., 2012) or shaped opportunities for goal scoring (Vilar et al., 2013) in the team sport of futsal. These studies provided understanding of how players interact with the performance environment to create and use information to support successful decision making and actions.

In this chapter we examine the topics of soccer performance that have been investigated in sport sciences literature. Here, an important task is to understand how constraints can channel information sources used to regulate upcoming actions and how the influence of these constraints is expressed in players' behavioural dynamics. As previously mentioned in this book, an ecological dynamics perspective can describe the properties observed at different levels of the system, capturing its scalability (Araújo & Davids, 2016; Araújo et al., 2015). This idea has important implications for understanding team sports performance since it captures the interdependence between individual and (sub)group levels of analysis. That is, changes at one level (individual) may influence performance at other levels (sub-groups and the team). Next, we present data from studies available in the literature that have exemplified how performance in soccer has been analysed from more local (individual) to more global (team) performance (see Araújo & Davids, 2016; Araújo et al., 2015, for a review of how different levels of analysis are linked). Instead of providing simple statistics on the basics of soccer defending and attacking, we refer to the existing research on soccer defending and attacking information imbedded in the different interrelated levels of performance, from the micro- to the macro-level.

DYADIC BEHAVIOUR

A growing body of research has been dedicated to studying the performance of 1v1 match sub-phases, after the seminal work of Araújo and colleagues (Araújo et al., 2004; Davids et al., 2006). The 1v1 task in competitive sports can be considered as a dynamic dyadic system in which the performers' relationship is characterised by stable and unstable patterns that emerge from their ongoing interpersonal interactions.

114

Such performance dynamics is based on information that is more or less correlated with a player's movements, which can be used for regulating actions by an opposing player (Araújo et al., 2004). Researchers have approached this task from a variety of perspectives.

Headrick and colleagues (Headrick et al., 2012) investigated the influence of proximity-to-goal as a constraint on the relationship between players and the ball in attacker–defender dyads in soccer. They found effects of player–ball relations and provided player-to-ball distance patterns for different field locations. Results reflected the variability in the emergent behaviours through different player strategies to satisfy the performance task constraints. Differences observed in player-to-ball patterns among field locations suggested that proximity-to-goal provides a source of constraint on intentionality of individuals in 1v1 dyads. Dyad design and general performance objectives at each location remained identical; hence differences in emergent decision-making behaviour could be attributed to interpersonal interactions of dyads based on the proximity-to-goal. Headrick and colleagues' study contributed to research by encouraging participants to explore the performance environment without the need for specific instructions and in distinct field locations.

In turn, Vilar and colleagues (Vilar et al., 2012, 2013, 2014) tried to clarify the influence of informational constraints on dyadic behaviour in indoor football (futsal) matches. For example, Vilar and colleagues (Vilar et al., 2012) showed how the attacking team used spatial-temporal information from the performance environment to create instabilities in the opponent's defensive structure. They found that stable in-phase patterns of coordination (i.e., synchronised behaviour) emerged between the attackers' and defenders' distances and angles to the goal. Attackers sought to break unintentional coordination with the defender by using lateral displacement to increase the angle to the goal relative to the defender's position, while decreasing the distance to the goal. These results suggested that defenders sought to be always closer to, and between, the attacker and their own goal. In addition, Vilar et al. (2014) argued that a decrease in the attacker's distance to the goal seemed to have constrained the defender to move towards the immediate attacker. This would prevent the attacker from moving the ball forward in the field and allow the defender to be closer to a possible trajectory of the ball to the goal (i.e., to intercept a shot). Conversely, when the ball moved away from the attacker (e.g., after a pass), the defender decreased significantly his angle to the ball and his distance to the immediate attacker. These results imply that the teammates' perceptions of an opportunity for a defender to intercept the ball constrained them to move towards the ball carrier and offer him a possibility to pass the ball. Probably, the backward displacement of the furthest defender in the field is performed to ensure a new level of dyadic system stability in case the ball carrier successfully dribbled past a nearest defender. These results were confirmed in outdoor football by Duarte, Araújo, Travassos, Davids, Gazimba, & Sampaio (2012), who revealed that attacking players' success was associated with more irregular and unpredictable space-time synchronisation with the defender. That is, players frequently approach and move away from the target area in a synchronised mode, but in an irregular manner. On the other hand, the success of a defending player was attributed to a more predictable coordination mode developed with the attacker, displaying a frequent lead–lag relationship (i.e., the to-and-fro movement displacements of the defender preceded the moves of the attacking player). Therefore, these findings demonstrate that specific features associated with the mutual influence of each player on dyadic behaviours tend to shape different performance outcomes.

Moreover, Vilar, Araújo, Davids, Travassos, Duarte & Parreira (2014) provided further understanding on how opportunities to score emerged from the attacker's interactions with the nearest defender and the goal. Their results indicated that the attacker did not need to be completely ahead of a defender (i.e., closer to goal than the defender) to create an opportunity to score. Instead, promoting a misalignment in the defender's relative position between the goal and the attacker, by standing at the same distance to the goal at the moment of shooting, was enough to prevent defenders from intercepting the ball trajectory to the goal. Simultaneously, when a goal is scored the attacker is able to prevent the defender from approaching his location to ensure conditions to shoot at the goal by using his displacement velocity (being faster than the defender). However, to score, attackers must also override the informational link that is established with the goalkeeper. To clarify this issue, Vilar et al. (2013) examined how the information from the locations of a nearest defender and the goalkeeper may constrain decision making when kicking the ball at the goal. Results showed that the defender's and the goalkeeper's required velocity to intercept the ball is significantly higher when a goal occurs than when a player intercepts the ball. This may imply that when a goal is scored, the attacker shoots the ball at such a direction and speed that the required velocity of a defender or the goalkeeper to arrive at the interception point at the same time as the ball is higher than their maximum movement velocities.

116

Penalty kick

Considering this relationship between attacker and goalkeeper, a major research focus has been on the penalty kick (see Lopes et al., 2014a, for a review), where the influence of several types of constraints, such as different performance strategies (e.g., Lopes et al., 2012), emotional pressure (e.g., Horikawa & Yagi, 2012) or the effects of an environment scaled to the body dimensions of the players (e.g., Dicks et al., 2010) were studied. A significant emphasis has been placed on identifying and establishing the influence of information for anticipation of players' performance in the penalty kick (e.g., Diaz et al., 2012).

Although performance in the penalty kick depends on ever-changing task and environmental constraints, performers can maintain their efficacy through their adaptive skill (Van der Kamp, 2006). This ability in skilled performers can be captured through using time-continuous measures, rather than recording discrete performance variables. For example, despite some research (e.g., Van der Kamp, 2006) relating a goalkeeper-independent strategy to higher success rates by penalty takers, there is evidence that the mere presence of a goalkeeper can influence the accuracy of a penalty taker (Navarro et al., 2013). The application of biophysical measures may clarify whether and how penalty takers change from a keeper-independent to a keeper-dependent strategy. For example, smaller run-up approaches are features related to a keeper-dependent strategy, and a keeper-independent strategy could influence the keeper's diving angle (Lopes et al., 2012).

Because of the penalty kick's role in the final score of a competitive match, individuals cope differently with the emotions related to performance pressure (Moll, Jordet & Pepping, 2010). Hence, recent investigations have addressed the particularities of these individual constraints as the event unfolds. Studies have shown an association between time spent by the penalty taker to initiate movement and penalty-kick outcome. Shorter response times by the penalty takers were linked to worse performances than longer times (Jordet et al., 2009). The manipulation of the level of pressure through (i) limited time for action (Navarro et al., 2011); (ii) comparison with other penalty takers' performances (Horikawa & Yagi, 2012); or (iii) highlighting players' individual focus on accomplishment and aspiration or prevention (Plessner et al, 2009) tend to be associated with penalty-kick outcomes.

Regarding personal and task constraint manipulations, Dicks and colleagues (2010) investigated the action timings of goalkeepers with different action capabilities (e.g., different displacement speeds, limb lengths or body statures). Distinct action capabilities influenced the timing for action initiation and an inverse relation between action capability and response initiation was reported (i.e., the faster the goalkeeper, the longer he waited before diving). Gaze behaviour has also been investigated, revealing that gaze and ball directions are highly related (i.e., the areas fixated on by penalty takers are closer to where they place the ball) when gaze was self-regulated (i.e., exclusively controlled by the penalty taker) (Dicks et al., 2010). Alternatively, when negative instructions have been imposed on gaze (e.g., 'Do not look at goalkeeper when approaching the ball'), penalty takers demonstrated a tendency to do the opposite (i.e., to look at goalkeepers) (Bakker et al., 2007). These findings reflect how different types of constraints interact during penalty-kick performance.

If the information that supports a player's actions is mainly based on his/her opponent's movements, then, at some moment prior to foot–ball contact, movement features should predict goal-directed behaviours. In terms of information sources, areas such as the torso, lower kicking leg, non-dominant leg (Dicks et al., 2010; Lees & Owens, 2011) head and ball (Piras & Vickers, 2011) have been reported as locations toward which goalkeepers direct their gaze. Although local information sources were identified by analyses of goalkeepers' gaze patterns, the sources that actually predict specific outcomes (e.g., ball direction) have yet to be identified. This distinction between sources towards which performers direct their gaze and sources that predict future events is not trivial. Even if one assumes that performers are looking at predictive sources, the perception of information from the performance environment does not signify the use of that information source for action guidance (Huys et al., 2009).

When related to performance and outcome, the differences in information usefulness (i.e., its relevance and the moment of its appearance during the time course of action) in the penalty kick led Lopes and colleagues (Lopes et al., 2014b) to profile which information source(s) is/are relevant at each moment. They found that several kinematic variables from the penalty taker were strongly correlated with shot direction, especially those related to the lower part of the body. Some of these variables, including the angle of the non-kicking foot, expressed high correlations at time intervals that are useful to goalkeepers. Compound variables, defined as linear combinations of variables, were found to be more useful than locally defined variables. Moreover, their findings indicated that, in trying to deceive the goalkeeper, penalty takers are

118

able to modify the predictive value of the local body kinematics to some extent, most particularly early in the approach, but for the majority of kinematic variables the deception is unsustainable at the final moments before ball contact, where players have to act genuinely in order to shoot the ball in the desired direction.

GROUP BEHAVIOUR

Recently, Sarmento et al. (2014) presented a review of a considerable number of studies on match analysis of adult male football. These studies are predominantly descriptive, presenting frequencies or sequences of group action and group outcomes. The observation of different actions performed by players, the locations on the pitch where they are performed as well as the timing of these actions during a match play are expressions of the strategy and tactics being applied. Further, Sarmento and colleagues found some studies that have developed their analysis by comparing categories such as final game score, Ramadan influence, levels of fatigue, different leagues, teams or tactical systems. Other studies analysed performance as contextualised by the influence of situational variables such as game location, quality of the opposition, match status and match half. Finally, increasing interest is being paid to understanding how performance in team sports is predicated on interpersonal interactions (coordination) between attackers and defenders as they act to satisfy spatio-temporal constraints of performance (Araújo et al., 2004). In this section we will address these points, starting with group coordination.

Group coordination

During the last years several studies were performed with positional data measuring the (sub)group behaviour in a team.

The influence of task constraints on small-sided and conditioned games

Duarte et al. (2012) studied emergent coordination processes displayed by two competing groups composed of three football players each. This study demonstrated how within- and between-group space-time relations influenced the creation of goal-scoring opportunities in small-group confrontations. The collective movement of the two sub-groups captured by the geometrical centre demonstrated a strong symmetrical relationship describing the coordinated actions in the approach to the scoring zones. Conversely, changes in the spatial areas covered by the sub-groups did not reveal a predominant nor stable pattern of coordination between them. However, attacking and defending sub-groups tended to increase the difference in their covered areas, particularly just before an assisted pass was made for the scoring zones. Silva and colleagues included other constraints such as field dimensions, number of players and numerical relations on small-sided and conditioned games (SSCG). Specifically, the variability of the players' movement trajectories during performance in SSCGs was analysed by varying performance area dimensions (Silva et al., 2014). Variability analyses of players' spatial distributions provided information about the width of each player's tactical role. On the other hand, variability in the distance to their trajectories' geometrical centre (i.e., the loci) over time provided information about the time-evolving nature of their movements on the field. Results confirmed distinct inter-individual coordination patterns according to field dimensions. As playing areas increased, the players' spatial distributions (i.e., their action zones) tended to become more restricted. Players also showed a near cyclical sinusoidal movement pattern across match play reflecting a tendency to travel around a preferred reference zone during the rhythmic ebb-and-flow of attacking and defending. The periodicity of these movements increased in larger fields, despite the fact that the distance to their positional locus had increased. In Silva et al. (2014) the effects of field dimension on tactical behaviours were extended to the intra- and inter-team level. The authors also tested the influence of players' level of expertise. Effective playing space was shown to augment effects of field dimension, with team players covering more ground when playing on larger fields. Teams whose players had higher levels of expertise showed elongated match shapes on larger fields, whereas teams with players with lower levels of expertise maintained similar length and width characteristics in all field dimensions. The available space between both teams concerning the players' nearest opponents also increased with field dimension without any differences between teams with players with different expertise levels, though, implying more available space and time for players to make decisions.

120

By manipulating numerical relations, Silva et al. (2014) tested the consequences on the areas of players' dominant regions and the predominant direction of their movements on the field. The dominant regions were larger and smaller for the overloaded and underloaded teams of players in a higher expertise level, respectively, when a difference of two players, in teams' numerical relation, was applied. The players in a lower expertise level presented larger dominant regions when a difference of one player was established. Skilled players displayed more similar movement amplitudes in the longitudinal and lateral directions than their less skilled counterparts. In general, overloaded teams also tended to advance up-field, whereas underloaded teams tended to retreat nearer their own goal and contract in order to protect it. However, players in a higher level of expertise showed a higher pressure on the underloaded team's defensive line, disturbing their defensive stability by shortening the distance between attacking and defending lines. Finally, in a series of studies, Silva, Esteves, Correia, Davids, Araújo, and Garganta (2015) showed that the establishment of the same relative space per player in SSCGs through manipulations of player numbers or field dimensions impacted differently on the players' interpersonal interactions during a game. Specifically, manipulations in player numbers induced larger playing areas allocated to each player and larger distances to nearest opponents per player than did manipulations on field dimensions. However, it was observed that different relative playing areas per player set by field dimensions promoted distinctive interpersonal coordination patterns. Furthermore, playing with fewer players in an area with fixed dimensions (i.e., on a larger relative space per player) or with a fixed number of players on smaller pitches (i.e., on a smaller relative space per player) seemed to induce broader spatial distributions of players on field, and vice-versa. This indicates that favourable or unfavourable contexts for attacking and defending can be recreated by simply manipulating such types of constraints.

Team coordination

In studying the entire team, Duarte et al. (2013) investigated emergent collective behaviours at the team level with positional data from entire matches. Five compound positional variables were used to capture changes in the coordinated behaviours of the teams as wholes (geometrical centre, stretch index, surface area, team length team width;

see Araújo et al., 2015 for a discussion of these variables). Those collective measures showed complementarity in capturing the global idiosyncratic behaviours of the opposing football teams, with high variations observed when a team scored a goal. Also, teams tended to became significantly more regular and predictable in their organisational shape over the natural course of a match, which can be attributed to the mutual adaptation between teams. A further question aimed to understand how the individual behaviour of each player influenced the synchronisation of the whole team.

Travassos et al. highlighted that the emergence of spatial-temporal patterns of coordination between players (Travassos et al., 2011) and teams (Travassos, Araújo, Duarte, McGarry, 2012) during an actual competitive performance setting of futsal were constrained by the goals of the attacking and defending teams, the ball dynamics and the position of the goal. At the team level, Travassos et al. (2012) revealed stronger relationships between the ball and the defending team than between the attacking team and the ball. The phase relations between the ball and the teams demonstrated complementary associations with each other. As an example, when the defending team presented a stable relationship with the ball it decreased the stability of the relationships with the attacking team. The opposite relation occurred when the defending team increased the stability of relationships with the attacking team. Furthermore, the strongest correlations were observed using angles to measure the associations between the defending team and the ball. Thus, the defending team continuously attempted to develop and maintain spatial-temporal coordination patterns with the attacking team, and with the ball, but importantly, it did so with respect to the goal line location. Duarte et al. (2013) investigated, by means of the cluster phase method, the relationship between these two levels of organisation – i.e., individual and team levels. Large synergistic relationships within each football team were observed, particularly in the longitudinal direction of the field. Moreover, increases in each team's synchrony were intimately related, revealing evidence of the mutual influence of each team's coordination. Concerning player–team synchronisation, footballers tended to be coordinated under near in-phase modes with the team behaviour. Their magnitudes of variations were lower, but more irregular in time, for the longitudinal than for the lateral direction of the field. Decreases of these synchronies were also observed from the first to the second halftime of the matches.

Another important topic to consider is the understanding of how this group coordination is formed – i.e., What is the information that guides group behaviour? (Travassos Araújo, Davids et al., 2012) showed how the behaviours of individuals were guided by the perception of action possibilities (affordances) during an indoor football (futsal) match. Results revealed how a decision to pass a ball to a teammate was regulated by the achievement of stable spatial constraints defined by the position of opponents in relation to the ball carrier. Moreover, initial distances between ball carrier and opponents constrained successful interceptions. Successful interceptions also seemed to be influenced by the continuous regulation of the performer's movement velocity as regarded the changing spatio-temporal constraints of the task. The variable of time to ball interception, based on spatial-temporal relationships between ball trajectory and opponents' actions, was instrumental in shaping the emergent functional behaviours of performers. The adjustment of an individual's velocity in relationship to the time required to intercept the ball is paramount for a ball interception. It is worth noting that the capture of kinematic data and the identification of changes in the dynamics of individual performances relative to the performance environment supported the view that passing decision-making processes are guided by the spatial-temporal relationship between the performers and the ball (see Silva et al., 2013, for an explanation of how shared affordances guide group behaviour).

Following a social network approach, Clemente and colleagues (2015) analysed successful and unsuccessful national teams that participated in the FIFA World Cup 2014.

Their results showed differences in network density total links (ball passes) for the teams that reached the later stages of the tournament.

COMPETITIVE ACTIVITY PROFILES AND SPECIFIC POSITION DEMANDS

When characterising profiles of competitive activity and specific position demands researches tend to describe the type of locomotion and related intensities, such as standing, walking, jogging, running (low speed, moderate speed and high speed) and sprinting, as well as the distance covered by these locomotion types (see the pioneer work of Reilly & Thomas, 1976). Some studies also considered path direction changes (Robinson et al., 2011) including accelerations, decelerations, turns and jumps. In the review of Sarmento and colleagues (2014), studies on activity profiles have shown that elite players normally covered distances between 9 and 14 km, and performed approximately 1,330 activities during a match, including 220 displacements at high speed (e.g., Lago et al., 2010). In the narrative review of Tenga (2013) it is indicated that outfield players cover 8 to 13 km during a match, distributed by 24 per cent walking, 36 per cent jogging, 20 per cent cruising sub-maximally (striding), 11 per cent sprinting, 7 per cent moving backwards and 2 per cent moving with possession of the ball. These players perform around 1,000 different activities in a game, and there is a break in the level or type of activity every six seconds, the majority of actions being 'off the ball' (Tenga, 2013). For example, Carling (2010) found that players ran a mean total distance of 191 ± 38 m with the ball, of which 34.3 per cent was covered at speeds of >19.1 km/hour. Moreover, mean time in possession, duration and touches per possession were 53.4 ± 8.1 s, 1.1 ± 0.1 s and 2.0 ± 0.2 s, respectively, with significant differences across playing positions for all variables.

In terms of specific position demands, researchers seek to find relationships that are established with physical activity patterns and efficacy of game actions (e.g., Dellal et al., 2010, 2011). For example, goalkeepers (De Baranda et al., 2008) covered a total distance of 5611 ± 613 m per match, of which 4025 ± 440 m were covered walking, 1223 ± 256 m jogging, 221 ± 90 m running and 56 ± 34 m at high intensity, while the distance covered in sprinting was 11 ± 12 m. In terms of outfielders, the results generally show that the demands on the physical and technical realms are different depending on the specific position the player takes in the field. Di Salvo and colleagues (2007) reported that midfield players cover a significantly greater total distance than defenders and forward players. Also, more distance was covered in the first half compared to the second at medium intensities, but there was not any difference between the two halves in either total distance or distances covered at submaximal and maximal intensities. Importantly, the players of more successful teams covered greater total distances with the ball, and at very high-intensity running; had a high average of goals for total shots on target; performed more involvements with the ball; and had a higher number of passes, tackles, dribbling and shots on target when compared with less successful teams (see Sarmento et al., 2014, for a detailed description). Recently, in studying the evolution of physical and technical performance parameters for various playing positions

124

in the English Premier League, Bush and colleagues (2015) found that high-intensity running distance increased in the final season versus the first season in all playing positions, with wide defenders displaying the greatest increase. Similar trends were observed for sprint distances with wide defenders, demonstrating the most pronounced increase across the last seven seasons. Central defenders and midfielders showed the most pronounced increases in total passes and pass success rates whilst wide defenders and midfielders demonstrated only small to moderate increases in total passes and pass success rates.

Tenga (2013) indicated that blood lactate concentration and heart rate varied with the work rate and differed among playing positions and between first and second halves. An interesting study by Bradley et al. (2011) showed that physical performance across playing positions is also dependent upon the team formation employed. These authors showed that attackers in 4–3–3 formations displayed about 30 per cent more high-intensity running than attackers in 4–4–2 and 4–5–1 formations. Further, the number of passes performed was higher for players in 4–4–2 formations compared with 4–3–3 and 4–5–1 formations. Tenga (2013) argues that an increase in the tempo of play over the years is the most likely reason behind the distances covered during matches in present soccer. These results provide guidelines for specific fitness training programmes which can enhance a player's baseline for performance and reduce the risk of injury during a match (Tenga, 2013).

Moreover, Dellal et al. (2011), in studying 5,938 matches of the English and Spanish Premier leagues, showed that there are differences in many physical and technical variables, suggesting that cultural differences may exist across leagues and playing positions. Other comparisons where these physical and technical variables are dependent variables focus on final ranking (e.g., Lago-Ballesteros & Lago-Peñas, 2010) and level of expertise (Bradley et al., 2010). There were also other studies analysing the influence of fatigue (Lago-Peñas et al., 2010), of an over-filled calendar (Lago-Peñas et al., 2011; Rey et al., 2010), of the Ramadan (Zerguini et al., 2007) and of substitutes and replaced players (Carling et al., 2010) on performance. It seems that players' performance is not influenced by short recovery between matches, whereas playing formation influences performance. For example, Carling and Dupont (2011) suggest that playing formation only influence the activity profiles of attackers, but skill-related demands vary substantially according to the opponent's formation and may have consequences for tactical and technical aspects and team-selection policies.

Group outcomes

Several authors have attempted to identify which game-related statistics are related to winning, drawing and losing. In a study conducted with 380 games of the Spanish First league, Lago-Peñas et al. (2010) inferred that discriminant functions correctly classified 55.1 per cent of these teams. Similarly, through the analysis of 288 of the UEFA Champions League matches, Lago-Peñas et al. (2011) concluded that the discriminant functions correctly classified 79.7 per cent of winning, drawing and losing teams. The variables that had a higher discriminatory power tended to be shots on goal, crosses and ball possession. On the other hand, Liu et al. (2015) studied the group stage of the FIFA World Cup (2014, Brazil) and found that for all the games, shots, shots on target, shots from counter-attacks, shots from inside area, ball possession, short passes, average pass streak, number of aerial advantages and tackles had positive effects on the probability of winning; however, shots blocked, crosses, dribbles and red cards had negative effects. While for the close games, the effects of aerial advantages and yellow cards turned to non-existent and negative, respectively. Also, in trying to clarify whether longer or shorter passing sequences are more effective in goal scoring (e.g., Bate, 1988; Olsen & Larsen, 1997; Reep & Benjamin, 1968), recent studies indicated that more goals were scored from shorter passing sequences, but also that there were more instances of shorter passing sequences than longer ones (Hughes & Franks, 2005; Tenga et al., 2010a, 2010b). Additionally, team possessions originating from the final third of the playing field were found to be effective in goal scoring (Bate, 1988; Garganta et al., 1997; Tenga et al., 2010a, 2010b). However, in comparison to unsuccessful teams, successful teams score more goals from possessions started in zones behind the attacking third (Tenga & Sigmundstad, 2011). Also, several studies have reported that possessions with relatively longer duration were related to successful teams (Hughes & Churchill, 2004; Jones et al., 2004; Tenga & Sigmundstad, 2011).

In terms of opposition interaction, Harris and Reilly (1988) showed that defence against attacks with a shot on target, compared to the ones without a shot, tended to involve higher attacker-to-defender ratios and greater average distances between the attacker in possession and the nearest defender throughout the attack. Bloomfield et al. (2005), Jones et al. (2004), Lago and Martin (2007) and Taylor et al. (2008) reported the influence of match status and opposition quality on ball possession and frequency of technical behaviours. Tenga et al. (2010a, 2010b) presented empirical evidence of opposition interaction between offensive and defensive soccer-playing tactics by using analytical study designs. For example, counter-attacks were associated with a higher odds ratio for producing a score box possession than elaborate attacks when playing against an imbalanced defence, but not against a balanced defence (Tenga et al., 2010a). Similarly, counter-attacks were associated with a higher odds ratio for producing a goal than elaborate attacks when playing against an imbalanced defence (Tenga et al., 2010b).

CONTEXTUALISING PERFORMANCE

Physical and technical variables have lower values in the second half of the match (Carling, 2011; Carling & Bloomfield, 2010; Carling & Dupont, 2011; Di Salvo et al., 2007; O' Donoghue et al., 2001; Vigne et al., 2010). The explanation for this effect is that fatigue negatively influences the physical and technical performance of the players. However, this decrement (total distance covered and distances covered at high and very high intensities) is not a phenomenon that occurs systematically; it has instead been associated with the distance covered by players during the first half. The results demonstrated that when players are required to carry out a more intense first half, total distance covered is decreased in the second half. In instances of a less intense first half, total distance and high-intensity running distance did not change, and very high–intensity running even increased on the second half. Regarding the technical aspects, Rampinini et al. (2009) observed a decline between the first half and second half in the Italian league, since players were less involved with the ball, had less short passes and had less successful short passes. These data are in contrast with the study by Carling and Dupont (2011), who concluded that there were no significant differences in performance shown by French league midfield players.

When investigating the effects of game location commonly referred to as 'home advantage', several studies (Jacklin, 2005; Lago & Martín, 2007; Lago-Peñas & Lago-Ballesteros, 2011; Lago-Peñas et al., 2011; Pollard, 2006; Sánchez et al., 2009; Thomas et al., 2006) have confirmed indicators pointing to a more favourable outcome when teams play at home. There is a tendency for teams playing home games to score more goals (Poulter, 2009), as well as perform more shots on goal (Lago-Peñas & Lago-Ballesteros, 2011; Poulter, 2009; Taylor et al., 2008), more crossings (Lago-Peñas & Lago-Ballesteros, 2011; Taylor et al., 2008), more passes, more successful passes, more dribbles with success, and also to take more corners (Lago & Martín, 2007; Lago-Peñas & Dellal, 2010; Lago-Peñas & Lago- Ballesteros, 2011; Poulter, 2009) compared with teams playing away. In regard to disciplinary behaviour, teams playing at home commit fewer fouls (Poulter, 2009) and receive fewer yellow cards (Lago-Peñas & Lago-Ballesteros, 2011; Poulter, 2009; Thomas et al., 2006). In general, the results showed that a home advantage effect exists for most performance and discipline measures at a team level. These findings indicate that strategies in soccer are influenced by match location and teams may alter their playing style accordingly.

Apart from the aspects related to home advantage and match half, researchers have attempted to study the influence of other contextual aspects, particularly those related to quality of opposition and match status. The results showed that there are significant differences based on the quality of the opposition and the ongoing result of the game: when losing the teams had more ball possessions (Lago, 2009; Lago & Martín, 2007; Lago-Peñas & Dellal, 2010) and performed more crosses (Taylor et al., 2008) and dribbles (Taylor et al., 2008). On the other hand, when winning the teams performed (1) more interceptions, clearances and aerial challenges (Taylor et al., 2008); (2) fewer passes and dribbles (Taylor et al., 2008); (3) and fewer high-intensity exercises (Lago, 2009; Lago-Peñas et al., 2011).

The studies that focused their analysis on the quality of the opposing teams showed that when playing against strong opponents, they performed more passes (Taylor et al., 2008) and less dribbling (Taylor et al., 2008) and covered greater distances (Castellano et al., 2011; Lago et al., 2010; Lago-Peñas et al., 2011). In addition, playing against strong opponents is associated with a reduction in ball-possession time (Lago & Martín, 2007; Lago-Peñas & Dellal, 2010). These findings may be important for coaches when developing strategic and tactical approaches in order to improve the performance of their team in relation to the diversity of situational variables that their teams may encounter.

128

THE ANALYSIS OF PERFORMANCE DEVELOPMENT

When looking at performance analysis for finding answers to practical problems, Travassos and colleagues (2012) required players to perform a passing task, in the team sport of futsal, in which uncertainty of passing direction for the player in possession of the ball was increased under four distinct conditions and compared with passing data observed during a competitive match. Higher levels of regularity were observed in pre-determined passes (distance and direction of pass verified) compared to passes made under practice conditions which included more uncertainty for performers (i.e., distance, angle and direction of pass varied). Importantly, passing speed regularity and accuracy were more similar between practice tasks with higher levels of uncertainty and during competitive performance. The data convincingly demonstrated that only the design of the more uncertain passing tasks *represented* the speed, accuracy and success found in passing circumstances performed during a competitive match. These data show how the informational constraints of practice tasks can be designed to correspond to the informational constraints of a competitive performance environment in team sports. In another study, Silva, Chung, Carvalho, Cardoso, Davids, Araújo, & Garganta (2016) provided further evidence for this assumption by analysing the effects of 13 weeks of practice on synergy formation of two teams of recreational players during performance. Team synchronisation resulting from the rhythmic ebb-and-flow movements during performance was shown to emerge from a continuous process of synergy formation that rapidly oscillated between peaks of player couplings, suggesting that moving players provide informational properties that invite actions from other members of the complex adaptive system (players) over different timescales. As some players advanced up-field, remaining teammates were compelled to follow their movements in correspondence to team patterns of play. Practice was shown to improve team synchronisation speed, captured as reduced time delays in the players' co-positioning re-adjustments, resulting in faster re-establishment of synergies. This process emerged after just two hours of practice per week in two newly formed football teams.

CONCLUSIONS AND SUGGESTIONS

Some researchers argue that it is difficult if not impossible to have valid data unless sports performance is considered as a complex dynamic process with self-organising properties (e.g., Araújo et al., 2004; Fister Jr. et al., 2015; McGarry et al., 2002). In this chapter we showed recent studies that address soccer as a complex dynamic match. Manipulation of specific key task constraints such as field dimensions, player numbers, numerical relations, etc., was observed to channel individual and team tactical behaviours into stable and functional coordination patterns during goal-directed team activities without the necessary need of prescriptive instructions (Silva et al., 2015). Slight changes in task constraints can influence the adaptive coordinative structures that emerge as individuals search, discover and exploit functional coordination solutions (Davids et al., 2005). For instance, when manipulations in field dimensions were applied, skilled players showed increased movement variabilities on small pitches and higher unpredictable distance values to nearest opponents than their less skilled counterparts, showing different negotiations of constraints influenced by skill level (Silva et al., 2014, 2015).

Team tactical behaviours are sustained (and must be understood) at the level of the player–player environment system, where practice can improve team synchronisation speed translated in faster re-establishment of synergies (i.e., when players act as a cohesive unit). Moreover, tactical behaviours are malleable and can be shaped during practice in SSCGs by simply manipulating key task constraints to promote different tactical adaptations. Players' individual characteristics, like skill level, and contextual factors, such as Ramadan, impact team performance and tactical coordination tendencies.

Match coordination tendencies emerging between individual players with specific skills characterise a team entity the same way in which genes, personality or physical capabilities interact to define each individual player's intrinsic dynamics. This idea implies that each team expresses its own idiosyncratic dynamics, which are shaped by many constraints, such as the club's history, playing philosophy, the players' learning and playing experiences, etc. This is especially important for coaches because tactical behaviours can shape the emergence of different collective coordination patterns (i.e., playing styles) that may or may not suit a team's intrinsic dynamics.

Tactical behaviours may then be shaped through manipulations of team constraints such as (i) off-field changes, (ii) selection of players with different characteristics (i.e., different constraints), (iii) the team's dispositional structure (e.g., from 1–4–3–3 to 1–4–4–2), or (iv) through substitution of players. The selection of constraints to be manipulated and

130

practiced should be grounded on the results of the performance analysis, as we have presented along this chapter. For instance, manipulations of field dimensions in SSGCs can be used to shape the breadth of tactical roles. Smaller fields constrain players to play in more variable zones of the field and, thus, assume more diversified functions in the team (e.g., playing in the left and right corridors; playing as the last player on a defensive line or as a forward). This also requires players to be constantly aware of the positioning of other teammates (i.e., higher tactical awareness) and opponents in order to constantly re-adjust their own positioning to ensure a balanced occupation of the field. On the other hand, larger fields appeal to a more structured playing style, according to specific positions (e.g., playing on the left side of the pitch). Furthermore, SSCGs played in larger fields allow for more space between attackers and defenders (Silva, Aguiar et al., 2014; Silva, Duarte et al., 2014). These findings are particularly useful for coaches of youth football. For instance, larger field SSCGs seem to be more appropriate to introduce the game to novice players, since in these performance contexts they mainly have to focus on covering a restricted territory following attacking and defending phases while having more space and time to make decisions. Manipulations of numerical relations can be used to facilitate attacking actions of overloaded teams, since with a numerical difference of one and two players there was a tendency to approach the underloaded team's goal. More space was also created at the back of the overloaded team and on the wings, providing good conditions for stimulating build-up play. Moreover, the underloaded teams tended to contract, probably because they spent more time engaged in defending actions due to difficulties of maintaining ball possession when playing with fewer players. Thus, an exacerbation of defending skills can be obtained by placing a team under a numerical disadvantage. The relative space per player in SSCGs should not be considered as a guideline for designing practice tasks, since the same areas per player can be obtained by manipulating field dimensions or player numbers, but, in turn, have been shown to promote distinct tactical adaptations of players. For instance, the same relative areas of play established by each one of these constraints have been shown to promote different individual spatial distributions and numerical relations near the vicinity of each player. Finally, performance analysis in SSCGs can be used as an evaluation tool of emerging talent in football. More skilled players display higher levels of movement variability and are more difficult to mark during performances in SSCGs played in small fields. They are also more tactically balanced in respect to the division and coverage of specific zones of the field.

131

REFERENCES

Araújo, D., Davids, K., Bennett, S., Button, C., & Chapman, G. (2004). Emergence of sport skills under constraints. In M. Williams & N. Hodges (Eds.), *Skill Acquisition in Sport Research, Theory and Practice* (pp. 409–433). UK: Routledge.

Araújo D., Passos, P. Esteves, P., Duarte, R., Lopes, J., Hristovski, R., & Davids, K., (2015). The micro-macro link in understanding sport tactical behaviours: Integrating information and action at different levels of system analysis in sport. *Movement Sport Science, 89,* 53–63.

Araújo, D., Silva, P., & Davids, K. (2015). Capturing group tactical behaviors in expert team players. In J. Baker & D. Farrow (Eds.), *Routledge Handbook of Sport Expertise* (pp. 209–220). New York: Routledge.

Araújo, D., & Davids, K. (2016). Team synergies in sport: Theory and measures. Frontiers in Psychology. DOI: 10.3389/fpsyg.2016.01449

Bakker, F. C., Oudejans, R. D., Binsch, O., & Kamp, J. van der. (2007). Penalty shooting and gaze behaviour: Unwanted effects of the wish not to miss. *International Journal of Sport Psychology, 37*(2), 265–280.

Bate, R. (1988). Football chance: Tactics and strategy. In T. Reilly, A. Lees, K. Davids, & W. J. Murphy (Eds.), *Science and Football* (pp. 293–301). London: E and FN Spon.

Bloomfield, J. R., Polman, R. C. J., & O'Donoghue, P. G. (2005). Effects of scoreline on team strategies in FA premier league soccer. *Journal of Sports Sciences, 23,* 192–193.

Bradley, P. S., Carling, C., Archer, D., Roberts, J., Dodds, A., Di Mascio, M., . . . Krustrup, P. (2011). The effect of playing formation on high-intensity running and technical profiles in English FA premier league soccer matches. *Journal of Sports Sciences, 29,* 821–830.

Bradley, P., Di Mascio, M., Peart, D., Olsen, P., & Sheldon, B. (2010). High-intensity activity profiles of elite soccer players at different performance levels. *Journal of Strength and Conditioning Research, 24*(9), 2343–2351.

Bush, M., Barnes, C., Archer, D., Hogg, B., & Dradley, P. (2015). Evolution of match performance parameters for various playing positions in the English premier league. *Human Movement Science, 39,* 1–11.

Carling, C. (2010). Analysis of physical activity profiles when running with the ball in a professional soccer team. *Journal of Sports Sciences, 28*(3), 319–326.

Carling, C. (2011). Influence of opposition team formation on physical and skill-related performance in a professional soccer team. *European Journal of Sport Science, 11*(3), 155–164.

Carling, C., & Bloomfield, J. (2010). The effect of an early dismissal on player work-rate in a professional soccer match. *Journal of Science and Medicine in Sport, 13*(1), 126–128.

Carling, C., & Dupont, G. (2011). Are declines in physical performance associated with a reduction in skill-related performance during professional soccer match-play? *Journal of Sports Sciences, 29*(1), 63–71.

132

Carling, C., Espié, V., Le Gall, F., Bloomfield, J., & Jullien, H. (2010). Work-rate of substitutes in elite soccer: A preliminary study. *Journal of Science and Medicine in Sport, 13*(2), 253–255.

Castellano, J., Blanco-Villaseñor, A., & Álvarez, D. (2011). Contextual variables and time-motion analysis in soccer. *International Journal of Sports Medicine, 32*(6), 415–421.

Clemente, F., Martins, F., Kalamaras, D., del Wong, P., & Mendes, R., (2015). General network analysis of national soccer teams in FIFA world cup 2014. *International Journal of Performance Analysis in Sport, 15*, 80–96.

Davids, K., Araújo, D., & Shuttleworth, R. (2005). Applications of dynamical systems theory to football. In T. Reilly, J. Cabri, & D. Araújo (Eds.), *Science and Football V* (pp. 547–560). London: Routledge.

Davids, K., Button, C., Araújo, D., Renshaw, I., & Hristovski, R. (2006). Movement models from sports provide representative task constraints for studying adaptive behaviour in human movement studies. *Adaptive Behavior, 14*, 73–94.

De Baranda, P., Ortega, E., & Palao, J. (2008). Analysis of goalkeepers' defence in the World Cup in Korea and Japan in 2002. *European Journal of Sport Science, 8*(3), 127–134.

Dellal, A., Chamari, K., Wong, D., Ahmaidi, S., Keller, D., Barros, R., . . . Carling, C. (2011). Comparison of physical and technical performance in European soccer match-play: FA Premier League and La Liga. *European Journal of Sport Science, 11*(1), 51–59.

Dellal, A., Wong, D. P., Moalla, W., & Chamari, K. (2010). Physical and technical activity of soccer players in the French First League – With special reference to their playing position. *International Sportmed Journal, 11*(2), 278–290.

Di Salvo, V., Baron, R., Tschan, H., Calderon Montero, F., Bachl, N., & Pigozzi, F. (2007). Performance characteristics according to playing position in elite soccer. *International Journal of Sports Medicine, 28*(3), 222–227.

Diaz, G. J., Fajen, B. R., & Phillips, F. (2012). Anticipation from biological motion: The goalkeeper problem. *Journal of Experimental Psychology: Human Perception and Performance, 38*(4), 848–864.

Dicks, M., Button, C., & Davids, K. (2010). Examination of gaze behaviors under in situ and video simulation task constraints reveals differences in information pickup for perception and action. *Attention, Perception, & Psychophysics, 72*(3), 706–720.

Dicks, M., Davids, K., & Button, C. (2010). Individual differences in the visual control of intercepting a penalty kick in association football. *Human Movement Science, 29*(3), 401–411.

Duarte, R., Araújo, D., Correia, V., Davids, K., Marques, P., & Richardson, M. (2013). Competing together: Assessing the dynamics of *team-team* and *player-team* synchrony in professional association football. *Human Movement Science, 32*(4), 555–566

Duarte, R., Araújo, D., Folgado, H., Esteves, P., Marques, P., & Davids, K. (2013). Capturing complex, non-linear team behaviours during competitive football performance. *Journal of System Science and Complexity, 26*(1), 62–72.

Duarte, R., Araújo, D., Freire, L., Folgado, H., Fernandes, O., & Davids, K. (2012). Intra- and inter-group coordination patterns reveal collective behaviours of football players near the scoring zone. *Human Movement Science, 31*(6), 1639–1651.

Duarte, R., Araújo, D., Travassos, B., Davids, K., Gazimba, V., & Sampaio, J. (2012). Interpersonal coordination tendencies shape 1vs1 sub-phase performance outcomes in youth soccer. *Journal of Sports Sciences, 30*(9), 871–877.

Fister Jr., I., Ljubic, K., Suganthanc, P. N., Percd, M., & Fister, I. (2015). Computational intelligence in sports: Challenges and opportunities in a new research domain. *Applied Mathematics and Computation, 262*, 178–186.

Garganta, J., Maia, J. & Basto, F. (1997). Analysis of goal-scoring patterns in European top level soccer teams. In T. Reilly, J. Bangsbo, & M. Hughes (Eds.), *Science and Football III* (pp. 246–250). London: E and FN Spon.

Harris, S., & Reilly, T. (1988). Space, teamwork and attacking success in soccer. In T. Reilly, A. Lees, K. Davids, & W. Murphy (Eds.), *Science and Football* (pp. 322–328). London: E&F Spon.

Headrick, J., Davids, K., Renshaw, I., Araújo, D., Passos, P., & Fernandes, O. (2012). Proximity-to-goal as a constraint on patterns of behaviour in attacker–defender dyads in team games. *Journal of Sports Sciences, 30*(3), 247–253.

Horikawa, M., & Yagi, A. (2012). The relationships among trait anxiety, state anxiety and the goal performance of penalty shoot-out by university soccer players. *PLoS One, 7*(4), e35727.

Hughes, M., & Churchill, S. (2004). Attacking profiles of successful and unsuccessful teams in Copa America 2001. *Journal of Sports Sciences, 22*, 505.

Hughes, M., & Franks, I. M. (2005). Analysis of passing sequences, shots and goals in soccer. *Journal of Sports Sciences, 23*, 509–514.

Huys, R., Cañal-Bruland, R., Hagemann, N., & Willams, A. M. (2009). Global information pickup underpins anticipation of tennis shot direction. *Journal of Motor Behavior, 41*(2), 158–171.

Jacklin, P. (2005). Temporal changes in home advantage in English football since the second world war: What explains improved away performance? *Journal of Sports Sciences, 23*(7), 669–679.

Jones, P. D., James, N., & Mellalieu, S. D. (2004). Possession as a performance indicator in soccer. *International Journal of Performance Analysis in Sport, 4*, 98–102.

Jordet, G., Hartman, E., & Sigmundstad, E. (2009). Temporal links to performing under pressure in international soccer penalty shootouts. *Psychology of Sport Exercise, 10*, 621–627.

Lago, C. (2009). The influence of match location, quality of opposition, and match status on possession strategies in professional association football. *Journal of Sports Sciences, 27*(13), 1463–1469.

Lago, C., Casais, L., Dominguez, E., & Sampaio, J. (2010). The effects of situational variables on distance covered at various speeds in elite soccer. *European Journal of Sport Science, 10*(2), 103–109.

Lago, C., & Martín, R. (2007). Determinants of possession of the ball in soccer. *Journal of Sports Sciences, 25*, 969–974.

Lago-Ballesteros, J., & Lago-Peñas, C. (2010). Performance in team sports: Identifying the keys to success in soccer. *Journal of Human Kinetics, 25*, 85–91.

Lago-Peñas, C., & Dellal, A. (2010). Ball possession strategies in elite soccer according to the evolution of the match-score: The influence of situational variables. *Journal of Human Kinetics, 25*, 93–100.

Lago-Peñas, C., & Lago-Ballesteros, J. (2011). Game location and team quality effects on performance profiles in professional soccer. *Journal of Sports Science and Medicine, 10*(3), 465–471.

Lago-Peñas, C., Lago-Ballesteros, J., Dellal, A., & Gomez, M. (2010). Game-related statistics that discriminated winning, drawing and losing teams from the Spanish soccer league. *Journal of Sports Science and Medicine, 9*(2), 288–293.

Lago-Peñas, C., Rey, E., Lago-Ballesteros, J., Casáis, L., & Domínguez, E. (2011). The influence of a congested calendar on physical performance in elite soccer. *Journal of Strength and Conditioning Research, 25*(8), 2111–2117.

Lees, A., & Owens, L. (2011). Early visual cues associated with a directional place kick in soccer. *Sports Biomech, 10*(2), 125–134.

Liu, H., Gomez, M., Lago-Peñas, C., & Sampaio, J. (2015). Match statistics related to winning in the group stage of 2014 Brazil FIFA world cup. *Journal of Sports Sciences, 33*, 1205–1213.

Lopes, J. E., Araújo, D., & Davids, K. (2014a). Investigative trends in understanding penalty-kick performance in association football: An ecological dynamics perspective. *Sports Medicine, 44*(1), 1–7.

Lopes, J. E., Araújo, D., Duarte, R., & Fernandes, O. (2012). Instructional constraints on movement and performance of players in the penalty kick. *International Journal of Performance Analysis in Sport, 12*(2), 331–345.

Lopes, J. E., Jacobs, D. M., Travieso, D., & Araújo, D. (2014b). Predicting the lateral direction of deceptive and non-deceptive penalty kicks in football from the kinematics of the kicker. *Human Movement Science, 36*, 199–216.

McGarry, T., Anderson, D. I., Wallace, S. A., Hughes, M. D., & Franks, I. M. (2002). Sport competition as a dynamical self-organizing system. *Journal of Sports Sciences, 20*, 771–781.

Moll, T., Jordet, G., & Pepping G. (2010). Emotional contagion in soccer penalty shootouts: Celebration of individual success is associated with ultimate team success. *Journal of Sports Sciences, 28*(9), 983–992.

Navarro, M., Miyamoto, N., Van der Kamp, J., Morya, E., & Ranvaud, R. (2011). The effects of high pressure on the point of no return in simulated penalty kicks. *Journal of Sport and Exercise Psychology, 34*(1), 83–101.

Navarro, M., Van der Kamp, J., Ranvaud, R., & Savelsbergh, G. J. P. (2013). The mere presence of a goalkeeper affects the accuracy of penalty kicks. *Journal of Sports Science, 9*, 921–929.

O'Donoghue, P., Boyd, M., Lawlor, J., & Bleakley, E. (2001). Time-motion analysis of elite, semi-professional and amateur soccer competition. *Journal of Human Movement Studies, 41*(1), 1–12.

Olsen, E., & Larsen, O. (1997). Use of match analysis by coaches. In T. Reilly, J. Bangsbo, & M. Hughes (Eds.), *Science and Football* (pp. 209–220). London: E and FN Spon.

Piras, A., & Vickers, J. N. (2011). The effect of fixation transitions on quiet eye duration and performance in the soccer penalty kick: Instep versus inside kicks. *Cognitive Process*, *12*(3), 245–255.

Plessner, H., Unkelbach, C., Memmert, D., Baltes, A., & Kolb, A. (2009). Regulatory fit as a determinant of sport performance: How to succeed in a soccer penalty-shooting. *Psychology of Sport and Exercise*, *10*(1), 108–115.

Pollard, R. (2006). Worldwide regional variations in home advantage in association football. *Journal of Sports Sciences*, *24*(3), 231–240.

Poulter, D. (2009). Home advantage and player nationality in international club football. *Journal of Sports Sciences*, *27*(8), 797–805.

Rampinini, E., Impellizzeri, F., Castagna, C., Coutts, A., & Wisløff, U. (2009). Technical performance during soccer matches of the Italian series a league: Effect of fatigue and competitive level. *Journal of Science and Medicine in Sport*, *12*(1), 227–233.

Reep, C., & Benjamin, B. (1968). Skill and chance in association football. *Journal of the Royal Statistical Society. Series A (General)*, *134*, 581–585.

Reilly, T., & Thomas, V. (1976). A motion analysis of work rate in different positional roles in professional football match play. *Journal of Human Movement Studies*, *2*, 87–97

Rey, E., Lago-Peñas, C., Lago-Ballesteros, J., Casais, L., & Dellal, A. (2010). The effect of congested fixture period on the activity of elite soccer players. *Biology of Sport*, *27*(3), 181–185.

Robinson, G., O'Donoghue, P., & Wooster, B. (2011). Path changes in the movement of English premier league soccer players. *Journal of Sports Medicine and Physical Fitness*, *51*(2), 200–226.

Sánchez, P., García-calvo, T., Leo, F., Pollard, R., & Gómez, M. (2009). An analysis of home advantage in the top two Spanish professional football leagues. *Perceptual and Motor Skills*, *108*(3), 789–797.

Sarmento, H., Marcelino, R., Anguera, M. T., Campaniço, J., Matos, N., & Leitão, J. C., (2014). Match analysis in football: A systematic review. *Journal of Sports Sciences*, *32*, 1831–1843.

Silva, P., Aguiar, P. Duarte, R., Davids, K., Araújo, D., & Garganta, J. (2014). Effects of pitch size and skill level on tactical behaviours of association football players during small-sided and conditioned games. *International Journal of Sports Science & Coaching*, *9*(5), 993–1006.

Silva, P., Chung, D., Carvalho, T., Cardoso, T., Davids, K., Araújo, D., & Garganta, J. (2016). Practice effects on emergent intra-team synergies in sports teams. *Human Movement Science*, *46*, 39–51.

Silva, P., Duarte, R., Sampaio, J., Aguiar, P., Davids, K., Araújo, D., . . . Garganta, J. (2014). Field dimension and skill level constrain team tactical behaviours in small-sided and conditioned games in football. *Journal of Sports Sciences*, *10*, *32*(20), 1–9.

Silva, P., Esteves, P., Correia, V., Davids, K., Araújo, D., & Garganta, J. (2015). Effects of manipulating player numbers vs. field dimensions on inter-individual coordination during youth football small-sided games. *International Journal of Performance Analysis of Sport*, *2*, 641–659.

136

Silva, P., Garganta, J., Araújo, D., Davids, K., & Aguiar, P. (2013). Shared knowledge or shared affordances? Insights from an ecological dynamics approach to team coordination in sports. *Sports Medicine, 43*, 775–772.

Silva, P., Travassos, B., Vilar, L., Aguiar, P., Davids, K., Araújo, D., . . . Garganta, J. (2014). Numerical relations and skill level constrain co-adaptive behaviors of agents in sports teams. *PLoS ONE, 9*(9), e107112, 1–12.

Taylor, J., Mellalieu, S., James, N., & Shearer, D. (2008). The influence of match location, quality of opposition, and match status on technical performance in professional association football. *Journal of Sports Sciences, 26*(9), 885–895.

Tenga, A. (2013). Soccer. In T. McGarry, P. O'Donoghue, & J. Sampaio (Eds.), *Routledge Handbook of Sports Performance Analysis* (pp. 323–337). London & New York: Routledge Taylor & Francis Group.

Tenga, A., Holme, I., Ronglan, L., & Bahr, R. (2010a). Effect of playing tactics on achieving score-box possessions in a random series of team possessions from Norwegian professional soccer matches. *Journal of Sports Sciences, 28*(3), 245–255.

Tenga, A., Holme, I., Ronglan, L., & Bahr, R. (2010b). Effect of playing tactics on goal scoring in Norwegian professional soccer. *Journal of Sports Sciences, 28*(3), 237–244.

Tenga, A., & Sigmundstad, E. (2011). Characteristics of goal-scoring possessions in open play: Comparing the top, in-between and bottom teams from professional soccer league. *International Journal of Performance Analysis in Sport, 11*, 545–552.

Thomas, S., Reeves, C., & Smith, A. (2006). English soccer teams' aggressive behaviour when playing away from home. *Perceptual and Motor Skills, 102*(2), 317–320.

Travassos, B., Araújo, D., Davids, K., Vilar, L., Esteves, P., & Correia, V. (2012). Informational constraints shape emergent functional behaviors during performance of interceptive actions in team sports. *Psychology of Sport & Exercise, 13*, 216–223.

Travassos, B., Araújo, D., Duarte, R., & McGarry, T. (2012). Spatiotemporal coordination patterns in futsal (indoor football) are guided by informational game constraints. *Human Movement Science, 31*, 932–945.

Travassos, B., Araújo, D., Vilar, L., & McGarry, T. (2011). Interpersonal coordination and ball dynamics in futsal (indoor football). *Human Movement Science, 30*, 1245–1259.

Travassos, B., Duarte, R., Vilar, V., Davids, K., & Araújo, D. (2012). Practice task design in team sports: Representativeness enhanced by increasing opportunities for action, *Journal of Sports Sciences, 30*, 1447–1454.

Van der Kamp, J. (2006). A field simulation study of the effectiveness of penalty kick strategies in soccer: Late alterations of kick direction increase errors and reduce accuracy. *Journal of Sports Sciences, 24*(5), 467–477.

Vigne, G., Gaudino, C., Rogowski, I., Alloatti, G., & Hautier, C. (2010). Activity profile in elite Italian soccer team. *International Journal of Sports Medicine, 31*(5), 304–310.

Vilar, L., Araújo, D., Davids, K., & Button, C. (2012). The role of ecological dynamics in analysing performance in team sports. *Sports Medicine, 42*(1), 1–10.

Vilar, L., Araújo, D., Davids, K., Correia, V., & Esteves, P. (2013). Spatial-temporal constraints on decision-making during shooting performance in the team sport of futsal. *Journal of Sports Sciences, 31*(8), 840–846.

Vilar, L., Araújo, D., Davids, K., & Travassos, B. (2012). Constraints on competitive performance of attacker-defender dyads in team sports. *Journal of Sports Sciences, 30*, 459–469.

Vilar, L., Araújo, D., Davids, K., Travassos, B., Duarte, R., & Parreira, J. (2014). Interpersonal coordination tendencies supporting the creation/prevention of goal scoring opportunities in futsal. *European Journal of Sport Science, 14*, 28–35.

Vilar, L., Araújo, D., Travassos, B., & Davids, K. (2014). Coordination tendencies are shaped by attacker and defender interactions with the goal and the ball in futsal. *Human Movement Science, 33*, 14–24.

Zerguini, Y., Kirkendall, D., Junge, A., & Dvorak, J. (2007). Impact of Ramadan on physical performance in professional soccer players. *British Journal of Sports Medicine, 41*(6), 398–400.

138

CHAPTER 7

RESEARCH TOPICS IN OTHER FOOTBALL CODES (RUGBY UNION, RUGBY LEAGUE, AUSSIE RULES AND AMERICAN FOOTBALL)

Leading author: Pedro Passos

INTRODUCTION

This chapter is focused on research issues in rugby union, rugby league, American football and Aussie rules as team sports distinguished by intense physical contact allowed by the rules of the game, and a continuous behaviour that aims to invade the opponent's pitch and, consequently, gaining territory over the opponent. These special features justify the use of distinct performance indicators.

Rugby is a team game played by two teams of 15 players (rugby union version) or 13 players (rugby league), each on a rectangular field 110 yards long with score lines and goal posts at either end. The objective of the rugby match is to run with an oval ball across the opponent's goal line (scoring a five-points try) or kick it between the goal posts above the crossbars (scoring three points, or two due to a conversion after scoring a try). As a main rule of the game forward passing is not permitted, and to stop the ball carrier intense physical contact is allowed within the rules of the game.

Australian rules football (aka Aussie rules) is a team sport played in Australia between teams of 18 players each on an oval pitch, with goal posts (these without crossbars) placed at either end of the pitch; the ball is also oval but larger than that used in rugby. Players attempt to kick the ball between goal posts, scoring six points for a goal (between the two main posts) and one point for a behind (between either of two outer posts and the main posts). They may punch or kick the ball and run with it provided that they bounce it/pass it every 10 yards. Similar to rugby intense physical contact with the ball carrier is also allowed within the rules of the game.

American football is a team sport played by two teams of 11 players on a rectangular field 100 yards long. Teams try to get possession of the ball and advance it across the opponent's goal line in a series of running and/or passing plays. Unlike rugby, forward passing is allowed and planned strategies for play are decided during the course of the game. To stop the attacker's actions the defenders can tackle him/her within the rules of the game. Points are scored by advancing the ball into the opponent's end zone for a *touchdown* (scoring six points), or by kicking the ball from the playing field through the goal posts above the crossbar (scoring three points).

This chapter is separated in two parts. The first part is dedicated to the most up-to-date research methods, variables and results that characterise performance analysis in other football codes. The second part presents some trends for future research in performance analysis in rugby union, rugby league, American football and Aussie rules.

PART I – METHODS AND VARIABLES

In rugby union, rugby league and Australian football an effective way to avoid allowing the attacking players to gain territory and get closer to the score line or area is by tackling the ball carrier. This is the reason that a main issue under research in these team sports is the tackle contest.

Hendricks and his colleagues (2012) classified the studies on tackling as grounded on four main aspects: (i) injury prevention (usually more related with medical sciences); (ii) technique analysis and its relation to performance variables and physiological demands (Deutsch et al., 2007; Gabbett et al., 2011); (iii) factors that may predict success in the tackle contest (Passos et al., 2008; van Rooyen et al., 2014; K. Wheeler & Sayers, 2009); and (iv) analysis of dynamics of ball carrier/tackle interactive behaviour (Hendricks et al., 2012; Passos et al., 2008; Passos et al., 2009).

Movement patterns, behavioural specificity and physiological demands

Concerning the association between technical and tactical skills with physiological demands, a study developed by Deutsch et al. (2007) aimed to quantify the movement patterns of rugby union players. For that purpose aerobic and anaerobic pathways were analysed according

140

to players' positions (i.e., forwards and backs). The method used was video analysis, and to set the physiological demands each player's movement was coded according to one of six speeds of displacement (standing still, walking, jogging, cruising, sprinting or utility), three states of non-running intensive exertion (rucking/mauling, tackling or scrummaging) and three discrete activities (kicking, jumping or passing). To characterise the positional group movement pattern the authors used the frequency of occurrences (number that each movement was performed in each match), average time and relative time that each player spent in each match (Deutsch et al., 2007). Results revealed a significant difference of movement patterns between forwards and backs, but also (and with more relevance) it was shown that each positional group of players had its own unique physiological demands (e.g., front row forwards display different demands when compared with back row forwards). This means that training sessions should be planning considering differences in physiological demands within positional groups, and not solely between backs and forwards (Deutsch et al., 2007).

A very similar study was developed by Dawson and colleagues in Australian football. The authors used video analysis to describe movement patterns coded as six different movements (stand, walk, jog, fast-run, sprint, change of direction) and game activities coded as six different actions (ball possessions, ruck duels, ground ball contests, shepherds, spoils, bumps and tackles) of elite players from five different positions (full forward/full back, centre half forward/centre half back, small forward/small back, midfielders and ruckmen) (Dawson et al., 2004). Results revealed that physiological demands and players' movement patterns along with players' positions were also relevant issues for performance analysis. The descriptive analysis from the Dawson and colleagues' study of Aussie rules players suggested differences in movement patterns and game activities among players' positions (e.g., full backs/full forwards stand more and jog less than players in other positions) (Dawson et al., 2004). A key message from both studies is that each role/position requires behavioural specificity, which has implications also for performance analysis (please see Table 7.1).

Variables that lead to success in tackle contests

Notational analysis can be used to identify key performance indicators in match play situations; however, most of the research was only focused

Table 7.1 Exemplar variables used in performance analysis in rugby union and Aussie rules

	Movement patterns/game activities	Player positions	Physiological demands
Rugby union	Rucking/mauling, tackling and scrummaging; kicking, jumping and passing, standing still, walking, jogging, cruising, sprinting and utility	Forwards and backs; being more specific: front row forwards and back row forwards	Aerobic and anaerobic
Aussie rules	Ball possessions, ruck duels, ground ball contests, shepherds, spoils, bumps and tackles; stand, walk, jog, fast-run, sprint, change of direction	Full forwards/full backs, centre half forwards/centre half backs, small forwards/small backs, midfielders and ruckmen	Aerobic and anaerobic

on reporting the frequency of events (e.g., the number of tackle-breaks that occur) as an index of performance, without considering parameters that could be related to performance effectiveness. With the purpose of addressing this Wheeler and colleagues (2010) used notational analysis in rugby union, seeking to associate attacking patterns of play (i.e., width, depth, velocity, direction) with agility skills (i.e., evasive step type; change of running line direction angle) that lead the ball carrier to desirable outcomes, such as off-loading, tackle-breaks or line-breaks (Wheeler et al., 2010). The data were collected from commercial television that was distributed in the public domain. One of the most relevant results from the Wheeler and colleagues' study was that 72 per cent of the tackle-breaks (as a performance indicator) occur due to a side-stepping attacking strategy performed within a moderate change of angle direction (i.e., between 20° and 60°) (Wheeler et al., 2010). This finding is in line with results of previous research that revealed the side-stepping manoeuvres with a moderate change in the running line trajectory afford the ball carrier to maintain horizontal momentum and thus increase the ability to penetrate the defensive line (Sayers & Washington-King, 2005). Both studies are good examples of the need of associating relevant variables with performance indicators to strive for a better understanding of team sports performance and the factors that lead to success. Results of Passos and colleagues (2008), Wheeler and colleagues (2010) and Sayers & Washington-King (2005) highlight the relevance for considering the co-adaptive behaviors in performance analysis, as well as reveal a set of variables that might help to describe, explain and, perhaps, predict attacker–defender behavioral outcomes.

Michele van Rooyen and colleagues studied tackles from the tackler's perspective. The authors aimed to understand the characteristics of tackler behaviour as regards contact with the ball carrier and relate those characteristics with tackle 'effectiveness' (van Rooyen et al., 2014). This concept was defined in the literature as a ball carrier territorial gaining after being tackled. Basically, if the ball carrier was closer the score line after the contact point with the tackler, then this tackle was not effective; on the contrary, if the ball carrier distance to the score line remained or even increased, then an effective tackle occurred (Passos et al., 2006; van Rooyen et al., 2014). To characterise the tackler behaviour the following variables were previously defined: (i) tackler body position (e.g., lean forward or upright); (ii) angle of approach between tackler and ball carrier (i.e., front, oblique, side-on, behind); (iii) weight distribution (i.e., front foot, rear foot). Tackler behaviour and outcome (i.e., effective or non-effective) were compared between winning and losing teams in an elite rugby tournament. The data were collected from the video recording of 15 matches of the 2007 Six Nations Tournament. Tackle situations were observed and categorised by a single analyst (intra-operator reliability procedures revealed acceptable values). As an example of the statistical analysis that can be used on similar studies the tackle frequencies were displayed with means and standard deviation, and the comparisons between tackle effectiveness of winning and losing teams used t tests or ANOVA (with post hoc Tukey's test) with significance values of $P=0.05$. To analyse the magnitude of the influence of tackle effectiveness on the match outcome effect sizes were also calculated (van Rooyen et al., 2014).

Ball carrier/tackler contests have been studied within two different performance conditions, match play and controlled conditions; a common method to support further analysis is the use of video recording to capture opposing players' performances. The analysis of players' performances in match play conditions is the most representative situation, but lacks objectivity in two aspects: (i) in the search for a linear association between independent and dependent variables; and (ii) in subjective estimations of kinematic variables (e.g., velocity), instead of using controlled situations, which allow a sharp accuracy in measurement of these sorts of variables. On the other side, controlled conditions may support the independent/dependent variables association, but the experimental task may lack representativeness, which is the 'arrangement of conditions of an experiment so that they represent the behavioural setting to which the results are intended to apply' (Araújo et al., 2007, p.72).

However, the improvements in technological devices in the last decades may change this trend, and nowadays it is possible to make an accurate analysis in match play situations. We are looking forward for what is going to happen in the next decade.[6]

A suitable example of the use of technological devices which will rule the next decades of research is the study of Hendricks and colleagues (2012), where the ball carrier's and tackler's running line path were tracked for the purpose of comparing players' velocity and acceleration before contact in front-on and side-on tackles in three different levels of competition. For that purpose the authors used video analysis and computer-generated algorithms to create a 2D image (x, y) of the playing field. The requirements for these procedures are the known coordinates (x, y) of four points of the field that must be permanently visible on the cameras; also the cameras must be fixed for the entire recording session (Hendricks et al., 2012). Hendricks et al. (2012) in rugby union aimed to analyse how the velocity and acceleration profiles of the ball carrier and defender may predict who will succeed and also be injury free. The results revealed no differences in the ball carrier's and tackler's velocity and acceleration between different levels of competition. But an intra-competition analysis unravels significant differences between the ball carrier's and tackler's velocity in the intermediate level of competition (semi-professional players), with the tacklers being faster than ball carriers in front-on tackles, but only at further distances from the point of contact between players (i.e., 0, 5 s before contact); as the time to contact decreases (i.e., below 0, 5 s to contact) this difference disappears, which means that within shorter distances (i.e., less time to contact) the ball carrier manages the running line speed in order to create some advantage over the tackler. These results seem to provide a good argument in favour of the 'critical regions' (or critical periods) which have a significant influence for each match 'history'. Critical periods (regions) have been characterised as brief time and space windows during which a system's organisation (such as a dyadic ball carrier–defender system) is most open to changes due to external and internal influences (Anderson, 2002). For the Hendricks et al. (2012) study the ball carrier–defender system may change its organisation (for instance the ball carrier goes

144

past the defender) due to such internal influences as changes in the relative velocity values.

A similar study developed in Australian football, which also favours the critical regions, was carried out by Gastin and colleagues (2013), where the authors aimed to analyse players' peak velocity and acceleration before tackling point of contact. The methods used were a combination of video analysis and GPS devices and the data were collected from 20 elite-level players in four matches. For data analysis the tackles were subjectively grouped into low-, medium- and high-intensity tackles. This study also aimed to compare players' peak velocity and acceleration regarding tackles made by the players and against the player; tri-axial accelerometers were used for that purpose. The comparative analysis was performed with analysis of variance (Gastin et al., 2013). The results reveal significant differences in peak velocity and acceleration immediately before contact among the three intensity tackle groups, which means that tacklers run faster and speed up when they performed high-intensity tackles, as compared to medium- or low-intensity tackles (Gastin et al., 2013). Speeding up immediately before the contact point with the ball carrier only makes sense within short interpersonal distances; otherwise, the tackler's behaviour may become predictable, allowing the ball carrier to make an 'easy' evasive manoeuvre. It is interesting to note the fact that several studies are supportive concerning the notion of 'critical regions'. This concept was characterised in a previous work of Passos and colleagues (2008) in rugby union, and is related with opponent players' contextual dependency. Critical regions can be characterised by time to contact as was done by Hendricks and colleagues, or by opponent players' interpersonal distances, as was done by Passos and colleagues (2008). However, the main issue is that within those regions each player's behaviour is no longer independent of the other players' behaviour. These results highlight the importance of analysing contests within critical regions. Being able to clearly identify and characterise 'critical regions' seems to be a good challenge for performance analysis in team sports.

Both previous studies were based on analysis of variance of players' velocity and acceleration. Nevertheless if we would like to collect data that may support behavioural prediction we should move forward to a dynamic analysis using variables that describe and explain players' behaviour, such as relative velocity, defined as the difference between the tackler's velocity and the ball carrier's velocity (Passos et al., 2008). However, relative velocity has a predictive feature only within critical regions that can be set using the time scale before impact, as suggested by Hendricks and colleagues.

The need of investigating co-adaptive behaviours between opponent players was also suggested by Wheeler and colleagues (2010) when they stated, regarding further research, the 'needs to investigate defensive decision-making against an attacking ball carrier displaying evasive agility skill' (Wheeler et al., 2010, p. 242). Perhaps for further research it would interesting to investigate the effect of ball carriers' evasive agility skills on the ball carrier–defender dyadic stability. If no actions occur the ball carrier–defender dyad remains stable. Nevertheless ball carriers' evasive skills aim to destabilise the relative positions of the ball carrier and defender. When this occurs the ball carrier–defender stability is disturbed and enters into fluctuations; within a certain range these fluctuations become critical, which means that the ball carrier is gaining an advantage and opportunities to overtake the defender are emerging.

The physical contact in team sports, such as rugby union, is indeed a main focus of research. The effectiveness of that contact in elite rugby union teams was studied by van Rooyen and colleagues, whose results showed that less effective tackles were on average 34 per cent more prevalent than effective tackles (van Rooyen et al., 2014). Regarding the analysis of tackle effectiveness in relation to individual technique, it was noted that effective tackles occurred when players lean their torso forward and consequently the body weight is placed predominantly in the front foot. An upright body positioning was more prevalent in less effective tackles. When the tackle effectiveness was related to the match outcome, results revealed that losing teams performed on average 4 per cent more less effective tackles and 3 per cent fewer effective tackles, when compared with winning teams. Despite the non-significance of these results, the effect size revealed a small difference between winning and losing teams regarding tackle effectiveness (van Rooyen et al., 2014). This study highlights that the use of effect size may be relevant to verify how some performance indicators may contribute to (even small) differences between winning and losing a match. Thus, an important issue this study stresses is that when we are looking for differences between winners and losers we need to go beyond variance analysis.

Also when searching for performance indicators that might explain an outcome, it seems more relevant to look for the effectiveness of the actions, rather than for the frequency of their occurrences (van Rooyen et al., 2014).

146

Another study in rugby union is a suitable example of an experimental study that provided interesting results of performance analysis to be explored in rugby practice. Aiming to analyse if the defenders' initial interpersonal distance influences the ball carrier's decisions a rugby union study used an experimental design with task constraints manipulation (Correia et al., 2012). In this study youth rugby players performed a 1v2 situation (i.e., one ball carrier vs two defenders). Aiming to analyse how the ball carrier's adaptive behaviour changes due to task constraints manipulation, the authors continuously decreased the defenders' interpersonal distance. Dependent variables under analysis were performance outcome, players' mean speed, and time between the first crossover and the end of the trial. Results revealed that a shorter defender interpersonal distance was associated with an increase on the tackle frequency and also with a decrease in players' mean speed. These results were in line with results from previous studies that highlighted the relevance of relative velocity within critical regions (i.e., defined as ball carrier–defender interpersonal distances below 4 m). The results revealed that within critical regions the player who was increasing his running line speed had an advantage over the opponent. But if both players decrease running line speeds, the defender may gain advantage (Passos et al., 2008). Correia and colleagues' study provided interesting insights for performance analysis in rugby. Defenders' proximity seems to be a crucial variable to explain performance outcomes, such as tackles, or going forward and getting closer to the try line.

As expected, most of the studies on field sports that feature tackles are focused on variables that describe and explain what happen within physical contact areas. The most commonly used variables in these studies are time to contact, players' velocity and acceleration before impact. This highlights one main issue in performance analysis of interactive behaviours, which is the identification of critical regions (periods) of performance. These critical regions are where opposing players' behaviour becomes mutually dependent. Previous studies suggest that these critical regions could be bound to time to contact between players (Hendricks et al., 2012) or to players' interpersonal distances (Passos et al., 2008; Passos et al., 2009; Passos et al., 2011).

In this section two perspectives of performance analysis were addressed: a *subject-based* analysis usually focused on the frequency of events performed by each player (or team); for instance, how many side-on tackles were performed. On the other hand, there was an *interaction-based* analysis, commonly centred on variables that describe and explain players' interactive behaviour. This second perspective may reveal the reasons for a successful or unsuccessful tackle; for instance, the relative velocity between the ball carrier and tackler, or defenders' interpersonal distance.

Performance indicators and the attempt to discriminate winners from losers

A key issue for notational analysis is to identify performance indicators that discriminate between winning and losing matches (Bishop & Barnes, 2013; Ortega et al., 2009; van Rooyen et al., 2014; Vaz et al., 2011). For example, the study developed by Bishop and Barnes (2013) aimed to characterise winning and losing teams in the knockout stages of the 2011 Rugby World Cup. The research design allowed for the comparing the eight winning teams with the eight losing teams. For that purpose a coding template was designed using 10 technical and tactical actions as performance indicators. This study is an example of the need to relate performance indicators with contextual constraints as the format of the competition (e.g., knockout stage) and also with task constraints such as the location on the pitch where the actions occur (Bishop & Barnes, 2013).

An interesting result was obtained on this study, where only 2 of 10 performance indicators significantly discriminated winners from losers. One of the findings suggests that winning teams use the kicks out of hand significantly more often than losing teams. However, the quality of kicks was not considered in the study; for instance, it would be interesting to relate the kicks out of hand with territorial gain. The authors only measured the frequency of the events and did not relate this frequency with the match outcome, something that was suggested by Wheeler and colleagues in their paper from 2010 when they assessed the quality of decision-making. Perhaps this is the reason that only 2 out of 10 performance indicators appeared as significant to discriminate between winners and losers. This suggests that the frequency of the event, without considering usefulness, might not discriminate clearly between winners and losers; subcomponents of performance indicators and dynamic variables (e.g., changes in players' relative positions; changes in players' location on the pitch) may also be needed to be considered; for instance, explore

148

the relationship between frequency of successful passes and the changes in players' positions on the pitch. Another result which also must be emphasised is that in the knockout matches the winning teams used more of a territory-based strategy (through kicking and high pressure on the pitch) than a ball possession–based strategy (Bishop & Barnes, 2013). A similar result was previously reported for IRB Six Nations and S12 matches between 2003 and 2006 (Bishop & Barnes, 2013; Vaz et al., 2011).

Vaz and colleagues used a similar approach in order to discriminate between winners and losers in close matches at elite-level competition in rugby union (Vaz et al., 2011). The authors hypothesised that differences in style of play due to geographical issues (i.e., southern vs northern hemisphere competitions) may hide significant differences in performance indicators on match-play situations (Vaz et al., 2011). This might suggest that, when the level of competition of the teams under analysis is close (e.g., when using data only from elite-level matches), performance indicators are not sensitive (i.e., didn't capture differences) to task and environmental constraints (e.g., geographical). Thus, to avoid bias due to these constraints, data should be collected and analysed for each specific situation (e.g., team, region, location). That's what Vaz and colleagues did. In this study a digital video analysis system was used to collect data from IRB tournaments (i.e., Six Nations and Super12) between 2003 and 2006. The matches were grouped accordingly the final score using cluster analysis. To avoid the different styles of play between the northern (Six nations) and from the southern (S12) hemispheres influencing the cluster analysis, the data from Six Nations and S12 matches were analysed separately. The results from this study highlight that team styles of play may hide significant differences between performance indicators of winners and losers. Supported on a cluster analysis were identified 'close' (i.e., matches in which the final score was a difference of 15 points or less) and 'balance' games accordingly with the final score differences. The data collected in the Six Nations Tournament revealed no differences between winners and losers in close matches (i.e., matches where the difference in the final score was 15 points or less) and only two significant differences in balanced matches (i.e., matches with a difference in the final score between 16 and 34 points), whereas in Super 12[7] matches eight performance indicators that significantly discriminated winners from losers in close matches were found (i.e., matches where the difference in the final score was 11 points or less), and nine performance indicators were found in balanced matches (i.e., matches with a difference in the final score between 12 and 25 points) (Vaz et al., 2011). However, when we compare data from different tournaments, performance indicators seem not to be sensitive to the level of competition, leading to some different results. For instance, Vaz and colleagues found that winning teams in Six Nations and Super 12 tournaments won fewer turnovers than losing teams, whereas Jones and colleagues have the opposite result from data collected in a domestic season of a professional rugby union team (Jones et al., 2004; Vaz et al., 2011). This was an issue that was later reinforced by van Rooyen and colleagues (van Rooyen et al., 2014).

Notational analysis and decision-making

A team's successful outcomes are quite dependent on how players decide and act. Notational analysis systems were used to evaluate players' decision-making. A recent study of Lorains and colleagues (2013) created and tested a custom-designed method to evaluate players' decision-making using a coding system. The aim was to assess the amount of information players transferred from video-based training to four matches of Australian football (Lorains et al., 2013). The coding system allowed the authors to quantify the players' decision-making abilities in match play.

For the off-the-field sessions a video-based training used a pre-test, five training sessions and a post-test as well as a custom design to assess information retention. In each training session the participants' decision-making was assessed using an AFL video clip showing attacking. Before key actions the video was paused and the participants were asked to point out on the screen where they should pass the ball. The decision-making was assessed based on the same coding system used in match-play situations. An advantage of this method was the use of sub-components to measure decision quality that went further than the traditional methods, which assess decision-making separate from skill execution.

For the coding system three factors were taken in consideration: (i) game context; (ii) decision making; and (iii) execution (for more details please, see Lorains et al., 2013). For instance, the decision quality was measured considering game context factors such as 'ball carrier number of options' and the 'defensive pressure'. Usually the coded systems created

150

for notational analyses were developed after consulting field experts, such as coaches (Lorains et al., 2013; Wheeler et al., 2010).

Concerning the analysis of match-play situations, the study of Lorains and colleagues (2013) in Australian football revealed an increase in the quality of players' decision-making and skill execution – i.e., players became more effective with using free space and retaining ball possession as the season progressed. An implication from the coding system applied in this study was an increase in the level of detail in decision-making, game context and skill execution, highlighting the areas for improvement. However, the transfer from the off-the-field decision-making training to match play situations revealed no significant results, which reinforces the suggestions of other research, that decision-making must be assessed in match-play situations (Araújo et al., 2006).

Take home messages

The majority of studies that aimed to discriminate winning from losing teams in football, rugby union and Aussie rules were not very successful. One of the possible reasons for this may lie in the recording of frequency of actions without considering the outcome. Thus, in order to make the results of performance analysis more relevant it is important to do the following: (i) assess the effectiveness of the actions, rather than the frequency of occurrence of actions; and (ii) associate the relevant variables that describe players' behaviours which might contribute to players' performances (e.g., players' location on the pitch, proximity to goal, relative positions) to performance indicators which characterise players' levels of performance (e.g., frequency of successful passes; number of tackles) to strive for a full understanding of team performance (Figure 7.1).

Additionally there are several issues that should be considered in performance analysis in football, rugby union and Aussie rules. First, there should be an awareness about the influence of task constraints over performance indicators that might bias the results of performance analysis. For example, the upgrade of game rules in rugby union has considerably changed the tactical approaches used by coaches and teams. Being more specific the ball-in-play time increase from an average of 21 to 23 minutes per match in the 1980s to a 35-minute average in the 2007 World Cup (Bishop & Barnes, 2013; Board, 2005, 2007). Another example of the

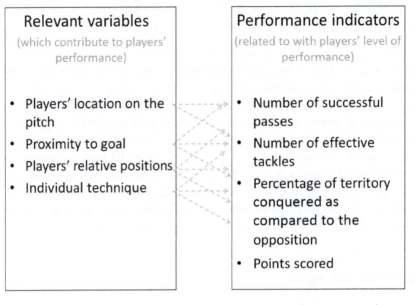

Relevant variables	Performance indicators
(which contribute to players' performance)	(related to with players' level of performance)
• Players' location on the pitch • Proximity to goal • Players' relative positions • Individual technique	• Number of successful passes • Number of effective tackles • Percentage of territory conquered as compared to the opposition • Points scored

Figure 7.1 An example of the 'needed' linkage for performance analysis between relevant variables and performance indicators.

influence of task constraints on the performance indicators is the specificity of players' positions, each of which has different physiological, technical and tactical requirements. Thus task constraints demand that performance analysis should be specific to each player's position.

Second, geographical and cultural constraints, as well as competition level, may influence the performance indicators due to different teams' styles of play. Thus, the different interpretations of results of performance analysis according to these kinds of constraints are required. For instance, in rugby union southern and northern hemisphere teams use different styles of play. Vaz and colleagues (2011) compared performance indicators of winning and losing teams from both hemispheres and verified that cultural and geographical issues bias the results. This means that performance indicators are not sensitive to differences in styles of play, a limitation that can bias the results (Vaz et al., 2011).

Third, when analysing opponent players' interactive behaviour the action to report should be performed within critical regions; that is an important issue when relating the actions (such as a tackle) to effectiveness. Due to a behavioural dependency we suggest that players' action effectiveness can only be assessed within critical regions.

152

PART II – FUTURE TRENDS FOR PERFORMANCE ANALYSIS

This section is comprised of two parts: (i) methodological issues and data analysis; and (ii) changes in performance analysis due to technological improvements.

Concerning suggested issues for data analysis, the main idea is to go beyond a descriptive analysis quantifying the number of occurrences of an event (which is for sure very useful) and go a step further, relating variables that might add some explicative power to performance analysis. For instance, as suggested by van Rooyen and colleagues, it is important to relate the effectiveness of performance indicators such as tackle effectiveness to the odds of scoring or at least creating conditions that will lead to an attempt to score (van Rooyen et al., 2014).

Other trends, presented in the first part of this section, are related to methodological issues in performance analysis. Aiming to analyse the effectiveness of a technical skill (e.g., tackle) some studies pointed out that team sports that feature physically intense contact require an assessment of the tackle dynamics in match-play situations (Hendricks et al., 2012). This means that an experimental task design created for assessment of technical skill effectiveness should represent the same task constraints that are present in match-play situations.

The second part of this section deals with technological improvements that might change performance analysis. An interesting example of a 'new' technological device that has already been tested in sports science research is the player-mounted camera (PMC), which was developed by Croft and colleagues to capture the player's movement from his/her own perspective. A PMC is a non-intrusive player-mounted camera that transmits footage in real time. This device captured images that were immediately available for viewing on a laptop with coaches' comments regarding the most relevant visual cues for the player (Croft et al., 2013).

Online data and real-time footage appear to be a trend to be considered in the near future. What changes could be expected in the performance analysis due to the possibility of assessing players' performances and providing feedback online? What if beyond images a PMC allowed us to capture players' verbal communications, a crucial issue in rugby? How can we relate communication to performance effectiveness? These are only a few questions that might prove interesting to explore.

Online data open the gate to 'new' methods and variables that might be useful for performance analysis. Already used in football (soccer in the U.S.), heat maps and network analysis are not currently used in performance analysis in other football games. Another question to be considered for further studies is: How do we relate network analysis to performance indicators and thus to performance effectiveness?

Virtual reality devices are also an interesting trend to follow especially due to the human–machine interactive opportunities that these devices may allow in a near future. Aiming to analyse whether gaps opening in specific running channels promote changes in the actions performed by the ball carrier, Correia and colleagues developed interesting studies with virtual reality devices in rugby union (Correia et al., 2012). As stated by the authors an advantage of the use of virtual reality devices 'lies in the fact that experimentally controlled information that could not be normally controlled in situ can be controlled in the virtual environment, allowing for an in depth examination of how information shapes action' (Correia et al., 2012, p. 319).

In summary research in other football games can be split into two different trends. A first trend is related to relevant variables that lead to success, with a particular emphasis on relating the relevant variables to performance indicators, particularly within the tackle contests. That way it is possible to display how a performance variable that seems to be relevant contributes to a certain level of performance. This first trend was very successful and highlights the existence of critical regions/periods where players' performances become highly relevant to the outcome of the contest. Therefore performance analysis should be focused on the relationship between relevant variables and performance indicators within these critical regions. A second trend, which has not been so successful, is concerned with finding the differences in performance indicators between winning and losing teams. Match outcome is influenced by a huge quantity of variables (technical, tactical, physiological, psychological), which then might also change due to geographical and cultural constraints. This perhaps explains why these studies have yet to be very successful.

Finally, research in other football games already make use of the most up-to-date technology to collect data of players' performances (e.g., rugby union teams already use GPS devices). The improvements in sports technology, informatics and engineering will result in smaller, lighter and

154

more powerful devices that players will use in competitive matches. In a near future these improvements will allow performance analysis to go to another level of detail.

REFERENCES

Anderson, D. I. (2002). Do critical periods determine when to initiate sport skill learning? In F. L. Smoll & R. E. Smith (Eds.), *Children and Youth in Sports: A Biopsychosocial Perspective* (2nd ed., pp. 105–148). Indianapolis, IN: Brown & Benchmark.

Araújo, D., Davids, K., & Hristovski, R. (2006). The ecological dynamics of decision making in sport. *Psychology of Sport and Exercise, 7*(6), 653–676.

Araújo, D., Davids, K., & Passos, P. (2007). Ecological validity, representative design, and correspondence between experimental task constraints and behavioral setting: Comment on Rogers, Kadar, and Costall (2005). *Ecological Psychology, 19*(1), 69–78.

Bishop, L., & Barnes, A. (2013). Performance indicators that discriminate winning and losing in the knockout stages of the 2011 rugby world cup. *International Journal of Performance Analysis in Sport, 13*(1), 149–159.

Board, I. R. (2005). *Changes in the Playing of International Rugby Over a 20-Year Period*. Dublin, Ireland: IRB.

Board, I. R. (2007). *Statistical Review and Match Analysis: IRB Game Analysis*. Dublin, Ireland: IRB.

Correia, V., Araújo, D., Cummins, A., & Craig, C. M. (2012). Perceiving and acting upon spaces in a VR rugby task: Expertise effects in affordance detection and task achievement. *Journal of Sport and Exercise Psychology, 34*(3), 305–321.

Correia, V., Araújo, A., Duarte, R., Travassos, B., Passos, P., & Davids, K. (2012). Changes in practice task constraints shape decision-making behaviours of team games players. *Journal of Science and Medicine in Sport, 15*(3), 244–249.

Croft, H., Suwarganda, E. K., & Omar, S. F. S. (2013). Development and application of a live transmitting player-mounted head camera. *Sports Technology, 6*(2), 97–110.

Dawson, B., Hopkinson, R., Appleby, B., Stewart, G., & Roberts, C. (2004). Player movement patterns and game activities in the Australian Football League. *Journal of Science and Medicine in Sport, 7*(3), 278–291.

Deutsch, M. U., Kearney, G. A., & Rehrer, N. J. (2007). Time – motion analysis of professional rugby union players during match-play. *Journal of Sports Science, 25*(4), 461–472.

Gabbett, T. J., Jenkins, D. G., & Abernethy, B. (2011). Relationships between physiological, anthropometric, and skill qualities and playing performance in professional rugby league players. *Journal of Sports Science, 29*(15), 1655–1664.

Gastin, P. B., McLean, O., Spittle, M., & Breed, R. V. P. (2013). Quantification of tackling demands in professional Australian football using integrated wearable athlete tracking technology. *Journal of Science and Medicine in Sport, 16*(6), 589–593.

Hendricks, S., Karpul, D., Nicolls, F., & Lambert, M. (2012). Velocity and acceleration before contact in the tackle during rugby union matches. *Journal of Sports Sciences, 30*(12), 1215–1224.

Jones, N., Mellalieu, S., & James, N. (2004). Team performance indicators as a function of winning and losing in rugby union. *International Journal of Performance Analysis in Sport, 4*, 61–71.

Lorains, M., Ball, K., & MacMahon, C. (2013). Performance analysis for decision making in team sports. *International Journal of Performance Analysis in Sport, 13*(1), 110–119.

Ortega, E., Villarejo, D., & Palao, J. M. (2009). Differences in game statistics between winning and losing rugby teams in the six nations tournament. *Journal of Science and Medicine in Sport, 8*(4), 523–527.

Passos, P., Araújo, D., Davids, K., Gouveia, L., Milho, J., & Serpa, S. (2008). Information-governing dynamics of attacker-defender interactions in youth rugby union. *Journal of Sports Sciences, 26*(13), 1421–1429.

Passos, P., Araújo, D., Davids, K., Gouveia, L., & Serpa, S. (2006). Interpersonal dynamics in sport: The role of artificial neural networks and 3-D analysis. *Behavior Research Methods, 38*(4), 683–691.

Passos, P., Araújo, D., Davids, K., Gouveia, L., Serpa, S., Milho, J., & Fonseca, S. (2009). Interpersonal pattern dynamics and adaptive behavior in multiagent neurobiological systems: Conceptual model and data. *Journal of Motor Behavior, 41*(5), 445–459.

Passos, P., Milho, J., Fonseca, S., Borges, J., Araújo, D., & Davids, K. (2011). Interpersonal distance regulates functional grouping tendencies of agents in team sports. *Journal of Motor Behavior, 43*(2), 155–163.

Sayers, M. G. L., & Washington-King, J. (2005). Characteristics of effective ball carries in Super 12 rugby. *International Journal of Performance Analysis in Sport, 5*(3), 92–106.

van Rooyen, M., Yasin, N., & Viljoen, W. (2014). Characteristics of an 'effective' tackle outcome in Six Nations rugby. *European Journal of Sport Science, 14*(2), 123–129.

Vaz, L., Mouchet, A., Carreras, D., & Morente, H. (2011). The importance of rugby game-related statistics to discriminate winners and losers at the elite level competitions in close and balanced games. *International Journal of Performance Analysis in Sport, 11*(1), 130–141.

Wheeler, K. W., Askew, C. D., & Sayers, M. G. (2010). Effective attacking strategies in rugby union. *European Journal of Sport Science, 10*(4), 237–242.

Wheeler, K., & Sayers, M. (2009). Contact skills predicting tackle-breaks in rugby union. *International Journal of Sports Science & Coaching, 4*(4), 535–544.

CHAPTER 8

RESEARCH TOPICS IN ICE HOCKEY

Leading author: Anna Volossovitch

INTRODUCTION

This chapter aims to review some issues regarding performance analysis in ice hockey, providing some insights into skating and shooting performance analysis, physical and physiological game demands, positional profiling, players' and teams' performance evaluation based on game statistics, prediction of games outcomes and assessment of team strategies in different match contexts.

A brief description of ice hockey

Ice hockey is one of the most popular winter sports practiced in Canada, United States and Northern Europe at the amateur and professional levels. The game is played by two teams composed by six players (five outfield skaters and a goaltender), who use their sticks and try to score by shooting the puck into the opposing team's goal. The match consists of three 20-minute periods of actual play with a rest intermission between periods. The game requires from players a complex set of playing skills, such as skating, shooting, passing, receiving, faking, hitting, blocking and body checking, performed in varying context-dependent conditions.

Scientific research on performance in ice hockey has involved analysis of hockey skills, statistical performance evaluation and probabilistic modelling, as well as physiological profiles and specific position demands.

ANALYSIS OF ICE HOCKEY SKILLS

Analysis of skating characteristics and mechanics

All the offensive and defensive skills in ice hockey are performed while players are skating. Skating is a complex motor ability which requires good motor coordination; it is considered as one of the most important technical skills in ice hockey (Bracko, 2004; Bracko et al., 1998).

Biomechanical and kinematic aspects of ice skating performance have been studied in off-ice experimental tasks (Upjohn et al., 2008) and during on-ice non-game trials (Fortier et al., 2014; Lafontaine, 2007). The individual performance skating characteristics have also been analysed during a game play (Bracko et al., 1998).

The stride rate and stride length have been identified as two principal factors that affect skating performance (Farlinger et al., 2007). The findings through three-dimensional skating motion analysis emphasised the importance of enlargement of the stride during the acceleration phase and a greater range of motion throughout the forward skating stride (Lafontaine, 2007; Upjohn et al., 2008). Left and right stride width, width between strides and hip abduction angle have been identified as characteristics that distinguish fast skaters from slow skaters (Bracko, 2004).

The study of ice skating mechanics of change-of-direction manoeuvres in the ice environment demonstrated that players exhibit asymmetric behaviours; that is, they produced dissimilar forces on outside and inside legs when turning in left or right directions. This might be related to leg dominance (Fortier et al., 2014). Thus, the equal competence for both turning directions regardless of leg dominance should be developed during the training process.

Individual performance ice skating characteristics, collected in real game play, have been analysed by Bracko and co-authors (1998). The two-foot glide has been identified as the most common characteristic of game performance (on average 39 per cent of time spent by a player in a game), followed by cruise stride (16.2 per cent), medium-intensity skating (10.0 per cent), a struggle for puck or position (9.8 per cent) and low-intensity skating (7.8 per cent). The ability to make left and right gliding turns as well as crossover turns from a two-foot glide position have also been reported as important skills for a player's performance.

158

The comparison between ice skating characteristics of high and low point scorers have shown the differences not in striding intensity, as might be expected, but in the time spent on the ice (Bracko et al., 1998). High point scorers spent more time in a two-foot glide with and without the puck. Using the definition of skills suggested by Bracko et al. (1998), Lafontaine and colleagues (1998) compared the frequency of ice skating skills of different playing positions. As could be predicted, to protect their own area from the opposite team, the defensemen spent more time travelling backwards and modified more frequently their skating directions than did the forward players (Lafontaine et al., 1998).

Shooting performance

Shooting is one of the most important technical skills in ice hockey, and it is directly related to a player's ability to score goals. The shooting techniques of two of the most commonly used types of shots – the slap shot and wrist shot – have been analysed. The slap shot is characterised by a greater width of the hand placement; it also generates maximum puck velocity (Lomond et al., 2007; Pearsall et al., 1999; Wu et al., 2003). The wrist shot is considered to be quicker and more accurate and requires a shorter swing movement (Worobets et al., 2006). The players' features, such as technical skills, body dimensions and strength, have been identified as the critical factors that determine puck velocity in both the slap and wrist shots (Pearsall et al., 1999; Wu et al., 2003). Skilled and unskilled players with similar physical strength characteristics demonstrated significant differences in shot technique, which was reflected in different vertical force, stick bending and deflection angle measures (Wu et al., 2003).

Regarding the shooting accuracy, it was found that very few kinematic variables allow the prediction of wrist shot accuracy. However, it was noted that the accuracy measures for shooting at the bottom or top corners were significantly different; that is, predicting variables varied according to target heights (Michaud-Paquette et al., 2011). The results of kinematic analysis suggest that a better stability of the base of support, momentum cancellation, proper trunk orientation and a more dynamic control of the lead arm throughout the wrist shot movement are the principal characteristics that improve wrist shot accuracy (Michaud-Paquette et al., 2011).

Information relating to how the skills are performed in experimental trials and game play conditions is crucial for the optimisation of practice and players' development. The results of analysis of ice skating and shooting performance suggest that practicing these skills in the tasks and under conditions similar to the real game (with goaltender and opposition) favours skill improvement.

STATISTICAL RESEARCH IN ICE HOCKEY

Like in other team sports, the range of data collected during ice hockey matches has increased considerably over the last decades. For instance, the NHL compiles comprehensive statistics on players, collecting data in 18 different categories (Mason & Foster, 2007). However, these extensive numbers are not completely suitable for the individual players' evaluation if they are not processed and interpreted properly. Hockey players coordinate their individual actions according to the specific game situation and team strategy for the game. The players' behaviours emerge from the complex dynamic interactions between teams on the ice, and a player's performance is always related to the quality of his/her team and the opponents. Factoring frequent substitutions and playing at full strength,[8] with a power play advantage[9] or short-handed[10] make the player and team evaluations even more difficult. Therefore, identifying statistics, which measure the contributions of each player to the overall performance of the team, the evaluation of team strategy in different competitive contexts and the use of the most appropriate way of data analysis are the critical issues in performance analysis during game play. In recent decades the application of the methods of mathematical statistics to hockey match analysis has grown significantly. Statistical research in ice hockey has covered the following issues:

1   players' and teams' performance evaluations based on game statistics (Bedford & Baglin, 2009; Mason & Foster, 2007; Williams & Williams, 1998);
2   prediction of game outcomes (Pischedda, 2014; Thomas, 2007);
3   assessment of strategies to attempt to tie the game (Beaudoin & Swartz, 2010; Thomas, 2007; Zaman, 2001);
4   analysis of the effect of rule changes on strategic behaviour in competition (Banerjee et al., 2007); and

160

5   the influence of home team advantage on teams' performances (Dennis & Carron, 1999; Doyle & Benjamin, 2012; Jones, 2009; Liardi & Carron, 2011).

Players' and teams' performance evaluations based on game statistics

A clear and comprehensive multivariate analysis of individual hockey statistics was suggested by Williams and Williams (1998). Using basic player statistics (shots on goal, penalty minutes, plus–minus, goals and assists) and considering the numerical relationship of players on the ice (playing at even strength, on a power play or short-handed), the authors proposed to use principal components analysis to evaluate the players' performances, quantified by the Offensive Performance Index (which measures the performance of the offence) and the Efficiency Performance Index (which measures how efficient the player is in preventing the opponent from having scoring opportunities). These measures provide well-established and proven ways of using data, collected per game or per season, and ensure an objective and sustainable comparison among players.

The search for an effective way to record accurately appropriate information from a game has led to the creation of novel tracking technologies for collecting data, new statistical measures and new methods of data analysis and presentation. For instance, Hexagonal Plots of NHL Data (see Figure 8.1) are used to display the success rate of taking shots from each position on the ice, binned by general shooting region (Thomas, 2015). In this method the overall width of 31 units represents the 85 feet in a regulation hockey rink. Sizes of the hexagons are scaled with the number of observations, and a colour scheme shows the fraction of shots that scored. The data presented in Hexagonal Plots can be analysed by specific competitive contexts (team is playing at home or away, at full strength or at an advantage/a disadvantage) and also may be used for comparison of team performance with and without a particular player.

Predicting game outcomes

For evaluation of the player and team performance the analysts usually use the summarised data per game or per season, applying the

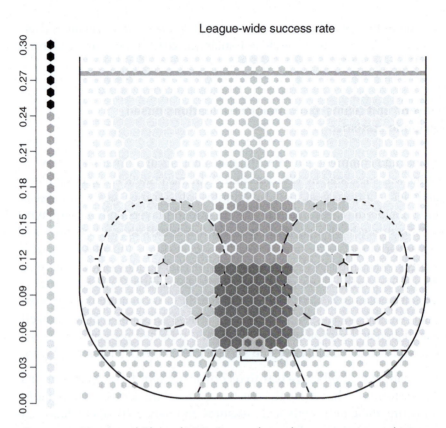

Figure 8.1 Hexagonal Plots of NHL Data, where shots are aggregated into hexagonal bins. Sizes of the hexagons scaled with the number of observations and a colour scheme for the hexagons signifies the fraction of shots that score, either as an absolute percentage or relative to the league mean at each position (from Thomas, 2015, p. 44).

retrospective analysis that aims to identify individual and collective performance indicators. The research regarding the prediction of game outcome is based on the analysis of score evolution and considers the team performance during the match. Several studies have shown that goals in ice hockey follow the Poisson process. This means that a probability of goal scoring is constant during the game and that goals are independent (Buttrey et al., 2011; Williams & Williams, 1998; Zaman, 2001). Thomas (2007) analysed the data from about 4,700 games played in four NHL seasons and identified three trends in goal scoring: (1) the number of goals scored at even strength does not vary much for every minute in the game, except in the last minute; (2) teams scored a lower number of goals at the beginning of each of three periods, regardless of even strength or power play; and (3) the lowest number of power play goals were scored at the first minutes of a first period.

In order to determine which class of distributions best describe the time of goals in ice hockey, Thomas (2007) considered Weibull and Plateau-Hazard distributions. It was concluded that Plateau-Hazard and Poisson models have predicted values most consistent with the observed data. In addition Thomas (2007) analysed a concept of goal value, defined as the change in the probability of victory caused by the goal. According to the winning probabilities estimated from the Plateau-Hazard model, the goals scored near the end of regulation time to even the score have been identified as the most valuable, even more valuable than goals that increased the point difference at the end of regulation time.

Assessment of strategies attempted to tie the game

The evaluation of strategies of resolving games tied at the end of regulation time was discussed in several statistical research projects (Beaudoin & Swartz, 2010; Zaman, 2001). One of the most frequently used strategies when a team is losing by one goal is to replace the goaltender with an extra skater to enhance the probability of scoring a tying goal. Frequently NHL coaches pull the goaltender during the last two minutes of regulation time. However, the question regarding the proper time to make this risky decision persists because the opposing team may score a goal on an empty net thereby extending their lead. Using the Markov chain model, Zaman (2001) calculated the probabilities of scoring a goal during a given state of the game, characterised by the puck location. The parameters of the model suggest the goaltender should be replaced earlier than was verified in competitive game contexts. This result was confirmed by more recent and comprehensive study by Beaudoin and Swartz (2010), which took into account specific game situations (penalties and home-ice advantage) and demonstrated that teams behind in score should pull their goaltenders much earlier when taking an advantage of a power play than when playing at even strength (5-on-5).

Analysis of the effect of rule changes on strategic behaviour in competition

In most cases rule changes in team sports aim to enhance the attractiveness of the game for spectators. In the 1999–2000 season the NHL implemented a new point structure for the tied games and overtime in an attempt to make the games more exciting by stimulating a more aggressive style of play in the overtime (Banerjee et al., 2007). According to the new rule, both teams receive one point if they draw in regulation time regardless of the outcome in overtime. A team that scores in sudden-death overtime earns an additional point, but the team that loses still keeps its one point. Banerjee et al. (2007) evaluated the effect of this rule change on the play of NHL teams during regulation time and in overtime. Beginning with the estimations of the theoretical model for optimal team strategies under the new point system, which was later supported by the empirical results, the statisticians found that the new rule had an ambiguous impact on the teams' playing style. On the one hand, the new rule really stimulated more offensive play in overtime, but, on the other hand, it provoked more defensive play during regulation time. This effect of the rule change was not expected and showed that some altered factors that affect players' behaviour don't necessarily have the intended outcome.

The influence of home advantage on teams' performances

The effect of home advantage on performance in ice hockey was investigated from different perspectives. The studies analysed the influence of game venue (home or away) on the probability of (1) winning the game (Liardi & Carron, 2011; Loughead et al., 2003), (2) scoring the first goal in the match (Jones, 2009), (3) wining by shootouts (Depken et al., 2012; Swartz & Arce, 2014), and (4) winning offensive, defensive and neutral zone face offs (Liardi & Carron, 2011). Furthermore, the variation in home advantage across teams and during the season (Doyle & Benjamin, 2012) and long-term trends in professional hockey home advantage (Pollard & Pollard, 2005), as well as the coaches' strategies in home and away games (Dennis & Carron, 1999) have also been studied.

The proportion of all points that were won by home teams (Pollard & Pollard, 2005), the difference in scoring and the difference in the fraction

164

of games won (Stefani, 2008) are the indicators most commonly used for measuring home advantage. Since the mid-1990s to 2002 the home advantage in professional ice hockey (NHL) was around 55 per cent (proportion of all points won by home teams) (Pollard & Pollard, 2005), and during the last five seasons up to January 1, 2012, it became a little bit smaller – 54.1 per cent (Gómez et al., 2013).

According to the difference in the fraction of games won,[11] the home advantage in the NHL (9.7 per cent) is lower than it is in other professional leagues, such as rugby union (25.1), the National Basketball Association (NBA) (21.0), the National Football League (NFL) (17.5), the Australian Football League (AFL) (18.8) and soccer (21.7). Only in Major League Baseball (MLB) was the home advantage (7.5 per cent) smaller than in the NHL (Stefani, 2008).

For instance, Doyle and Benjamin (2012) verified that the home advantage varies over the season, being the highest at the beginning and end of the season, and very small in the middle of the season. The home advantage does not vary across teams, but at the end of the season it is larger, when two opposing teams are highly ranked. Analysing the games from three NHL seasons (2003–04, 2005–06 and 2006–07) Jones (2009) confirmed the home advantage in winning the match (56.05 per cent), as well as in scoring the first goal (53.01 per cent) and in goals scored after the first (52.37 per cent).

Among the main factors that explain the home advantage, the following are usually mentioned: crowd factor, familiarity with venue, travel factor and rule factor[12] (Carron et al., 2005). Stefani (2008) explained the relatively low home advantage in ice hockey using the three following factors: (1) frequent substitutions (every 40–50 seconds), which allow for the management of the players' fatigue during the game and reduce the effect of travel fatigue; (2) the protective glass that surrounds the rink and abates the crowd influence; and (3) insignificant differences in venue conditions, which results in not providing relevant tactical advantages for the home team.

Depken et al. (2012) reported that after overtime in tied games with great attendance the home team had a tendency to choose to shoot first in shootouts, although it could have a negative effect on the match outcome because the second shooting team tended to win more often. The authors suggest that home team coaches choose to shoot first to try to satisfy home-team fans by avoiding the risk of not winning because of choosing to shoot after the away team.

Home advantage has also been registered in face off success. Home teams won 51.9 per cent of face offs, from which 52.3 per cent are in offensive, 52.1 per cent in defensive and 51.4 per cent in neutral zones (Liardi & Carron, 2011). Dennis and Carron (1999) found that coaches used different strategies for home and away games, giving preference to a more active and assertive forechecking strategy at home and a more defensive approach in away games.

POSITIONAL PROFILES AND SPECIFIC POSITION DEMANDS

Hockey is very intense contact game, characterised by frequent acceleration, fast intermittent skating, changes in direction and execution of different playing skills, that requires from players a high level of power, speed, strength and coordination, as well as specifically trained anaerobic and aerobic fitness (Cox et al., 1995; Potteiger et al., 2010; Quinney et al., 2008). Match demands depend on a player's position, game strategy, quality of opposition and the match result evolution. On average game duration is 150 to 170 minutes and players spend about 15 to 30 minutes on ice. Each on-ice shift lasts between 30 and 80 s interspersed with 2 to 5 minutes of less intense recovery intervals (Cox et al., 1995; Montgomery, 2000). The time-motion analysis of hockey indicates that the average heart rate during a professional match is about 85 to 90 per cent, suggesting that average oxygen uptake of players lies between 80 and 90 per cent (Twist & Rhodes, 1993). Similar heart rates have been also registered for youth hockey players (Stanula & Roczniok, 2014).

Anthropometric, physical and physiological profiles of elite hockey players are well reported (Cox et al., 1995; Montgomery, 2000; Twist & Rhodes, 1993). Longitudinal testing of male elite hockey players has confirmed the progressive increase of their height, lean body mass, muscular strength and maximal oxygen uptake over the last decades (Cox et al., 1995; Montgomery, 2006; Quinney et al., 2008). In female hockey the very high level of upper and lower body strength of players has been verified (Ransdell & Murray, 2011).

Body index (height, lean mass, muscular development), percentage of body fat, isokinetic leg strength, anaerobic power, standing long jump and especially off-ice 30-m sprints have been identified as measures that better

166

predict on-ice skating speed and power in elite hockey (Behm et al., 2005; Burr et al., 2008; Farlinger et al., 2007; Potteiger et al., 2010). However, the off-ice test results demonstrated neither effect on draft selection for the NHL (Vescovi, Murray, Fiala, & VanHeest, 2006) nor a significant relationship with successful and unsuccessful seasons of NHL teams (Quinney et al., 2008). These findings once again confirmed that performance in ice hockey is multidimensional, and in addition to highly developed physiological attributes of players, the game requires other specific skills related to playing ability and psychological factors, which are crucial for each player's success and should be considered in performance assessments.

Detailed knowledge of the physical and activity profiles of different playing positions provides a basis for accurate player assessments and helps coaches to design effective training and conditioning programs. Time-motion hockey analysis demonstrated that defensemen generally skated slower than forwards, spent more time on the ice and had shorter recovery phases between shifts (Twist & Rhodes, 1993). The specific position demands explain the differences verified in physical and physiological traits among defensemen, forwards and goaltenders in men's ice hockey. The majority of studies characterised defensemen as taller, heavier and stronger than forwards, who generally were reported as lighter, more able to manoeuvre and fast-moving (Burr et al., 2008; Vescovi, Murray, & VanHeest, 2006). In elite women's ice hockey the significant differences among players positions have been found not for body size, but rather for body composition, on-ice anaerobic capacity and skating performance (Geithner et al., 2006). These findings possibly could be explained by less body contact and the more skilled style of female play.

Some studies reported significant differences between defensemen and forwards in peak anaerobic power and $VO_{2\,max}$, with the advantage in peak anaerobic power and absolute $VO_{2\,max}$ for defensemen and in relative $VO_{2\,max}$ for forwards (Burr et al., 2008; Peyer et al., 2011). Other researchers have not confirmed the differences between defensemen and forwards in relative $VO_{2\,max}$ (Agre et al., 1988; Vescovi, Murray, & VanHeest, 2006). Since findings related to position comparison for aerobic power are inconsistent, this factor, even being important for the hockey performance, could not be considered as appropriate for positional profiling (Vescovi et al., 2006).

The goaltenders have a greater percentage body fat as compared to the outfield positions and in general revealed inferior results in all physiological tests, having an advantage only in flexibility tests. These findings confirm that physiological characteristics are not decisive for the

167

goalkeeper's success, which is mostly related to specific skills, high levels of coordination, decision-making skills, quickness and flexibility (Bell et al., 2008).

Some studies attempted to identify relationships between the results of off-ice and on-ice testing and individual game performance of players, assessed by three general measures: total minutes played,[13] net scoring chances[14] (Green et al., 2006) and the plus–minus statistic[15] (Peyer et al., 2011). Physiological variables were found to be related to the on-ice players' performance registered throughout a competitive season. For instance, lactate accumulation and percentage of body fat have shown a significant relationship with total minutes played per game, and $VO_{2\,max}$ with scoring opportunities (Green et al., 2006); additionally, repeat sprint and strength ability significantly correlated with the plus–minus statistic (Peyer et al., 2011). The different results reported by researches concerning the physical and physiological predictors of players' game performances pointed out some problems with this kind of analysis that should be acknowledged. Since the defensemen and forwards play different roles during the game, it would be more appropriate to consider the position differences in a performance assessment and use more consistent offensive and defensive performance variables (goals, assists, penalties, etc.). Scoring opportunities and the plus–minus score are variables that reflect collective rather than individual performance. Besides, the plus–minus score has been reported as one of the less consistent hockey statistics, as it may be highly influenced by the opposite goaltender's performance (Berri & Schmidt, 2010). Furthermore, future studies should aim to estimate more complex models that relate several fitness and performance indicators instead of establishing correlations between two variables.

CONCLUSIONS AND SUGGESTIONS

Future studies should continue to analyse how the results of off-ice and on-ice testing are related to players' performances during match-play. It is necessary to examine different levels of players to determine factors that influence and better predict the on-game performance in professional, amateur and youth ice hockey. Further research should provide more accurate tools for evaluation of on-ice specific skills and playing ability. Recording of players' movement trajectories during match-play would

168

provide objective information about specific position demands and allow the description of the inter- and intra-team collective behaviour in different game contexts. More data and more substantial research efforts are required for evaluation of teams' behaviours and optimal team strategy. Given the scarcity of studies conducted on female players, the women's game should continue to be analysed.

REFERENCES

Agre, J. C., Casal, D. C., Leon, A. S., McNally, C., Baxter, T. L., & Serfass, R. C. (1988). Professional ice hockey players: Physiologic, anthropometric, and musculoskeletal characteristics. *Archives of Physical Medicine and Rehabilitation, 69*, 188–192.

Banerjee, A. N., Swinnen, J. F. M., & Weersink, A. (2007). Skating on thin ice: Rule changes and team strategies in the NHL. *The Canadian Journal of Economics, 40*(2), 493–514.

Beaudoin, D., & Swartz, T. B. (2010). Strategies for pulling the goalie in hockey. *The American Statistician, 64*(3), 197–204.

Bedford, A., & Baglin, J. (2009). Evaluating the performance of an ice hockey team using interactive phases of play. *IMA Journal of Management Mathematics, 20*(2), 159–166.

Behm, D. G., Wahl, M. J., Button, D. C., Power, K. E., & Anderson, K. G. (2005). Relationship between hockey skating speed and selected performance measures. *Journal of Strength & Conditioning Research, 19*, 326–331.

Bell, G. J., Snydmiller, G. D., & Game, A. B. (2008). An investigation of the type and frequency of movement patterns of National Hockey League goaltenders. *International Journal of Sports Physiology and Performance, 3*, 80–87.

Berri, D. J., & Schmidt, M. B. (2010). *Stumbling on Wins: Two Economists Expose the Pitfalls on the Road to Victory in Professional Sports.* Upper Saddle River, NJ: FT Press.

Bracko, M. (2004). Biomechanics powers ice hockey performance. *Biomechanics* (September), 47–53.

Bracko, M. R., Fellingham, G. W., Hall, L. T., Fisher, A. G., & Cryer, W. (1998). Performance skating characteristics of professional ice hockey forwards. *Sports Medicine, Training and Rehabilitation, 8*(3), 251–263.

Burr, J. F., Jamnik, R. K., Baker, J., Macpherson, A., Gledhill, N., & McGuire, E. J. (2008). Relationship of physical fitness test results and hockey playing potential in elite-level ice hockey players. *Journal of Strength and Conditioning Research, 22*(5), 1535–1543.

Buttrey, S. E., Washburn, A. R., & Price, W. L. (2011). Estimating NHL scoring rates. *Journal of Quantitative Analysis in Sports, 7*(3), Article 24.

Carron, A. V., Loughhead, T. M., & Bray, S. (2005). The home advantage in sport competitions: Courneya and Carron's (1992) conceptual framework a decade later. *Journal of Sports Sciences, 23*(4), 395–407.

Cox, M. H., Miles, D. S., Verde, T. J., & Rhodes, E. C. (1995). Applied physiology of ice hockey. *Sports Medicine, 19*(3), 184–201.

Dennis, P. W., & Carron, A. V. (1999). Strategic decisions of ice hockey coaches as a function of game location. *Journal of Sports Sciences, 17*, 263–268.

Depken, C. A., Sonora, R. J., & Wilson, D. P. (2012). Performance under pressure: Preliminary evidence from the National Hockey League. *International Journal of Sport Finance, 7*, 213–231.

Doyle, J., & Benjamin, L. (2012). Variations in home advantage: Evidence from the National Hockey League. *Journal of Quantitative Analysis in Sports, 8*(2), 1–27.

Farlinger, C., Kruisselbrink, L., & Fowles, J. (2007). Relationships to skating performance in competitive hockey players. *Journal of Strength and Conditioning Research, 21*(3), 915–922.

Fortier, A., Turcotte, R. A., & Pearsall, D. J. (2014). Skating mechanics of change-of-direction manoeuvres in ice hockey players. *Sports Biomechanics, 13*(4), 341–350.

Geithner, C. A., Lee, A. M., & Bracko, M. R. (2006). Physical and performance differences among forwards, defensemen, and goalies in elite women's ice hockey. *Journal of Strength and Conditioning Research, 20*(3), 500–505.

Gómez, M. A., Peñas, C., & Pollard, R. (2013). Situational variables. In T. McGarry, P. O'Donoghue, & J. Sampaio (Eds.), *Routledge Handbook of Sports Performance Analysis* (pp. 259–269). London: Routledge.

Green, M. R., Pivarnik, J. M., Carrier, D. P., & Womack, C. J. (2006). Relationship between physiological profiles and on-ice performance of a national collegiate Athletic association division I hockey team. *2006, 20*(1), 43–46.

Jones, M. B. (2009). Scoring first and home advantage in the NHL *International Journal of Performance Analysis of Sport, 9*, 320–331.

Lafontaine, D. (2007). Three-dimensional kinematics of the knee and ankle joints for three consecutive push-offs during ice hockey skating starts. *Sports Biomechanics, 6*(3), 391–406.

Lafontaine, D., Lamontagne, M., & Lockwood, K. (1998). *Time-motion analysis of ice-hockey skills during games.* Paper presented at the 16 International Symposium on Biomechanics in Sports, Konstanz – Germany. https://ojs.ub.uni-konstanz.de/cpa/article/view/1232/1119

Liardi, V. L., & Carron, A. V. (2011). An analysis of National Hockey League face-offs: Implications for the home advantage. *International Journal of Sport and Exercise Psychology, 9*(2), 102–109.

Lomond, K. V., Turcotte, R., & Pearsall, D. J. (2007). Three-dimensional analysis of blade contact in an ice hockey slap shot, in relation to player skill. *Sports Engineering, 11*(3), 103–107.

Loughead, T. M., Carron, A. V., Bray, S. R., & Kim, A. J. (2003). Facility familiarity and the home advantage in professional sports. *International Journal of Sport and Exercise Psychology, 1*(3), 264–274.

Mason, D. S., & Foster, W. M. (2007). Putting moneyball on ice? *International Journal of Sport Finance, 2*, 206–213.

Michaud-Paquette, Y., Magee, P., Pearsall, D. J., & Turcotte, R. (2011). Whole-body predictors of wrist shot accuracy in ice hockey: A kinematic analysis. *Sports Biomechanics, 10*(1), 12–21.

Montgomery, D. L. (2000). Chapter 52. Physiology of ice hockey. In W. E. Garrett & D. T. Kirkendall (Eds.), *Exercise and Sport Science* (pp. 815–828). Philadelphia: Lippincott Williams & Wilkins.

Montgomery, D. L. (2006). Physiological profile of professional hockey players – a longitudinal comparison. *Applied Physiology, Nutrition and Metabolism, 31*, 181–185.

Pearsall, D. J., Montgomery, D. L., Rothsching, N., & Turcotte, R. A. (1999). The influence of stick stiffness on the performance of ice hockey slap shots. *Sports Engineering, 2*, 3–11.

Peyer, K. L., Pivarnik, J. M., Eisenmann, J. C., & Vorkapich, M. (2011). Physiological characteristics of national collegiate Athletic association division I ice hockey players and their relation to game performance. *The Journal of Strength & Conditioning Research, 25*(5), 1183–1192.

Pischedda, G. (2014). Predicting NHL match outcomes with ML models. *International Journal of Computer Applications, 101*(9), 15–22.

Pollard, R., & Pollard, G. (2005). Long-term trends in home advantage in professional team sports in North America and England (1876–2003). *Journal of Sports Sciences, 23*(4), 337–350.

Potteiger, J. A., Smith, D. L., Maier, M. L., & Foster, T. S. (2010). Relationship between body composition, leg strength, anaerobic power, and on-ice skating performance in division I men's hockey athletes. *Journal of Strength & Conditioning Research, 24*(7), 1755–1762.

Quinney, H. A., Dewart, R., Game, A., Snydmiller, G., Warburton, D., & Bell, G. (2008). A 26-year physiological description of a national hockey league team. *Applied Physiology, Nutrition and Metabolism, 33*, 753–760.

Ransdell, L. B., & Murray, T. (2011). A physical profile of elite female hockey players in the United States. *Journal of Strength and Conditioning Research, 25*(9), 2358–2363.

Stanula, A., & Roczniok, R. (2014). Game intensity analysis of elite adolescent ice hockey players. *Journal of Human Kinetics, 44*, 211–221.

Stefani, R. (2008). Measurement and interpretation of home advantage. In J. Albert & R. H. Koning (Eds.), *Statistical Thinking in Sports* (pp. 203–216). Boca Raton, FL: Chapman & Hall/CRC.

Swartz, T., & Arce, A. (2014). New insights involving the home team advantage. *International Journal of Sports Science and Coaching, 9*(4), 681–692.

Thomas, A. C. (2007). Inter-arrival times of goals in ice hockey. *Journal of Quantitative Analysis in Sports, 3*(3), Article 5.

Thomas, A. C. (2015). A Statistician reads the sports pages: Pucksberry: What we can learn from hexagonal plots of NHL data. *Chance, 28*(1), 43–50.

Twist, P., & Rhodes, T. (1993). A physiological analysis of ice-hockey positions. *National Strength and Conditioning Association Journal, 15*(6), 44–46.

Upjohn, T., Turcotte, R., Pearsall, D. J., & Loh, J. (2008). Three-dimensional kinematics of the lower limbs during forward ice hockey skating. *Sports Biomechanics, 7*(2), 206–221.

Vescovi, J. D., Murray, T. M., Fiala, K. A., & VanHeest, J. L. (2006). Off-ice performance and draft status of elite ice hockey players. *International Journal of Sports Physiology and Performance, 1*, 207–221.

Vescovi, J. D., Murray, T. M., & VanHeest, J. (2006). Positional performance profiling of elite ice hockey players. *International Journal of Sports Physiology and Performance, 1*, 84–94.

Williams, B., & Williams, D. (1998). Performance indices for multivariate ice hockey statistics. In J. Bennett (Ed.), *Statistics in Sport* (pp. 141–155). London: Arnold.

Worobets, J. T., Fairbairn, J. C., & Stefanyshyn, D. J. (2006). The influence of shaft stiffness on potential energy and puck speed during wrist and slap shots in ice hockey. *Sports Engineering, 9*(4), 191–200.

Wu, T.-C., Pearsall, D. J., Hodges, A., Turcotte, R. A., Lefebvre, R., Montgomery, D., . . . Bateni, H. (2003). The performance of the ice hockey slap and wrist shots: The effects of stick construction and player skill. *Sports Engineering, 6*, 31–40.

Zaman, Z. (2001). Coach Markov pulls Goalie Poisson. *Chance, 14*(2), 31–35.

172

CHAPTER 9

RESEARCH TOPICS IN BASKETBALL

Leading author: Anna Volossovitch

INTRODUCTION

Basketball is one of the most popular indoor sports, played at professional and amateur levels. It is a time-dependent, high-scoring game with detailed rules, which were advanced and developed during the last century. Performance in basketball is strongly dependent on the anthropometric characteristics, fitness and technical and tactical skills of players, as well as team strategy and tactics. Most of these factors should be regarded during the training process in a way representative of the competition demands to ensure the transfer of the developed skills and capacities to the on-court performances. Therefore, the information collected from a match is very important to organise the training sessions and prepare for the forthcoming contests. Performance analysis in basketball is a powerful tool that is largely used by coaches, scouts, sport scientists and technical staff and allows gathering valid and reliable information.

Available research on basketball performance has covered the following topics:

- shooting performance analysis,
- individual and team performances using game-related statistics,
- scoring dynamics,
- dynamic analysis of space–time coordination and interactions between players and teams, and
- competitive activity profiles and specific position demands.

Focusing on these issues the present chapter aims to survey the literature regarding performance analysis in basketball.

SHOOTING PERFORMANCE ANALYSIS

Shooting performance is a critical factor for success in basketball. Research on game-related statistics has consistently reported the field goal percentage as one of the most important performance indicators that distinguishes between winning and losing teams (Gómez et al., 2008; Malarranha et al., 2013). The development of shooting drills represents an essential goal of training sessions. Hence, several studies have addressed the characterisation of the best release conditions and identifying the factors that influence the shooting skill acquisition process. Shooting skills were analysed from biomechanical (Bartlett & Robins, 2008) and perception-action coupling perspectives (Oliveira et al., 2006; Oliveira et al., 2008; Oudejans et al., 2012; Stöckel & Fries, 2013). Research has mainly focused on three types of shots: free throws (Button et al., 2003; Hamilton & Reinschmidt, 1997; Mullineaux & Uhl, 2010; Uchida et al., 2014), jump shots (Oliveira et al., 2006; Robins et al., 2006) and three-point shots (Stöckel & Fries, 2013).

Biomechanical analysis of shooting performance and movement variability

A free throw in basketball is an accuracy-dominated skill that has been largely analysed by measuring kinematic variables, such as release height of the ball, linear and angle displacements and velocities of the articulations of the kinematic chain (Button et al., 2003; Schmidt, 2012); and release height, release speed, launch angle, side angle and back spin (Tran & Silverberg, 2008). The optimal relationship between release speed and release angle has been reported as crucial for shooting accuracy for a given height of release and distance from the basket (Bartlett & Robins, 2008). However, the idea of an optimal uniform movement pattern or ideal technique has been countered by studies that analysed the intra- and inter-individual movement variability in basketball shooting performance. Large inter-individual variability reported by several authors suggests that players use considerably different shooting techniques (Bartlett & Robins, 2008; Mullineaux & Uhl, 2010).

174

Changes in the shot kinematics have been examined as a function of skill levels (Button et al., 2003; Schmidt, 2012), distance (Robins et al., 2006) and shot outcome (Mullineaux & Uhl, 2010). Button and colleagues (2003) examined multiple joint displacement variabilities during the free throw performed by female players of different expertise levels, ranging from very little experience to under-18 national team and senior national team players. The findings of Button et al. (2003) demonstrated that contrary to what was expected, trajectory variability did not reduce with increasing playing expertise. Trajectory variability was measured by the standard deviation of linear elbow displacement at discrete points during the throwing action. However, the elbow and wrist joints coupling of the skillful players was more consistent than that of the less skilled counterparts. The coordination (angular motions) of elbow and wrist joints was found to be more variable towards the end of the throw. The expert players also showed a greater range of motion about the wrist than the less skilled players, confirming that biomechanical degrees of freedom are released to skill acquisition (Vereijken et al., 1992). This compensatory or functional variability ensured the joint–space adaptation to changing ball release parameters.

Robins and co-authors (2006) analysed the variability of discrete and continuous variables collected in the five standardised successful shots performed by six skilled basketball players from distances of 4.26, 5.25 and 6.25 m from the basket. The angles of the shoulder, elbow and wrist joints were calculated in the study. The joint angle variability did not increase with an increment of shot distance, while an increase has been observed in the proximal to distal variability of joint angle along the kinematic chain at ball release (Robins et al., 2006). These findings are in line with those reported by Button et al. (2003) and provide further evidence for the compensatory variability that is essential for the adaptive and corrective behaviour and optimal functioning in shooting tasks.

The coordination variability in joint kinematics between misses and swishes of basketball free throw shots has been analysed by Mullineaux and Uhl (2010), who found that lower ball release speed discriminated between failed and successful free throw shots. It was observed that independent of shot outcome the synergy between the elbow and wrist angles reduced until one frame before ball release and only after this instant. The significant differences between missed and swished shots have been reported. While the coordination variability did not change for successful free throw shots, it increased statistically for missed ones.

These differences have been explained by an interaction between perceptual and motor components (Mullineaux & Uhl, 2010). Skilled players were able to anticipate shot results and tried to correct their actions when it was perceived that they would miss the shot. They used more stable movement pattern when the shot technique was perceived as a correct.

Previous research of Schmidt (2012) examined the movement patterns of free throw shooting as a function of individuality and the skill level of players by using the Dynamically Controlled Net-works (DyCoN), the net analysis developed by Perl (2004). Angle displacements and velocities of the articulations of the kinematic chain were used to characterise and classify throwing patterns of three groups of players – beginner, advanced and experts. Contrary to the previous studies, Schmidt (2012) analysed the whole movement organisation of basketball free throw shots, including the preparing phase. The movement organisation has been found to be very individual and fitting with specific characteristics of each player, but not representing the typical skill level pattern. Some different movement patterns have also been identified in each expertise level. According to findings of Button et al. (2003), the skilful and more successful players revealed a higher intra-individual and inter-trial stability compared to low-level shooters, who demonstrated a high variability in their movement patterns.

Perception-action analysis of basketball shooting

The gaze behaviour plays a very important role in the control of basketball shooting. Several studies have investigated players' visual behaviours in static (free throw shot) and dynamic (jump shot) shooting tasks using eye-tracking systems (Vickers, 1996; Oliveira et al., 2008) and visual occlusion techniques (Oudejans et al., 2002; Oliveira et al., 2006).

In the static free throw shot, where the positions of thrower and basket are stationary, players used long target fixations. This gaze behaviour was called 'quiet eye' phenomenon (Vickers, 1996). The duration of the final fixation on the target combined with an earlier fixation offset during the shooting action has been reported as a distinctive feature of an experts' performance. In the dynamic task of jump shooting, the gaze behaviour of skilled players seems to be different. Oliveira et al. (2006) and Oudejans et al. (2002) provided evidence that when performing a

176

jump shot, players mostly picked up the late optical information – that is, just before ball release – and this information was considered to be crucial for the guidance of player's movement and shooting success.

Uchida et al. (2014) studied the eye movements of basketball players while they were observing a basketball free throw to predict the success or failure of shots. The anticipation of shot result is very important for gaining the favourable rebounding position; obtaining the rebound is one of the most important performance indicators in basketball, frequently associated to the game outcome (Berri & Schmidt, 2010; Oliver, 2004). Uchida and co-authors (2014) found that novice and expert players used different visual references to predict shot success while observing basketball free throws in videos with different replay speeds. The novices mostly focused on the ball and shot trajectory, independently on video replay speeds, and could not predict free throw outcome at better than a chance level. Skilled players gazed more on the lower part of the shooter's body and moved their gaze according to the shooter's movements. They predicted the free throw outcomes more accurately and significantly better than novices. The patterns of gaze behaviour of experts changed when the video speed of the observed free throw was increased, suggesting that temporal information is also important for predicting shot results. These findings are in line with results of Wu et al. (2013), who also confirmed the significant differences between elite basketball players and novices in the process and accuracy of anticipating action while observing a free throw. Experienced players demonstrated significantly more stable gaze fixation with the reliable locus of fixation and showed more accurate results of anticipation. The differences between experts and novices have also been observed in the players' brain activity during the task (Abreu et al., 2012).

Analysis of player's visual activity during shooting tasks has clearly demonstrated that shooting skill places high demands on visual perception and perception–action coupling of players. Thus, the on-court training programmes in basketball should address visual attention and pick-up of relevant optical information. The task used for the optimisation of perceptual-motor coupling should stimulate the players to use more beneficial informational sources, but without providing explicit instructions in a prescriptive way. Learning to look at a relevant point at a proper time or to use only late optical information can be achieved by applying the appropriate task constraints; for example, shoot from behind a screen for the development of late viewing (Oudejans et al., 2002).

177

Despite the advances in the description of player gaze behaviour while performing or observing basketball shoots, further research is needed to better understand what critical visual information expert players use to organise and deliver a basketball shot, as well as to predict shot success.

MEASURING OF INDIVIDUAL AND TEAM PERFORMANCE USING GAME-RELATED STATISTICS

Statistics are traditionally used to measure individual and team performances in professional and amateur basketball matches, and play a major role in sports fan interest in the game. The meticulous way in which the on-court events are recorded by basketball statistics and the accessibility of statistical reports on the Internet have greatly contributed over the last two decades to the growth of scientific research in basketball match analysis. The research in this area addresses the following issues:

1   identifying the performance indicators that better discriminate between winning and losing teams (Gómez et al., 2008) and between teams' season-long success (Ibañez et al., 2008; Ziv et al., 2010);
2   evaluating of players' performances and their contribution to the match outcome (Berri & Schmidt, 2010; Casals & Martinez, 2013; Kubatko et al., 2007; Martinez, 2012); and
3   assessing of the home advantage (Pollard & Gómez, 2013).

Identifying the performance indicators that better discriminated between winning and losing teams

Identification of statistics that discriminate between the performance of winning and losing teams is one of the best-studied problems in basketball match analysis. The research, based on game-related statistics, aims to improve understanding of factors that influence game performance in different contexts. The context of the competition is commonly characterised by game location – home and away (Gómez et al., 2010; Sampaio et al., 2008); quality of opposition – better and worse ranked teams (Malarranha et al., 2013); final points difference – close, balanced and unbalanced (García et al., 2013; Gómez et al., 2008; Sampaio & Janeira, 2003); type of match – season or play-off (García et al., 2013); and pace of the game – fast or slow (Sampaio et al., 2010). Other criteria used in

178

comparative analysis of performance statistics in basketball were as follows: season-long success – better and worse teams (Ibañez et al., 2008); impact of fatigue – effect of consecutive games played (Ibáñez et al., 2009); the starting five of the team – starters and nonstarters (Gómez et al., 2009; Vescovi, Murray, & VanHeest, 2006); as well as gender of players and level of competition (Sampaio et al., 2004).

Oliver, an expert in the scientific evaluation of basketball performance and author of the book *Basketball on Paper*, which provides a large set of statistical tools to help coaches evaluate their teams and players, suggested that success in basketball is dependent on four factors: shooting percentage from the field, offensive rebounds, turnovers and free throws (Oliver, 2004). This opinion is aligned with research in basketball match analysis over the last two decades, which has identified defensive rebounds and two-point field goals as the most consistent statistics that better discriminate between winning and losing teams regardless of the competitive situation (Gómez et al., 2008; Ibáñez et al., 2009; Karipidis et al., 2001; Trninić et al., 2002). The relevance for the match outcome of other statistics, such as assists, successful free throws, three-point field goals, offensive rebounds, fouls, steals and blocks, has been found to change according to season, age and level of players, as well as context of the game. Furthermore, these variables have not been reported consistently as discriminators between winning and losing teams in specific game contexts. Ziv and collaborators (2010) explained this inconsistency based on the design of studies and methodological approaches, such as the following:

1 using samples from only one or two consecutive seasons;
2 recording only one type of game-related variable that not always reflects the complexity of factors (physical, psychological, technical) that may influence match result;
3 using different statistical methods to examine the relationship between on-court performance and different classifications of the analysed games; and
4 lacking in or even having no control for multicollinearity of variables used in analysis.

Most game-related statistics represent discrete players' actions or their results; this does not evaluate properly the interaction between teammates and does not take into account the particular course of the game, which greatly influences the team's tactics; i.e., the manner in which a team plays.

Ziv and co-authors (2010) analysed 12 commonly used game-related statistics from the seven consecutive seasons of all the teams that participated in the Israeli Basketball Super League and demonstrated that some of the on-court variables were highly correlated, and the set of these variables did not reliably predict team ranking at the end of season. To solve this problem the authors suggested the aggregation of game-related statistics in broader categories, which may contribute to the more consistent prediction of long-term team success.

Evaluating of players' performance and their contribution to the match outcome

Player performance evaluation is very important for coaches, managers, scouts and fans and represents a key element of team performance analysis. Over the last two decades numerous studies aimed to find the more reliable way to measure the player's effectiveness. Some of these studies focused on the development of expert systems (Swalgin, 1998; Trninić et al., 1999), and other used indexes, obtained from the official game statistics (Casals & Martinez, 2013; Kubatko et al., 2007; Oliver, 2004; Sampaio, Janeira, Ibáñez, & Lorenzo, 2006).

Typically on-court statistics of different basketball competitions are collected play-by-play and summarised in a box score, where basic statistics for each player are listed. For instance, the measures used for player evaluations in the NBA has been classified into three categories: (1) scoring factors, including field shot attempts, free throw attempts, field goal percentage, free throw percentages and points scored; (2) possession factors, incorporating rebounds, steals and turnovers; and (3) help factors derived from blocked shots, assists and personal fouls (Berri & Schmidt, 2010). Most of the basketball specialists concurred that it is not easy to separate the player from his/her team and measure an individual player's contribution to team performance. Thus, it should be assumed that all individual statistics are highly influenced by the teammates' performances and game environment (Berri & Schmidt, 2010; Oliver, 2004; Martinez, 2012).

A large amount of quantitative data related to players' performances and its accessibility has led to a proliferation of various systems for players'

180

performance assessments. A comprehensive review of these measurement systems was provided by Martínez (2010), who analysed more than 220 metrics, which are currently used for basketball player evaluation. The author proposed three criteria for the classification of players' ranking systems. According to the first criterion, ranking systems are classified as offensive, defensive or combined in function of the indicators used. The second criterion categorises ranking systems as simple, which are based on the data from the box-score, or complex, based on the more advanced mathematical calculations. The third criterion distinguishes the systems for player evaluation in a game-by-game scenario, or during a game set/entire competition. Concluding his analysis, Martinez (2010) suggests the combined use of different ranking systems.

Considering the concept of equal possessions for opponents in a game, Kubatko and colleagues (2007) suggested the improved and more general formulation for possession estimates, which was recommended as a common starting point for research in basketball (Kubatko et al., 2007). Authors indicated three ways in which teams can lose possession: (1) field goals or free throws that lead to other team taking a ball out of bounds; (2) defensive rebounds; and (3) turnovers. An offensive rebound does not start a new possession, but it starts a new play. Thus, a ball possession begins when a team gains control of the ball and ends when this control is lost. Explaining the relationship between possessions and commonly used game-related statistics Kubatko and collaborators (2007) demonstrated the importance of game pace adjustment for reliable performance analysis in basketball.

Berri and colleagues suggested the *Wins Produced Model* for estimating individual player contribution to team success (Berri, 1999; Berri, 2008; Berri & Schmidt, 2010). This model is based on the *Wins Produced* formula, which relates box-score statistics to team wins through regression analysis, overcoming other famous metrics such as 'Efficiency', 'PER', 'Plus–Minus' and 'Adjusted Plus–Minus'. The *Wins Produced* represents a mathematically developed version of the model proposed by Oliver (2004) for calculating the winning percentage based on the offensive efficiency (points scored per offensive possession) and defensive efficiency (points given up per defensive possession).

Recently Martinez (2012) introduced a metric called Factors Determining Production (FDP) to assess the players performance through non-scoring box-score statistics. This metric separates points made from other quantitative variables and provides a simple linear weight formula,[16] which together with the points made by each player, allows for the evaluation of player performance and reflects the result of a game with a high level of accuracy (72 per cent).

To better understand which variables influence individual performance in basketball and to explain why the players' performance vary from one game to another, Casals and Martinez (2013) estimated the mixed (or multilevel) model that took into account the heterogeneity between players and computed the relative contribution of player performance variables to explain two outcomes: points scored and winning outcome. As could be expected, the parameters of the model with random effects confirmed a significant impact of minutes played and usage percentage on point and win scores. The difference of quality between teams was also revealed as a relevant factor that influences players' performances during the game. Surprisingly, the interaction between age and position has shown a negative association with the points scored by a player. Home advantage, season period and quality of game, which previously has been shown to influence the team performance, have not been revealed as significant for an individual's performance. Casals and Martinez (2013) highlighted that use of models with random effects on players' characteristics may be a promising tool for the accurate assessment of factors that influence the variability of player performance from one game to another.

Assessment of the home advantage

The home advantage in professional North American and European basketball leagues is a well-documented issue. Since in basketball the tie is not allowed and the outcome of a game is either a win or a loss, home advantage is calculated as a 'winning percentage', defined as the number of games won by the home team expressed as a percentage of all games played. The influence of game location on game-related statistics analysed at the team level (García et al., 2009) and across playing positions (Sampaio et al., 2008) has also been confirmed.

Analysis of a year-by-year measurement of home advantage for the NBA from 1946 to 2002 has revealed the great variability in home advantage over the years, which was more expressive than in other professional sports (Pollard & Pollard, 2005). By the late 1980s, the NBA home advantage increased to around 65 per cent and then was decreasing, reaching about 60 per cent in the 2000s (Pollard & Pollard, 2005) and continuing to decrease to 53.7 per cent in 2014–2015 season (Haberstroh, 2015).

Haberstroh (2015) suggested three possible reasons that explain decreasing of the NBA home advantage. One is related to the growth of three-point attempts, which implies a reduced contact between opponents, fewer fouls and, therefore, greater difficulty for referees to influence the course and the outcome of the game. The increased oversight of NBA referees in recent years and the facility of spreading the videos of certain game situations by fans almost in real-time may also contribute to more objective arbitration, which does not favour the home team. The second possible reason is the changing of travel habits (teams travel less often) and technological advances, which help reduce the effect of travel on the players and accelerate the recovery process. Furthermore, new video scouting technologies contribute to a better opponent analysis and game preparation even during travel.

A change in fans' behaviour was identified as the third possible reason for reducing the NBA home advantage. HD television negatively influences game assistance, as well as social networks, accessible in places such as basketball stadiums, as these factors frequently deviate fans' attention from the pitch, affecting their support of the home team. Nevertheless, these reasons for the reduction of the NBA home advantage should be verified by scientific studies.

The comparison of the home advantage magnitude in the 35 national basketball leagues of Europe has confirmed the existence of a home advantage in all countries, with the highest values (above 70 per cent) being for the Balkan countries Bosnia-Herzegovina and Croatia, and the lowest value for Estonia and Georgia (under 52 per cent). The average home advantage for European national basketball leagues was 60.7 per cent (Pollard & Gómez, 2013). The territorial protection as a consequence of ethnic conflicts, which may affect the players' performance, game assistance and also referees' behaviour, was considered as the most probable factor that explains the high home advantage in the Balkans leagues. The multiple regression analysis used in this study also confirmed the importance of taking into account the competitive balance within a national league, when the home advantage between leagues is compared (Pollard & Gómez, 2013). Gómez and Pollard (2011) also demonstrated that for the most part home advantage is inferior for European basketball teams playing in the capital cities compared with teams that play in other locations. In general the clear evidence of the home advantage effect in European basketball leagues emphasises the importance of taking the venue into consideration when analysing teams' on-court performance.

ANALYSIS OF SCORING DYNAMICS

One of the major challenges for the analysis of competitive activity in sports is the estimation of the predictive models from the retrospective analysis of team performance. The current scientific trends in basketball match analysis revealed a growing interest in probabilistic modelling of game performance. To model the performance in team sports, what is needed first is to formally describe the scoring dynamics of teams during the game and then to identify the factors that influence the probability of scoring.

Using a comprehensive data set of points scored in NBA games played in the 2002 through 2010 seasons, Merritt and Clauset (2014) analysed the sequences of scoring events within matches, focusing on the scoring tempo (when scoring events occur), scoring balance (how often a team wins an event) and predictability. The same data from two football leagues – college and professional (CFB and NFL) – as well as one professional hockey league (NHL) were also analysed in the study. Scoring tempo was shown to follow a common Poisson-like process[17] with specificities for each sport and stable rate (Merritt & Clauset, 2014). The model estimated by Merritt and Clauset (2014) revealed the common dynamic pattern underlying scoring dynamics during the basketball game. This pattern is defined by three phases: (1) *early phase with non-linear increasing tempo*, which is characterised by a reduced probability of scoring relative to the game average, due to the need to know the opponent and 'warming up' when the match starts; (2) *middle phase with constant tempo*, which is described by a stable pattern of scoring, where scoring events occur independent of the game clock, with a slight increase of scoring probability in the second through fourth periods; and (3) *end phase with sharply increased tempo*, which is characterised by a sudden increase in the scoring rate in order to take advantage of the last opportunities to score. Results reported by Merritt and Clauset (2014), where the scoring balance of a particular game was quantified as a fraction of all the events in the game won by a randomly selected team, showed that lead size (the points difference)

184

negatively influences the probability of scoring in NBA games. Moreover, the teams that were slightly behind have won a game more often. Merritt and Clauset (2014) called this phenomenon the 'restoring force', which is facilitated by the unlimited number of substitutions permitted in basketball and various opportunities to manage team strategies controlling the score evolution. The 'restoring force' was considered one of the causes that makes NBA games less predictable as compared to professional football and hockey games. Further research is needed to investigate whether the 'restoring force' is also observed in college basketball and how the response to the current points difference is related to the team's level and the quality of player management.

One of the better-explored issues related to scoring dynamics is the statistical evaluation of the occasionality of success. The widely held beliefs that 'success breeds success and failure breeds failure' and that 'behaviour has momentum' have inspired many studies related to the 'hot hand' phenomena in basketball. This relationship between past and present performance has been tested through the formulation of hypotheses of independence and the identical distribution of points scored. Basically, the studies tried to verify if the points scored represent random sequences or result from the ability of a team or player to repeat the success.

The publication of studies by Gilovich et al. (1985) and Tversky & Gilovich (1989a) marked the beginning of the first generation of works which studied the problem of scoring in series and over the years has involved experts from various scientific fields and analysis of scoring dynamics in different sports. The systematisation and analysis of these studies has been carried out in comprehensive reviews by Bar-Eli et al. (2006) and Reifman (2012). Currently, research related to the phenomenon of the 'hot hand' includes work that can be grouped into the following categories:

1   Studies based on the binomial model,[18] applied to different contexts, which showed no change in the probability of scoring along the competitive activity and did not confirm the existence of the 'hot hand' phenomenon (Adams, 1992; Gilovich et al., 1985; Koehler & Conley, 2003; Tversky & Gilovich, 1989a; Tversky & Gilovich, 1989b; Vergin, 2000).
2   Studies that questioned the suitability of the methodology used by Gilovich and Tversky to identify the phenomenon (Forthofer, 1991; Miyoshi, 2000; Stern & Morris, 1993; Wardrop, 1999).

3   Studies that raised the problem of the adaptive players' behaviour and focused attention on the behavioural consequences of the belief in the 'hot hand' (Burns, 2004; Gula & Raab, 2004).
4   Studies that presented alternative models to the binomial and admitted the possibility of markings in series, under the proviso that it is difficult to detect (Larkey et al., 1989; Stern & Morris, 1993; Korb & Stillwell, 2002).

Most of the 'hot hand' analyses considered only the past performance of the player or team in order to test for independence of points. However, there is no doubt that the behaviour of a team is influenced by the opponent's achievements. It is commonly assumed that a team plays what the other team allows it to play. That is why Oliver (2004) shifted the problem of the 'hot hand' from statistical inconsistencies to the basketball game strategy. The author states that the best NBA shooters usually attract more attention from defenders who are able to detect and counteract the 'hot hand' trend before it becomes statistically significant, making the phenomenon very difficult to detect. This simple hypothesis about the lack of evidence of a serial scoring phenomenon is consistent with the findings of Burns (2001) and Burns and Corpus (2004).

DYNAMIC ANALYSIS OF SPACE–TIME COORDINATION AND INTERACTIONS AMONG PLAYERS AND TEAMS

During the last two decades the use of the framework and tools of the Dynamical System Theory in team sports analysis has grown considerably. From this theoretical perspective the game is understood as a self-organising and non-linear system, and the game dynamics are described and explained in terms of order and control parameters, perturbations, attractors and non-linear phase transitions (McGarry et al., 2002). For instance, Schmidt and colleagues (1999) suggested in a hypothetical way how the dynamic changes in interpersonal coordination could be studied in basketball. Although without experimental data support, the authors recommended to describe the dynamic patterns of players' coordination in two competitive situations: when the forces of the teams are counterbalanced and attacking players pass the ball to each other without the clear progression towards the opponents' basket, and when this stable pattern is broken down, and the attacking team gets the

186

opportunity to move forward in the opponent's midfield (Schmidt et al., 1999). In this proposal the distance between the ball and the opponent's basket has been suggested as a candidate for an order parameter and interpersonal distance between players as a control parameter.

The idea to conceptualise the basketball game as a complex, dynamic systems was developed in the several studies analysing players' behaviours at the dyadic level (Cordovil et al., 2009; Esteves et al., 2012; Fujii et al., 2014) and at the team level (Bourbousson et al., 2010b; Fewell et al., 2012; Kempe et al., 2015).

Cordovil and colleagues (2009) studied an emergent dyadic behaviour in a typical 1v1 sub-phase in basketball, evaluating the impact of the individual (player's height) and the task constraints (instruction given to the attacker) regarding the three following variables: (1) frequency of symmetry-breaking occurrences (measured by the distance of the players to the basket, complemented by the interpersonal distance within the dyad), (2) the time the attacker needs to cross the court mid-line, and (3) the variability of the attacker's trajectory (quantified by calculating the residual standard deviation to a straight line adjusted to the attacker's trajectory). The results confirmed the significant influence of both the instruction given to the players, as well as the ratio of the heights of the attacker and defender on the emergent players' behaviour in the 1v1 sub-phase in basketball.

Using relative-phase analysis, stabilities and instabilities in the phase relations and phase transitions, Bourbousson et al. (2010a) examined space–time patterns of intra- (between players from the same team) and inter-couplings (between players from opposing teams) of dyads in basketball. The results demonstrated strong in-phase relations in the longitudinal (basket-to-basket) direction, particularly for the player–opponent interaction, and less strong in the lateral direction. Only the wing players of the same team demonstrated an anti-phase behaviour in the lateral direction.

In the second study on space–time coordination dynamics in basketball, Bourbousson et al. (2010b) introduced three collective variables that reflected team behaviour based on the players' displacements: spatial centre,[19] stretch index[20] and relative stretch index.[21] By using these measures the interactions between two teams was examined in terms of relative phase in six game sequences. The strong in-phase relationship between the two teams in both the longitudinal and lateral directions has been reported for the spatial centre and relative stretch index, while for the stretch indexes an in-phase relationship has been observed only in the longitudinal direction. The results of both studies of Bourbousson and colleagues (2010a, 2010b) demonstrated that in basketball, both individual and collective behaviours follow the principles of self-organised complexity.

Esteves and colleagues (2012) demonstrated that the patterns of coordination in attacker–defender dyads changed according to the relative positions of players to the basket. It was suggested that relative positioning to the scoring target and a player's handedness might be relevant interacting constraints for the emergent dyadic behaviour.

The interaction between dribbler and defender was investigated in the study of Fujii and colaborators (2014), who identified three different defending patterns: 'early initiation' (when the defender had sufficient time to move properly), 'quick movement' (when the defender delayed his/her movement, but then moved much faster than the dribbler) and 'dribbler stop' (when the dribbler stopped on his/her own independent of other conditions). The initiation time and medio-lateral peak velocity between defenders and dribbles have been identified as crucial parameters that explained the outcome of the dribbler–defender interaction.

Recently network analysis became one of the widely used approaches in the study of dynamic interactions among players in team sports. For instance, Fewell et al. (2012) analysed the sequential ball movements for 16 NBA teams in games of 2010 play-offs. The analysis allowed for generating the weighted graph of ball movement, where the players' positions, start-of-play and possession outcomes were used as nodes, and ball movement between those nodes as directed edges. The relevance of two network metrics for capturing the team offensive coordination and strategy has been evaluated. One of the metrics – team entropy – measured the unpredictability of an individual's passing behaviour, and another – uphill/downhill flux[22] – was used to evaluate a team's ability to move the ball towards the better shooters. Furthermore, the measure of individual flow centrality was used to evaluate the importance of a player's position within the ball distribution network, and clustering analyses allowed for the examination of how the players of different positions are interconnected within teams. Results suggested that a combined use of entropy, centrality and clustering is valuable for characterisation of team offensive strategy. However, to evaluate the contribution of different network dynamics in team success it would be necessary to consider the defensive strategies used by opposing teams.

188

Cervone et al. (2014) proposed evaluating the quality of every player's decisions during whole possession by using modelling framework for player-tracking data from the NBA 2012–13 season. Authors estimated the metric called Expected Possession Value (EPV), which assigns a certain value to any moment of the possession, according to its estimated impact on the probability of scoring. The EPV framework not only simulates and forecasts an offensive play, but also provides an understanding of how players contribute to the entire possession and identifies the decisive moments for the possession outcome. This advanced framework has great potential for analysis of single matches and for improving player performances in the coaching context by quantifying objectively the quality of players' decisions.

COMPETITIVE ACTIVITY PROFILES AND SPECIFIC POSITION DEMANDS

Basketball is a fast, highly demanding, intermittent sport, which requires from players high levels of agility, speed, strength, power and aerobic capabilities. Motor activity of players includes running, jumping, shooting, dribbling, rebounding, blocking and quick changes of direction (Cortis et al., 2011). These high-intensity actions are performed in a relatively small playing area (15×28 m), which does not require covering great distances during the match (Ben Abdelkrim, Castagna, Jabri, et al., 2010; Scanlan et al., 2014).

In the last decade the research regarding basketball physiology has grown considerably. The physical attributes, physiological characteristics and on-court performances of players have been analysed according to gender (Delextrat & Cohen, 2009; Narazaki et al., 2009), playing position and skill level of players (Carter et al., 2005; Rodríguez-Alonso et al., 2003; Sallet et al., 2005).

Anthropometric, physical and physiological characteristics of basketball players according to playing positions

The differences in anthropometric characteristics among positions have been observed both in men's and in women's basketball. Centres tend to be taller and heavier than forwards and guards, while guards are smaller than forwards (Boone & Bourgois, 2013; Carter et al., 2005; Cormery et al., 2008; LaMonte et al., 1999; Ostojic et al., 2006). These differences clearly express the specific functions attributed to each of playing positions on the field. Guards can take an advantage from lighter weight because they cover the most distance at the fastest speed (Ben Abdelkrim et al., 2007), carry the ball and are in charge of the game organisation, whereas physical attributes of taller and heavier centres help them to support physical contact and to better accomplish their tasks (rebounding, picking and boxing-out) in a low-post position (Ostojic et al., 2006). Absolute size has been found to be related to skill level of female guards and forwards (Carter et al., 2005), although for professional male players this relationship has not been confirmed (Sallet et al., 2005).

Studies focused on the physical and physiological characteristics of basketball players confirmed the significant association between aerobic and anaerobic performance of players and their positional roles on court (Ostojic et al., 2006; Rodríguez-Alonso et al., 2003). The findings suggest that guards perform better in endurance, speed and agility tests, while centres and forwards had higher muscle strength (Boone & Bourgois, 2013). Anaerobic fitness was considered as one of the most important factors of players' performance (Castagna et al., 2007; Gonzalez et al., 2013; LaMonte et al., 1999); however, aerobic capacity is essential for the recovery of players from the anaerobic efforts during less intense periods and helps them to maintain a high pace and effectiveness of actions during the entire game (Delextrat & Cohen, 2009; Narazaki et al., 2009; Ziv & Lidor, 2009). Higher values of heart rates and $VO_{2\ max}$ have been reported for international female players comparatively to their national-level counterparts (Rodríguez-Alonso et al., 2003). However, basketball players do not show high levels of $VO_{2\ max}$, (44.0–54.0 for females and 50–60mLO_2/kg/min for males) (Ziv & Lidor, 2009) because during the match they perform much more short high-intensity actions.

Playing time during the season and physical fitness of players

The playing time during the season has been reported as influencing the physical fitness of players. Caterisano and collaborators (1997) verified that the playing time status (starters *vs.* reserves) influences the maximal aerobic capacity of college players during the season. While during the preseason no significant differences regarding the maximal aerobic capacity were observed between the two groups, the aerobic capacity of

190

reserves decreased throughout the season due to their small amount of playing time. Both groups of college players demonstrated the significant decreasing of strength parameters during the season, which was more expressive in the group of reserves (Caterisano et al., 1997). Studies conducted in professional basketball reported that starters were able to maintain their physical performance (strength, power and quickness) and showed better results than bench players during the NBA season (Gonzalez et al., 2013). This finding reinforces the importance of the in-season individual monitoring of players, especially nonstarters, to evaluate their need in strength and power improvement.

Time-motion, movement and metabolic analysis of players' activity

Video-based time-motion analysis has been employed to calculate the frequencies, durations and distances of various activities across men's and women's basketball games (Ben Abdelkrim, Castagna, Jabri, et al., 2010; Cánovas López et al., 2014; Scanlan et al., 2012). The players' activity has been characterised using sets of the most common types of basketball movements and calculating the frequency and duration of each movement category (Ben Abdelkrim, Castagna, El Fazaa, & El Ati, 2010; Narazaki et al., 2009; Scanlan et al., 2011). The motion profile (distance covered and work-to-rest ratio), heart rate, oxygen consumption and blood-lactate levels of basketball players have also been evaluated (Ben Abdelkrim, Castagna, Jabri, et al., 2010; Narazaki et al., 2009).

The frequent changes between different types of actions (every two to three seconds) suggest the high demands of the game with regard to speed and agility (Ben Abdelkrim et al., 2007; Scanlan et al., 2011). Guards and forwards spent a higher percentage of time performing high-intensity activities and guards also performed more movements than players in other positions (Ben Abdelkrim et al., 2007)

The total distance travelled during the match was 7.558 ± 575 m for elite youth male players, as well as 6.390 ± 48 m and 6.230 ± 26 m for elite backcourt and frontcourt male basketball players, respectively. In women's basketball the state-level players travelled on average 5214 ± 315 m during the match (Scanlan et al., 2012). Male players spend 50 to 72 per cent, 17 to 43 per cent, and 6 to 20 per cent of match time in low, moderate and high-intensity activities, respectively (Ben Abdelkrim, Castagna, El Fazaa, et al., 2010; Ben Abdelkrim et al., 2007; Scanlan et al., 2011). Side-ward movements, which are considered as metabolically demanding, were used in 22 per cent of total distance covered (Ben Abdelkrim, Castagna, Jabri, et al., 2010).

Narazaki et al. (2009) evaluated the average oxygen consumption during one half of a basketball match and reported the $VO_{2\ max}$ of 33.4 ± 4.0 (66.7 ± 7, 5 per cent $VO_{2\ max}$) and 36.9 ± 2.6 mL/kg/min (64.7 ± 7.0 per cent $VO_{2\ max}$) for female and male players, respectively. These results evidence the relative importance of aerobic fitness for basketball performance. The mean values of blood lactate concentration registered in match play were 3.7–5.2 mmol/l for females (Matthew & Delextrat, 2009; Rodríguez-Alonso et al., 2003; Scanlan et al., 2012) and 5.5–6.8 mmol/l for males, with a large variability among players (Ben Abdelkrim et al., 2007; Ben Abdelkrim, Castagna, El Fazaa, et al., 2010; Scanlan et al., 2012). Greater lactate concentrations and heart rates have been recorded for higher competitive levels in women's and men's basketball, suggesting the higher pace of the game at this level (Ben Abdelkrim et al., 2007; Rodríguez-Alonso et al., 2003; Scanlan et al., 2011).

Research has reported inconsistent results regarding the players' activities across the game (Ben Abdelkrim et al., 2007; McInnes et al., 1995; Narazaki et al., 2009). While some studies, conducted with male (McInnes et al., 1995) and female players (Matthew & Delextrat, 2009) have not found significant differences in players' activity profiles between the game quarters and halves, others have recorded a decrease in the number of high-intensity actions performed by elite youth players during the second and fourth quarters, comparatively, with those registered in the first and third quarters (Ben Abdelkrim et al., 2007). These conflicting findings suggest that game context and tactical factors may influence the physiological demands of basketball and further investigation is needed to better describe and explain this influence.

Time-motion analysis gives an understanding of the general physical and physiological demands of the game, but it does not really find itself used in day-to-day coaching. Further efforts are needed to better use the knowledge about players' activity profiles and specific position demands in designing of appropriate tasks from physiological, technical and tactical points of view.

CONCLUSIONS AND SUGGESTIONS

By reviewing research studies from recent literature, this chapter presented five main topics of research in basketball performance analysis, covering issues related to shooting performance, player and team performance evaluation, dynamic analysis of score evolution and space-time interactions among players, as well as competitive activity profiles. The contributions of each research topic to understanding factors that influence different aspects of performance in basketball are summarised in this narrative survey.

Although the current state of performance analysis in basketball is quite advanced, and the level of scientific research continues to increase, further work on developing appropriate offensive and especially defensive performance metrics and research methodologies for deeper tactical analysis is needed. The attention of researchers may be directed to the dynamic process of players' spatio-temporal interactions during the game using the data of automatic positional tracking of players instead of conventional notational approaches, based on the game-related statistics and outcomes of individual and team actions. However, it would be useful to capture the quantitative information about game performance with qualitative research and analysis of coaches' opinions that contribute to yielding of applicable findings.

REFERENCES

Abreu, A. M., Macaluso, E., Azevedo, R. T., Cesari, P., Urgesi, C., & Aglioti, S. M. (2012). Action anticipation beyond the action observation network: A functional magnetic resonance imaging study in expert basketball players. *European Journal of Neuroscience, 35*, 1646–1654.

Adams, R. (1992). The "hot hand" revisited: Successful basketball shooting as a function of intershot interval. *Perceptual and Motor Skills, 74*, 934.

Bar-Eli, M., Avugos, S., & Raab, M. (2006). Twenty years of "hot hand" research: Review and critique. *Psychology of Sport and Exercise, 7*, 525–553.

Bartlett, R., & Robins, M. (2008). Biomechanics of throwing. In Y. Hong & R. Bartlett (Eds.), *Routledge Handbook of Biomechanics and Human Movement Science* (pp. 285–296). Oxon: Routledge.

Ben Abdelkrim, N., Castagna, C., El Fazaa, S., & El Ati, J. (2010). The effect of players' standard and tactical strategy on game demands in men's basketball. *Journal of Strength and Conditioning Research, 24*(10), 2652–2662.

Ben Abdelkrim, N., Castagna, C., Jabri, I., Battikh, T., El Fazaa, S., & El Ati, J. (2010). Activity profile and physiological requirements of junior elite basketball players in relation to aerobic-anaerobic fitness. *Journal of Strength and Conditioning Research, 24*(9), 2330–2342.

Ben Abdelkrim, N., El Fazaa, S., & El Ati, J. (2007). Time–motion analysis and physiological data of elite under-19-year-old basketball players during competition. *British Journal of Sports Medicine, 41*(2), 69–75.

Berri, D. J. (1999). Who is most valuable? Measuring the player's production of wins in the National Basketball Association. *Managerial and Decision Economics, 20*(8), 411–427.

Berri, D. J. (2008). A simple measure of worker productivity in the national basketball association. In B. Humphreys & D. Howard (Eds.), *The Business of Sport* (pp. 1–40). Westport, CT: Praeger.

Berri, D. J., & Schmidt, M. B. (2010). *Stumbling on wins in Basketball. Two economists expose the pitfalls on the road to victory in professional sports.* Upper Saddle River, NJ: FT Press.

Boone, J., & Bourgois, J. (2013). Morphological and physiological profile of Elite basketball players in Belgium. *International Journal of Sports Physiology and Performance, 8*(6), 630–638.

Bourbousson, J., Sève, C., & McGarry, T. (2010a). Space-time coordination dynamics in basketball: Part 1. Intra- and intercouplings among player dyads. *Journal of Sports Sciences, 28*(3), 339–347.

Bourbousson, J., Sève, C., & McGarry, T. (2010b). Space–time coordination dynamics in basketball: Part 2. The interaction between the two teams. *Journal of Sports Sciences, 28*(3), 349–358.

Burns, B. (2001). *The hot hand in basketball: Fallacy or adaptive thinking?* Paper presented at the 23th Annual Meeting of the Cognitive Science Society Hillsdale, NJ.

Burns, B. (2004). Heuristics as beliefs and as behaviours: The adaptiveness of the "hot hand". *Cognitive Psychology, 48*, 295–311.

Burns, B., & Corpus, B. (2004). Randomness and inductions from streaks: "Gambler's fallacy" versus "hot hand". *Psychonomic Bulletin & Review, 11*(1), 179–184.

Button, C., MacLeod, M., Sanders, R., & Coleman, S. (2003). Examining movement variability in the basketball free-throw action at different skill levels. *Research Quarterly for Exercise and Sport, 74*(3), 257–269.

Cánovas López, M., Arias, J. L., García, M. P., & Yuste, J. L. (2014). Time-motion analysis procedure in team sports: Example for youth basketball. *Strength and Conditioning Journal, 36*(3), 71–75.

Carter, J. E. L., Ackland, T. R., Kerr, D. A., & Stapff, A. B. (2005). Somatotype and size of elite female basketball players. *Journal of Sports Sciences, 23*(10), 1057–1063.

Casals, M., & Martinez, J. A. (2013). Modelling player performance in basketball through mixed models. *International Journal of Performance Analysis in Sport, 13*, 64–82.

Castagna, C., Manzi, V., D'Ottavio, S., Annino, G., Padua, E., & Bishop, D. (2007). Relation between maximal aerobic power and the ability to repeat sprints

194

in young basketball players. *Journal of Strength and Conditioning Research, 21*(4), 1172–1176.

Caterisano, A., Patrick, B. T., Edenfield, W. L., & Batson, M. J. (1997). The effects of a basketball season on aerobic and strength parameters among college men: Starters vs. reserves. *Journal of Strength and Conditioning Research, 11*(1), 21–24.

Cervone, D., D'Amour, A., Bornn, L., & Goldsberry, K. (2014). *POINTWIse: Predicting points and valuing decisions in real time with NBA optical tracking data*. Paper presented at the MIT Sloan Sports Analytics Conference, Cambridge, MA. http://www.sloansportsconference.com/wp-content/uploads/2014/02/2014_SSAC_Pointwise-Predicting-Points-and-Valuing-Decisions-in-Real-Time.pdf

Cordovil, R., Araújo, D., Davids, K., Gouveia, L., Barreiros, J., Fernandes, O., . . . Serpa, S. (2009). The influence of instructions and body-scaling as constraints on decision-making processes in team sports. *European Journal of Sport Science, 9*(3), 169–179.

Cormery, B., Marcil, M., & Bouvard, M. (2008). Rule change incidence on physiological characteristics of elite basketball players: A 10-year-period investigation. *British Journal of Sports Medicine, 42*, 25–30.

Cortis, C., Tessitore, A., Lupo, C., Pesce, C., Fossile, E., Figura, F., . . . Capranica, L. (2011). Inter-limb coordination, strength, jump, and sprint performances following a youth men's basketball game. *Journal of Strength and Conditioning Research, 25*(1), 135–142.

Delextrat, A., & Cohen, D. (2009). Strength, power, speed, and agility of women basketball players according to playing position. *Journal of Strength and Conditioning Research, 23*(7), 1974–1981.

Esteves, P. T., Araújo, D., Davids, K., Vilar, L., Travassos, B., & Esteves, C. (2012). Interpersonal dynamics and relative positioning to scoring target of performers in 1 vs. 1 sub-phases of team sports. *Journal of Sports Sciences, 30*(12), 1285–1293.

Fewell, J. H., Armbruster, D., Ingraham, J., Petersen, A., & Waters, J. S. (2012). Basketball teams as strategic networks. *PLoS ONE, 7*(11), e47445. doi: 10.1371/journal.pone.0047445

Forthofer, R. (1991). Streak shooter – the sequel. *Chance: New Directions for Statistics and Computing, 4*(2), 46–48.

Fujii, K., Yamashita, D., Yoshioka, S., Isaka, T., & Kouzaki, M. (2014). Strategies for defending a dribbler: Categorisation of three defensive patterns in 1-on-1 basketball. *Sports Biomechanics, 13*(3), 204–214.

Gabel, A., & Redner, S. (2012). Random walk picture of basketball scoring. *Journal of Quantitative Analysis in Sports, 8*(1), ISSN (Online), 1559–0410.

García, J., Ibáñez, S. J., De Santos, R. M., Leite, N., & Sampaio, J. (2013). Identifying basketball performance indicators in regular season and playoff games. *Journal of Human Kinetics, 36*, 161–168.

García, J., Saéz, J., Ibáñez, S. J., Parejo, I., & Cañadas, M. (2009). Home advantage analysis in ACB League in season 2007–2008 *Revista de Psicología del Deporte, 18*(3), 331–335.

Gilovich, T., Vallone, R., & Tversky, A. (1985). The hot hand in basketball: On the misperception of random sequences. *Cognitive Psychology, 17*, 295–314.

Gómez, M. A., Lorenzo, A., Ibáñez, S. J., Ortega, E., Leite, N., & Sampaio, J. (2010). An analysis of defensive strategies used by home and away basketball teams. *Perceptual and Motor Skills, 110*, 159–166.

Gómez, M. A., Lorenzo, A., Ortega, E., Sampaio, J., & Ibáñez, S. J. (2009). Game related statistics discriminating between starters and nonstarters players in women's national basketball association league (WNBA). *Journal of Sports Science and Medicine, 8*, 278–283.

Gómez, M. A., Lorenzo, A., Sampaio, J., Ibáñez, S. J., & Ortega, E. (2008). Game-related statistics that discriminated winning and losing teams from the Spanish men's professional basketball teams. *Collegium Antropologicum, 32*(2), 315–319.

Gómez, M. A., & Pollard, R. (2011). Reduced home advantage for basketball teams from capital cities in Europe. *European Journal of Sport Science, 11*(2), 143–148.

Gonzalez, A. M., Hoffman, J. R., Rogowski, J. P., Burgos, W., Manalo, E., Weise, K., . . . Stout, J. R. (2013). Performance changes in NBA basketball players vary in starters vs. nonstarters over a competitive season. *Journal of Strength and Conditioning Research, 27*(3), 611–615.

Gula, B., & Raab, M. (2004). Hot hand belief and hot hand behaviour: A comment on Koehler and Conley. *Journal of Sport & Exercise Psychology, 26*, 167–170.

Haberstroh, T. (2015). Home-court advantage? Not so much. *ESPN.* http://espn.go.com/nba/story/_/id/12241619/home-court-advantage-decline

Hamilton, G. R., & Reinschmidt, C. (1997). Optimal trajectory for the basketball free throw. *Journal of Sports Sciences, 15*, 491–504.

Ibáñez, S., García, J., Feu, S., Lorenzo, A., & Sampaio, A. (2009). Effects of consecutive basketball games on the game-related statistics that discriminate winner and losing teams. *Journal of Sports Science and Medicine, 8*, 458–462.

Ibañez, S., Sampaio, J., Feu, S., Lorenzo, A., Gómez, M. Á., & Ortega, E. (2008). Basketball game-related statistics that discriminate between teams season-long success. *European Journal of Sport Sciences, 8*(6), 369–372.

Karipidis, A., Fotinakis, P., Taxildaris, K., & Fatouros, J. (2001). Factors characterising a successful performance in basketball. *Journal of Human Movement Studies, 41*, 385–397.

Kempe, M., Grunz, A., & Memmert, D. (2015). Detecting tactical patterns in basketball: Comparison of merge self-organising maps and dynamic controlled neural networks. *European Journal of Sport Science, 15*(4), 249–255.

Koehler, J., & Conley, C. (2003). The "hot hand" myth in professional basketball. *Journal of Sport & Exercise Psychology, 25*, 253–259.

Korb, K., & Stillwell, M. (2002). *The story of the hot hand: Powerful myth or powerless critique.* Paper presented at the International Conference on Cognitive Science, Sydney. http://www.csse.monash.edu.au/~korb/iccs.pdf

Kubatko, J., Oliver, D., Pelton, K., & Rosenbaum, D. T. (2007). A starting point for analyzing basketball statistics. *Journal of Quantitative Analysis in Sports, 3*(3), Article 1.

LaMonte, M. J., McKinney, J. T., Quinn, S. M., Bainbridge, C. N., & Eisenman, P. A. (1999). Comparison of physical and physiological variables for female college basketball players. *Journal of Strength and Conditioning Research, 13*(3), 264–270.

196

Larkey, P., Smith, R., & Kadane, J. (1989). It's okay to believe in the "hot hand". *Chance: New Directions for Statistics and Computing, 2*(4), 22–30.

Malarranha, J., Figueira, B., Leite, N., & Sampaio, J. (2013). Dynamic modeling of performance in basketball. *International Journal of Performance Analysis in Sport, 13*, 377–386.

Martínez, J. A. (2010). Una revisión de los sistemas de valoración de jugadores de baloncesto (I) descripción de los métodos existentes *International Journal of Sports Law & Management (Revista Internacional de Derecho y Gestión del Deporte), 10*, 37–77.

Martinez, J. A. (2012). Factors determining production (FDP) in basketball. *Economics and Business Letters, 1*(1), 21–29.

Matthew, D., & Delextrat, A. (2009). Heart rate, blood lactate concentration, and time–motion analysis of female basketball players during competition. *Journal of Sports Sciences, 27*(8), 813–821.

McGarry, T., Anderson, D. I., Wallace, S., Hughes, M., & Franks, I. (2002). Sport competition as a dynamical self-organizing system. *Journal of Sports Sciences, 20*(10), 771–781.

McInnes, S. E., Carlson, J. S., Jones, C. J., & McKenna, M. J. (1995). The physiological load imposed on basketball players during competition. *Journal of Sports Sciences, 13*(5), 387–397.

Merritt, S., & Clauset, A. (2014). Scoring dynamics across professional team sports: tempo, balance and predictability. *EPJ Data Science, 3*. http://www.epjdatascience.com/content/3/1/4

Miyoshi, H. (2000). Is the "hot-hands" phenomenon a misperception of random events? *Japanese Psychological Research, 42*(2), 128–133.

Mullineaux, D. R., & Uhl, T. L. (2010). Coordination-variability and kinematics of misses versus swishes of basketball free throws. *Journal of Sports Sciences, 28*(9), 1017–1024.

Narazaki, K., Berg, K., Stergiou, N., & Chen, B. (2009). Physiological demands of competitive basketball. *Scandinavian Journal of Medicine & Science in Sports, 19*, 425–432.

Oliveira, R., Oudejans, R., & Beek, P. J. (2006). Late information pick-up is preferred in basketball jump shooting. *Journal of Sports Sciences, 24*(9), 933–940.

Oliveira, R., Oudejans, R., & Beek, P. J. (2008). Gaze behavior in basketball shooting. *Research Quarterly for Exercise and Sport, 79*(3), 399–404.

Oliver, D. (2004). *Basketball on Paper. Rules and Tools for Performance Analysis.* Dulles, VA: Brassey's, Inc.

Ostojic, S. M., Mazic, S., & Dikic, N. (2006). Profiling in basketball: Physical and physiological characteristics of elite players. *Journal of Strength and Conditioning Research, 20*(4), 740–744.

Oudejans, R. R. D., Karamat, R. S., & Stolk, M. H. (2012). Effects of actions preceding the jump shot on gaze behavior and shooting performance in elite female basketball players. *International Journal of Sports Science & Coaching, 7*(2), 255–267.

Oudejans, R. R. D., van de Langenberg, R. W., & Hutter, R. I. (2002). Aiming at a far target under different viewing conditions: Visual control in basketball jump shooting. *Human Movement Science, 21*, 457–480.

197

Perl, J. (2004). A neural network approach to movement pattern analysis. *Human Movement Science, 23*, 605–620.

Pollard, R., & Gómez, M. A. (2013). Variations in home advantage in the national basketball leagues of Europe. *Revista de Psicología del Deporte, 22*(1), 263–266.

Pollard, R., & Pollard, G. (2005). Long-term trends in home advantage in professional team sports in North America and England (1876–2003). *Journal of Sport Science, 23*(4), 337–350.

Reifman, A. (2012). *Hot Hand: The Statistics Behind Sports' Greatest Streaks.* Washington, DC: Potomac Books.

Robins, M. T., Wheat, J., Irwin, G., & Bartlett, R. M. (2006). The effect of shooting distance on movement variability in basketball. *Journal of Human Movement Studies, 20*, 218–238.

Rodríguez-Alonso, M., Fernández-García, B., Pérez-Landaluce, J., & Terrados, N. (2003). Blood lactate and heart rate during national and international women's basketball. *Journal of Sports Medicine and Physical Fitness, 43*(4), 432–436.

Sallet, P., Perrier, D., Ferret, J. M., Vitelli, V., & Baverel, G. (2005). Physiological differences in professional basketball players as a function of playing position and level of play. *The Journal of Sports Medicine and Physical Fitness, 45*(3), 291–294.

Sampaio, J., Ibanez, S. J., & Feu, S. (2004). Discriminative power of basketball game-related statistics by level of competition and sex. *Perceptual and Motor Skills, 99*(3), 1231–1238.

Sampaio, J., Ibañez, S. J., Gómez, M. A., Lorenzo, A., & Ortega, E. (2008). Game location influences basketball players performance across playing positions. *International Journal of Sport Psychology, 39*(3), 43–50.

Sampaio, J., Ibáñez, S. J., Lorenzo, A., & Gomez, M. (2006). Discriminative game-related statistics between basketball starters and nonstarters when related to team quality and game outcome. *Perceptual and Motor Skills, 103*(2), 486–494.

Sampaio, J., & Janeira, M. (2003). Statistical analyses of basketball team performance: Understanding teams' wins and losses according to a different index of ball possessions. *International Journal of Performance Analysis in Sport, 3*, 40–49.

Sampaio, J., Janeira, M., Ibáñez, S. J., & Lorenzo, A. (2006). Discriminant analysis of game-related statistics between basketball guards, forwards and centres in three professional leagues. *European Journal of Sport Science, 6*(3), 173–178.

Sampaio, J., Lago, C., & Drinkwater, E. J. (2010). Explanations for the United States of America's dominance in basketball at the Beijing Olympic Games (2008). *Journal of Sports Sciences, 28*(2), 147–152.

Scanlan, A., Dascombe, B., & Reaburn, P. (2011). A comparison of the activity demands of elite and sub-elite Australian men's basketball competition. *Journal of Sports Sciences, 29*(11), 1153–1160.

Scanlan, A., Humphriesa, B., Tuckera, P. S., & Dalboa, V. (2014). The influence of physical and cognitive factors on reactive agility performance in men basketball players. *Journal of Sports Sciences, 32*(4), 367–374.

Scanlan, A. T., Dascombe, B. J., Reaburn, P., & Dalbo, V. J. (2012). The physiological and activity demands experienced by Australian female basketball players during competition. *Journal of Science and Medicine in Sport, 15*(4), 341–347.

198

Schmidt, A. (2012). Movement pattern recognition in basketball free-throw shooting. *Human Movement Science, 31*, 360–382.

Schmidt, R., O'Brien, B., & Sysko, R. (1999). Self-organization of between-person cooperative tasks and possible applications to sport. *International Journal of Sport Psychology, 30*(4), 558–579.

Stern, H., & Morris, C. (1993). Comment. *Journal of the American Statistical Association, 88*(424), 1189–1196.

Stöckel, T., & Fries, U. (2013). Motor adaptation in complex sports – The influence of visual context information on the adaptation of the three-point shot to altered task demands in expert basketball players. *Journal of Sports Sciences, 31*(7), 750–758.

Swalgin, K. L. (1998). The basketball evaluation system: A computerised factor-weighted model with measures of validity. *The International Scientific Journal of Kinesiology and Sport, 30*, 31–37.

Tran, C. M., & Silverberg, L. M. (2008). Optimal release conditions for the free throw in men's basketball. *Journal of Sports Sciences, 26*(11), 1147–1155.

Trninić, S., Dizdar, D., & Lukšić, E. (2002). Differences between winning and defeated top quality basketball teams in final tournaments of European club championship. *Collegium Antropologicum, 26*(2), 521–531.

Trninić, S., Perica, A., & Dizdar, D. (1999). Set of criteria for the actual quality evaluation of the elite basketball players. *Collegium Antropologicum, 23*(2), 707–721.

Tversky, A., & Gilovich, T. (1989a). The cold facts about the "hot hand" in basketball. *Chance, 2*(1), 16–21.

Tversky, A., & Gilovich, T. (1989b). The "hot hand" statistical reality or cognitive illusion? *Chance, 2*(4), 31–34.

Uchida, Y., Mizuguchi, N., Honda, M., & Kanosue, K. (2014). Prediction of shot success for basketball free throws: Visual search strategy. *European Journal of Sport Science, 14*(5), 426–432.

Vereijken, B., van Emmerick, R. E. A., Whiting, H. T. A., & Newell, K. M. (1992). Free(z)ing degrees of freedom in skill acquisition. *Journal of Motor Behavior, 24*, 133–142.

Vergin, R. (2000). Winning streaks in sports and the misperception of momentum. *Journal of Sport Behavior, 23*, 181–197.

Vickers, J. N. (1996). Visual control when aiming at a far target. *Journal of Experimental Psychology, 22*, 342–354.

Wardrop, R. (1999). Statistical tests for the hot-hand in basketball in a controlled setting. http://www.stat.wisc.edu/~wardrop/papers/tr1007.pdf

Wu, Y., Zeng, Y., Zhang, L., Wang, S., Wang, D., Tan, X., . . . Zhang, J. (2013). The role of visual perception in action anticipation in basketball athletes. *Neuroscience, 237*, 29–41.

Ziv, G., & Lidor, R. (2009). Physical attributes, physiological characteristics, on-court performances and nutritional strategies of female and male basketball players. *Sports Medicine, 39*(7), 547–568.

Ziv, G., Lidor, R., & Arnon, M. (2010). Predicting team rankings in basketball: The questionable use of on-court performance statistics. *International Journal of Performance Analysis of Sport, 10*, 103–114.

CHAPTER 10

RESEARCH TOPICS IN TEAM HANDBALL

Leading author: Anna Volossovitch

INTRODUCTION

Over the past decade, coaches and researchers have developed various strategies for observing, analysing and evaluating the performance of handball players and teams. Data collected by match analysis systems tend to capture technical, tactical or physical aspects of performance, and represent a strong argument for the organisation and evaluation of the training process. This chapter intends to identify the key facets of the game and the main research topics, methodologies and findings in handball, as well as outline trends that might influence further research. Moreover, the chapter aims to discuss the determinants of handball performance and to formulate recommendations regarding the appropriate methods for performance assessment of handball players and teams in match play. The studies reviewed were selected from the Web of Science™ All Databases using the following criteria (Moore et al., 2014; Sarmento et al., 2014; Wagner et al., 2014): (1) based on the match play data or on-court performance similar to competition; (2) carried out with elite or experienced team-handball players as subjects; (3) published from the year 2000 onwards.

A brief description of team handball

Team handball is an Olympic sport practiced on different continents, but it is particularly popular in Europe, where it is played at a high professional level. During the game two teams of seven players (six field players and a goalkeeper) try to get the ball into the opposing team's goal, alternating ball possessions. A handball match lasts 60 minutes, divided into two halves of 30 minutes each. The game is played on a court 40-by-20 meters consisting of two goal areas, where only the goalkeeper is allowed to stay, and a playing area. Handball is considered a complex, multifactorial, highly demanding intermittent sport that requires from players a high level of specific technical and tactical skills, good team coordination, and fitness to support frequent body contact and perform multiple high-intensity actions. This brief description of handball emphasises certain features of the game; this explains some concerns of match analysis in handball, discussed in this chapter.

TACTICAL ASPECTS OF MATCH ANALYSIS

Outcome-oriented approach based on cumulative data

The identification of individual or collective behavioural events that contribute significantly to the team's success is one of the major issues of tactical analysis in sports games. Three levels of success with a clear hierarchical inter-relationships among them could be distinguished in the research regarding tactical analysis in handball:

1   team's final ranking (Bilge, 2012; Gutiérrez & Ruiz, 2013);
2   match outcome, expressed by goal difference (Lago et al., 2013; Ohnjec et al., 2008; Srhoj et al., 2001; Vuleta et al., 2007) or victory and loss (Foretić et al., 2013; Rogulj et al., 2004); and
3   goal scoring (Lozano & Camerino, 2012; Rogulj et al., 2011).

Studies analysing tactical performance in relation to first two levels of success (team's final ranking and match outcome) has been carried out using predominantly the cumulative descriptive statistics from the national and international high-level competitions. These primary data represent discrete events (counts or frequencies) of previously coded individual or team actions focused mainly on players' activities with the ball and on the result of these activities (scoring, loss/gain ball possession). In these quantitative studies the performance variables are recorded by the following:

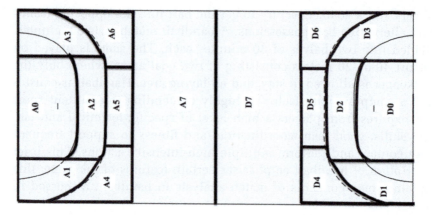

Figure 10.1 Court division in zones

A0 – goal area of defending team; D0 – goal area of attacking team; A1 and A3 – zone of attacking wing players; A2 – zone of attacking pivot; A4 and A6 – zone of attacking backcourt players; A5 – zone of attacking central player; D1 and D3 – zone of defending wing players; D2 – zone of defending pivot; D4 and D6 – zone of defending backcourt players; D5 – zone of defending central player; A7 – transition area of defending team midfield; D7 – transition area of attacking team midfield.

1   court zone (see Figure 10.1),
2   player's position (wing, backcourt, pivot or goalkeeper), and
3   game phase (positional play or fast break).

The analysis of technical and tactical aspects of performance has allowed for the identification of offensive and defensive key indicators, which better differentiate the performance of winning and losing teams and characterise the individual player's performance (Foretić et al., 2013) in elite handball. For the attacking performance the following variables have been identified:

1   total number of field shots and goals (Lago et al., 2013; Meletakos et al., 2011; Vuleta et al., 2003);
2   total number of 6-m shots and goals (Meletakos et al., 2011; Ohnjec et al., 2008; Oliveira et al., 2012; Vuleta et al., 2003);
3   total number of 7-m throws and goals (Oliveira et al., 2012; Vuleta et al., 2003);
4   total number of break-throughs (Foretić et al., 2013; Srhoj et al., 2001);
5   total number of fast breaks and goals in fast breaks (Gruić et al., 2006; Oliveira et al., 2012; Rogulj et al., 2004; Rogulj et al., 2011; Srhoj

et al., 2001; Teles, & Volossovitch, 2015) and total number of fast position attacks with up to 25-s duration (Rogulj et al., 2004);

6 ratio of fast break goals to all goals scored (Bilge, 2012);
7 ratio of goals scored by backcourt and pivot players to all goals (Bilge, 2012); and
8 field shot efficiency and shot efficiency of backcourt and wing players (Gómez et al., 2014; Srhoj et al., 2001; Teles & Volossovitch, 2015).

The set of defensive performance indicators included the following variables:

1 goalkeeper efficiency (Gómez et al., 2014; Gruić et al., 2006; Lago et al., 2013; Volossovitch & Gonçalves, 2003; Teles & Volossovitch, 2015);
2 turnovers (Lago et al., 2013);
3 steals (Lago et al., 2013); and
4 blocked shots (Foretić et al., 2013; Lago et al., 2013).

It should be noted that research findings have revealed considerable differences in the variables identified as most relevant for team performance and game outcome in handball. Some of the results are fairly obvious and converge on the importance of the field shot, the goalkeeper and fast break efficiency. However, the high number of fast breaks in handball as well as 6-m shots usually occurs in unbalanced games. Therefore, to better understand the factors that influence team performance it is necessary to take into account the context of the competition, typically characterised by game location, quality of opposition and match status.

The influence of contextual variables on teams' performance

In recent years several studies have evidenced a significant influence of competitive context on team performance in handball.

Game location

The existence of a home advantage effect was confirmed in the seven national European handball leagues. Based on the final scores of 10,358 games, played during the seven seasons from 2002–2003 to 2008–2009, Meletakos and Bayios (2010) registered the values ranging from 57.7 per cent in Denmark to 59.9 per cent in Germany. Strong evidence of home advantage (with values ranging between 61 and 64 per cent) has also been identified in Spanish handball (Gómez et al., 2011; Lago et al., 2013; Oliveira et al., 2012; Pollard & Gómez, 2012). The differences in magnitude of the home advantage effect have been verified among men's (61.6 per cent) and women's (59.2 per cent) competition (Pollard & Gómez, 2012), as well as among games with balanced (71 per cent) and unbalanced opposition (55 per cent) in men's handball (Oliveira et al., 2012).

More detailed analysis of the influence of contextual variables on the performance indicators has shown the higher shooting efficiency from 6 m (Oliveira et al., 2012; Lago et al., 2013), 9 m and fast breaks, as well as higher goalkeeper efficiency and total number of shots for home teams (Lago et al., 2013).

Interactive effect of game location and quality of opposition

Oliveira et al. (2012) also registered an interactive effect of the game location and quality of opposition on the 6-m shot efficiency. Home teams demonstrated higher line shot efficiency playing against weaker opponents. As far as the findings of Oliveira et al. (2012), Lago et al., (2013) and Gómez et al. (2014) have shown in matches sampled from one or two seasons of the Spanish Professional Men's Handball League, the extrapolation of their results for other seasons and competitions requires further research.

Gómez and colleagues (2014) analysed the interaction effects of contextual variables on the performance indicators in the particular case of close games (with the final goal differences of 1.98±1.37). In these matches the home teams performed more successful counter-attack shots, assists and blocks and recovered more balls. However, when the team's quality was considered, the superior teams had better results in the mentioned indicators when playing both at home and away; moreover the inferior teams obtained higher values when drawing or losing (Gómez et al., 2014). These results demonstrate that in close games it is really difficult to establish a direct and linear relationship between the frequency of actions, considered as performance indicators, and the match outcome. In order to understand how the final match result was achieved, it is necessary to look beyond the cumulative data and analyse the players' behaviours and score evolution during the match process.

204

Process-oriented approach based on sequential and score evolution data

Analysis of tactical patterns

One of the limitations of the outcome-oriented analysis, based on the cumulative data, is that it provides a static view of the game, with a restricted ability to describe the interactions among game events over time (Volossovitch, 2013; Volossovitch & Ferreira, 2013). This problem can be solved by using information about the match process (description of sequences of players' behaviours and the results during ball possession or collection and analysis of data by ball possession). The process-oriented approach is based on the recording of substantial tactical actions in a chronological, sequential order and provides a deeper insight into the tactical models used by a team during a match (Pfeiffer & Perl, 2006).

The efficient way of sequentially using different attacking tactical means was identified in the study of Lozano & Camerino (2012), who examined the behaviour patterns of four top-ranked teams in six games from the 2011 World Men's Handball Championship. The observation instrument (T-patterns sequential analysis) used in the study consisted of eight criteria, which categorised chronologically the attacking actions from the start to the end of the offensive sequence (ball possession), including the opponent's defence systems, numerical relationship between teams, the number of attempts within every possession and offensive system used in each attempt (structured, unstructured and fast break). Results of this study suggest that the efficiency of attack sequence (ball possession) is enhanced if it begins with a fast break or unstructured attack and continues with structured attacking actions. The shorter attacking sequences (with less than three configurations) and the sequences in which the attacking system is not changed were also recognised as more efficient.

The different types of offensive tactical structures in youth female handball have been identified by Pfeiffer and Perl (2006). Using an Artificial Neural Networks approach the authors analysed and afterwards made classifications according to the similarity of tactical organisation in 2,900 offensive attempts (processes) from 15 matches (12 teams) of the Women's Junior World Championship 2001. The content and the structure of the system of states used to analyse the tactical behaviour were based on handball-specific concepts, beginning with 'offence formation', continuing with the sequence of tactical actions and ending with 'goal throw'. The trained neural network identified typical tactics aggregated over several plays of three teams and thereby showed its great potential for analysing the interactions between different events in complex game processes.

Analysis of the dynamics of score evolution

Another example of research that used the process-oriented approach is represented by studies that analysed teams' performance according to time and score evolution during the match. A first step to understanding the processes that lead to winning or to losing is to describe the dynamics of the score evolution during the game and to identify the factors that influence it.

Vuleta and co-authors (2007) analysed the influence of the goals scored in four 15-minute periods during a game on the final outcome (defined by the final goal difference) of 60 matches from the 2003 Men's Handball World Championship. It was found that winning teams scored the greatest number of goals in the second quarter, while for losing teams the most productive period was the fourth quarter of a match. The average value of goals scored by victorious teams was higher in all quarters. The results of the study have shown that the goals scored in the second and in the first quarter of match better predicted the final score. In this study the specific context of each match (round of the championship, level of opposite teams and match equilibrium) was not considered and this limits the interpretation of the findings.

In turn, the contextual variables have been taken into account in the study conducted by Oliveira et al. (2012) with a sample of 480 regular season games (2007–2009) from the Spanish Men's Professional Handball League. In this paper the goals scored; the efficiency of the shots from 6 m, 7 m and 9 m; and the fast breaks were analysed by 5-minute game periods in matches played against balanced and unbalanced opponents. In accordance with Vuleta et al. (2007), Oliveira and colleagues (2012) registered that a lower number of goals is scored at the beginning of a match. The highest number of goals is counted in the last five-minute period of each half. Home teams scored more in the last five-minute period of the first half, while away teams performed more goals in the last five minutes of the second half. These results clearly indicate that the game period is one of the factors that influences teams' performance. For instance, Bar-Eli

206

et al. (1992) identified the final five minutes of the handball match as a potentially critical period, in which the probability of players experiencing a psychological crisis is higher than in all other game periods.

With exception to the mentioned studies, research in handball notation analysis has paid relatively little attention to the time dimension of the game. Furthermore, in the studies of Vuleta et al. (2007) and Oliveira et al. (2012) it was assumed that all periods of 15 and 5 minutes, respectively, were independent, and the possible relationship between the performances in subsequent game intervals was not considered. However, the analysis of variability of performance and score evolution during the match implies considering how prior events influence subsequent ones. The development of prospective mathematical models from the time series of data collected in the real context of the competition by ball possession could be one of the possible and promising consequences of this analysis. For example, the influence of a team's past performance on the team's present performance was evaluated throughout the match by Dumangane et al. (2009) and Volossovitch et al. (2009). The assessment considered the specific context of the game situation, the team's ranking, the match equilibrium and the number of ball possessions per match. It was analysed if the probability of scoring varied during the game and which factors influenced this probability; in other words, the study verified if the goals scored during the match are independent and identically distributed. The data from 32,273 observations of ball possessions from 224 matches from the 17th, 18th and 19th Men's World Handball Championships were used for the estimation of a linear probability model with time-varying parameters for the probability of scoring. The probability of scoring was estimated as a function of the past offensive performance of the opposing team and the current match result. The results of the model estimation confirmed that the probability of scoring did not depend directly on the past offensive performance of the team, but indirectly through the team's past defensive performance, and the current goal difference between the teams' scores; moreover the level of this dependence varied during the game.

COMPETITIVE ACTIVITY PROFILES AND SPECIFIC POSITION DEMANDS

Team handball is an intermittent, high-intensity sport characterised by complex movements, such as shooting, passing, catching, jumping, blocking, stealing and physical contact with the opponent. Handball rules allow unlimited substitutions of players throughout the match. Over recent years, the technological advances and the need for reliable information about competitive activity profiles led to an increase of scientific knowledge regarding the time-motion analysis, as well as the physical and physiological demands of elite handball. This knowledge is essential for the adequate design and application of specific training. The on-court physical and physiological requirements of handball have recently been addressed in several studies, based on the data collected during real match play (Michalsik et al. 2014; Póvoas et al., 2012; Póvoas et al., 2014) and in experimental games (Šibila et al., 2004; Barbero et al., 2014), with special emphasis on position-related demands in male (Karcher & Buchheit, 2014; Michalsik et al., 2013; Póvoas et al., 2014) and female games (Belka et al., 2014; Michalsik et al., 2014).

Manual coding systems of video recordings of competitive games were employed for time-motion analysis in the majority of handball studies, with the exception of one, conducted by Barbero et al. (2014), who used GPS devices. In manual coding systems the mean speed and the type of locomotion were determined by detailed analysis of match images using the lines of the playing court as reference (Michalsik et al., 2013; Póvoas et al., 2012).

The activity patterns and physiological demands in handball were examined as a function of the following variables: (1) total distance covered; (2) running pace; (3) distance covered in different speed zones; (4) time spent in different speed zones; (5) frequency and duration of different locomotor activities; (6) frequency of technical playing actions; (7) heart rate; (8) percentage of time spent at different interval percentages of players' maximal heart rate; (9) frequency and duration of maximal and high-intensity activities; (10) mean recovery time between high- and low-intensity activities; and (11) fluid loss and intake. Most of these variables have been analysed according to playing positions, game half or five-minute game periods, discriminating data for attack and defence phases.

Time-motion analyses in handball have shown that elite male handball players cover on average 3,600–4,500 m per match (Michalsik et al., 2013; Póvoas et al., 2012) and elite female players run around 4,000 m (Michalsik et al., 2014). With regard to average running pace, the studies reported that handball players move at a speed around 60–100 m/min (Barbero et al., 2014; Michalsik et al., 2013; Šibila et al., 2004).

208

To better describe the players' displacement profiles the total distance covered during the matches is generally broken down into different categories of movement according to intensity. The movement categories and speed zones of players' locomotion are defined as shown in Table 10.1.

In addition to the players' displacement profiles, other specific playing actions are usually registered to characterise position-related activity – for example, shots, jumps, side-cutting, one-on-one situations, fakes, tackles and body contacts (Karcher & Buchheit, 2014; Póvoas et al., 2012). These power-related actions do not require large displacements and therefore do not influence significantly the time-motion data (Póvoas et al., 2012). However, these technical playing actions that are considered as key factors for handball performance have great impact on the heart rate of players. For this reason researchers use the combined form of analysis that includes time-motion and heart rate monitoring (Barbero et al., 2014; Belka et al., 2014; Michalsik et al., 2014; Póvoas et al., 2012).

The effect of playing positions on the game's technical and physical demands has been confirmed by different studies and thus should be taken into account when evaluating players' activities (Barbero et al., 2014; Michalsik et al., 2013; Michalsik et al., 2014; Póvoas et al., 2014). The team-averaged data can be useful for characterising the general game requirements, but it has a little interest from the practical point of view because it does not provide detailed information for the prescription of position-specific training programs (Karcher & Buchheit, 2014).

The playing positions in handball include wings (right and left), back-court players (central, right and left), pivots and goalkeepers. There are significant position-related differences in the tactical/technical and loco-motor activities of handball players. Work activity position-related profiles, identified by different authors, vary considerably, as can be seen in Table 10.2 (for more detailed information, see the comprehensive review by Karcher & Buchheit, 2014). The differences in the methodology regarding the tracking systems used in the studies, speed zones and the consideration of players' substitutions make the comparison of the results of different studies quite difficult. Even so, the collected data allow for broadly characterising the position-related locomotion demands.

Time-motion data recorded during match play generally suggest that players spend large amounts of time standing still or walking (see Table 10.2). However, the physical demands of the game remain high because of numerous high-intensity and power-related actions

Table 10.1 Summary of movement categories and speed zones for time-motion analysis in handball

Reference	Standing still	Walking	Jogging	Running	Fast running	Sprinting	Backwards movement	Sideways medium-intensity movement	Sideways high-intensity movement
Men's handball									
Šibila et al., 2004	0 m·s⁻¹	up to 1.4 m·s⁻¹	1.4 to 3.4 m·s⁻¹		3.4 to 5.2 m·s⁻¹	above 5.2 m·s⁻¹			
Póvoas et al., 2012*	0 km·h⁻¹	6 km·h⁻¹	8 km·h⁻¹	12 km·h⁻¹	18 km·h⁻¹	above 18 km·h⁻¹	10 km·h⁻¹	10 km·h⁻¹	above 10 km·h⁻¹
Póvoas et al., 2014*	0 km·h⁻¹	6 km·h⁻¹	8 km·h⁻¹	12 km·h⁻¹	18 km·h⁻¹	above 18 km·h⁻¹	10 km·h⁻¹	10 km·h⁻¹	above 10 km·h⁻¹
Michalsik et al., 2013	0 km·h⁻¹	4 km·h⁻¹	8 km·h⁻¹	13 km·h⁻¹	17km·h⁻¹	above 24 km·h⁻¹	10 km·h⁻¹	10 km·h⁻¹	
Barbero et al., 2014	0 km·h⁻¹	0.5–4 km·h⁻¹	4.1–9 km·h⁻¹	9.1–14 km·h⁻¹	14.1–18 km·h⁻¹	above 18 km·h⁻¹			
Women's handball									
Michalsik et al., 2014	0 km·h⁻¹	4 km·h⁻¹	7 km·h⁻¹	12 km·h⁻¹	15.5 km·h⁻¹	22 km·h⁻¹	9 km·h⁻¹	9 km·h⁻¹	
Belka et al., 2014	0 m·s⁻¹	0–1 m·s⁻¹	1–3 m·s⁻¹	3–5 m·s⁻¹	5–7 m·s⁻¹	above 7 m·s⁻¹			

* The definitions of the locomotive categories were not described explicitly, but defined using the criteria of Bangsbo et al. (1991)

performed during the game, such as changing directions, throws, jumps, stops and duels with physical contact; these actions are performed in a limited space without large displacements. For instance, Póvoas et al. (2012) reported that during 53 per cent of the effective match time the players exercised at intensities higher than 80 per cent of the maximal heart rate, spending only a small amount (7 per cent) of total effective game time at heart rate values equal or below 60 per cent of maximal heart rate. In addition, the authors found that the mean recovery time between high- to low-intensity activities was 55 seconds. Barbero et al. (2014) found that on average high-intensity actions occur each 44 ± 17 seconds and sprints every 189 ± 95 seconds. Although in general the findings confirm the fast pace of handball game, the data regarding repeated high-intensity actions varied considerably. The reasons for this inconsistency need to be better clarified in further research.

The results concerning positional differences in the locomotion and physical demands are not consensual regarding the distance travelled per match by wing and backcourt players. Šibila et al. (2004) and Barbero et al. (2014) reported higher total distances covered by wing players, whereas Póvoas et al. (2014) and Michalsik et al. (2014) registered higher total distances for backcourt players. For the pivots, who run significantly less than other outfield positions, the data were more consistent. To be expected, the goalkeeper covers considerably shorter distances in comparison with outfield players. Barbero and colleagues (2014) also found that central players (playmakers) run more and had a higher frequency of sprint actions than lateral backcourt players. Therefore, a suggestion for future research would be to split the backcourt players into central and lateral, analysing them separately.

In all recent studies wing players have shown a more intensive activity profile, revealing the highest average speed of movements and high-intensity running distances (Barbero et al., 2014; Michalsik et al., 2013; Michalsik et al., 2014; Póvoas et al., 2014). Backcourt players moved predominantly with low and moderate intensities, performing a lot of sideways movements and spending less time standing still; they also demonstrated a higher mean speed than pivots. Pivots performed fewer displacements than backcourt players, but participated in the highest number of duels and body contacts, exercising longer periods of high-intensity activities

Table 10.2 Percentages of total playing time and total distance covered per match in different movement categories by male handball players of different playing positions

Reference	Playing position	Standing still		Walking		Jogging	
		% of total distance covered	% of total playing time	% of total distance covered	% of total playing time	% of total distance covered	% of total playing time
Šibila et al., 2004	Backcourt						57
	Wing						58
	Pivot						62
Michalsik et al., 2013	Backcourt	0	44.4	42.7	32.3	17.2	8.6
	Wing	0	39.7	46.7	34.5	11.5	9.1
	Pivot	0	41.8	46.0	31.4	14.3	9.7
Póvoas et al., 2014	Backcourt	0	34.6±5.9	48.5±7.1	40.9±4.5	24.6±7.3	10.5±4.3
	Wing	0	45.7±5.6	46.2±6.2	34.1±3.7	18.2±2.1	6.6±1.0
	Pivot	0	48.7±9.3	42.9±7.7	29.9±7.3	26.9±4.2	9.2±2.0

MI – medium-intensity movement; HI – high-intensity movement

Running		Fast running		Sprinting		Sideways movement		Backwards movement	
% of total distance covered	% of total playing time	% of total distance covered	% of total playing time	% of total distance covered	% of total playing time	% of total distance covered	% of total playing time	% of total distance covered	% of total playing time
	25		14		3				
	23		14		4				
	25		10		2				
12.8	4.0	4.7	1.0	1.6	0.2	15.5	8.4	5.5	1.1
11.6	5.4	7.3	1.6	5.0	0.4	11.2	8.2	6.7	1.1
11.3	4.9	7.0	1.3	3.7	0.2	12.7	9.7	5.0	1
		8.8±4.6	1.9±1.2	1.9±1.3	0.3±0.2	6.9±2.8 (MI) 3.1±2.2 (HI)	6.0±2.3 (MI) 0.9±0.7 (HI)	6.2±3.3	4.8±2.3
		16.4±5.2	3.0±1.2	3.9±2.4	0.6±0.4	3.9±1.8 (MI) 2.8±2.2 (HI)	3.1±1.7 (MI) 0.7±0.5 (HI)	8.6±1.8	6.2±1.7
		9.3±4.3	1.5±0.7	1.5±1.4	0.2±0.2	8.8±4.8 (MI) 7.1±5.5 (HI)	6.4±4.2 (MI) 1.6±1.3 (HI)	3.5±1.2	2.3±0.9

in defence (Michalsik et al., 2013; Póvoas et al., 2014). Backcourt players and pivots, compared to wings, executed a greater number of high-demand actions, such as stops, jumps and one-on-one situations, and they spent longer periods of time at intensities above 80 per cent of the maximal heart rate (Póvoas et al., 2014). Generally, the results of time-motion analysis in handball have shown that the isolated evaluation of players' displacement might not describe properly the real game demands, because the numerous high-intensity playing actions do not require to cover considerable distances, but remain physically highly demanding.

CONCLUSIONS AND SUGGESTIONS

Tactical aspects of match analysis in team handball have been studied according to outcome-oriented and process-oriented perspectives. The first perspective is a traditional form of analysis based on the cumulative statistics registered at the end of the match and associated with the game outcome. The advantage of this approach is that it identifies the relevant aspects of performance and defines 'roughly' the profiles of successful performance. However, despite the high amount of studies aimed at identifying the most relevant performance indicators, the lack of consensus on its findings is quite often. The main limitation of the outcome-oriented approach based on the cumulative data is the loss of information on changes in performance over time in different competitive contexts. For effective modelling of the game process it is necessary to obtain more data on the teams' activity during the game and on the strategies used in different competitive contexts. It would be appropriate to complete the notational analysis with variables related to defensive processes, which remains predominantly characterised by goalkeeper efficiency and by the actions with a low frequency of occurrences, such as interceptions, tackles and disciplinary sanctions.

Although the process-oriented approach has been gaining relevance for handball match analysis, the application of tools which capture accurately the space and temporal properties of team behaviour remains scarce. Future research should include the spatial and temporal analysis of players' and teams' behaviours based on the positional data from players' tracking in match play. This will ensure the better understanding of factors that influence the interpersonal and teams' coordination during the game.

214

Motion analysis helps to understand the physical and physiological requirements of match play that should be considered in the organisation of training for different playing positions. The information about positional demands in handball should be complemented by data regarding the influence of game tactics, playing style and contextual factors on the locomotor activity and work-rates. The use of more precise and accurate tools than video-based methods for estimating accelerations, velocities and distances is also desirable.

The different approaches to match analysis are not mutually exclusive; they serve different purposes and should be seen as complementary. The relevance of the research questions about the game, which, it is claimed, are to be answered by using one or another approach, is what really matters.

REFERENCES

Bangsbo, J., Norregaard, L., & Thorso, F. (1991). Activity profile of competition soccer. *Canadian Journal of Sport Sciences, 16*, 110–116.

Bar-Eli, M., Taoz, E., Levy-Kolker, N., & Tenenbaum, G. (1992). Performance quality and behavioral violations as crisis indicators in competition. *International Journal of Sport Psychology, 3*, 325–342.

Barbero, J. C., Granda-Vera, J., Calleja-González, J., & Del Coso, J. (2014). Physical and physiological demands of elite team handball players. *International Journal of Performance Analysis in Sport, 14*(3), 921–933.

Belka, J., Hulka, K., Safar, M., Weisser, R., & Samcova, A. (2014). Analyses of time-motion and heart rate in elite female players (U19) during competitive handball matches. *Kinesiology, 46*, 33–43.

Bilge, M. (2012). Game analysis of Olympic, world and European championships in men's Handball. *Journal of Human Kinetics, 35*, 109–118.

Dumangane, M., Rosati, N., & Volossovitch, A. (2009). Departure from independence and stationarity in a handball match. *Journal of Applied Statistics, 36*(7), 723–741.

Foretić, N., Rogulj, N., & Papić, V. (2013). Empirical model for evaluating situational efficiency in top level handball. *International Journal of Performance Analysis in Sport, 13*, 275–293.

Gómez, M. A., Lago, C., Viaño, J., & González, I. (2014). Effects of game location, team quality and final outcome on game-related statistics in professional handball close games. *Kinesiology, 46*(2), 249–257.

Gómez, M., Pollard, R., & Luis-Pascual, J. C. (2011). Comparison of the home advantage in nine different professional team sports in Spain. *Perceptual and Motor Skills, 113*(1), 150–156.

Gruić, I., Vuleta, D., & Milanović, D. (2006). Performance indicators of teams at the 2003 Men's World Handball Championship in Portugal. *Kinesiology, 38*, 164–175.

Gutiérrez, O., & Ruiz, J. L. (2013). Game performance versus competitive performance in the world championship of handball 2011. *Journal of Human Kinetics, 36*, 137–147. doi: 10.2478/hukin-2013–0014

Karcher, C., & Buchheit, M. (2014). On-court demands of elite handball, with special reference to playing positions. *Sports Medicine, 44*, 797–814. doi: 10.1007/s40279–014–0164-z

Lago, C., Gómez, M. A., Viaño, J., González-García, I., & Fernández, M. (2013). Home advantage in elite handball: The impact of the quality of opposition on team performance. *International Journal of Performance Analysis in Sport, 13*, 724–733.

Lozano, D., & Camerino, O. (2012). Effectiveness of offensive systems in handball. *Apunts. Educación Física y Deportes, 108*, 70–81.

Meletakos, P., & Bayios, I. (2010). General trends in European men's handball: A longitudinal study. *International Journal of Performance Analysis in Sport, 10*, 221–228.

Meletakos, P., Vagenas, G., & Bayios, I. (2011). A multivariate assessment of offensive performance indicators in Men's Handball: Trends and differences in the World Championships. *International Journal of Performance Analysis in Sport, 11*, 284–294.

Michalsik, L. B., Aagaard, P., & Madsen, K. (2013). Locomotion characteristics and match-induced impairments in physical performance in male elite team handball players. *International Journal of Sports Medicine, 34*, 590–599.

Michalsik, L. B., Madsen, K., & Aagaard, P. (2014). Match performance and physiological capacity of female elite team handball players. *International Journal of Sports Medicine, 35*, 595–607.

Moore, R., Bullough, S., Goldsmith, S., & Edmondson, L. (2014). A systematic review of futsal literature. *American Journal of Sports Science and Medicine, 2*(3), 108–116.

Ohnjec, K., Vuleta, D., Milanovic, D., & Gruic, I. (2008). Performance indicators of teams at the 2003 world handball championship for women in Croatia. *Kinesiology, 40*(1), 69–79.

Oliveira, T., Gómez, M. A., & Sampaio, J. (2012). Effects of game location, period, and quality of opposition in elite handball performances. *Perceptual and Motor Skills, 114*(3), 783–794.

Pfeiffer, M., & Perl, J. (2006). Analysis of tactical structures in team handball by means of artificial neural networks. *International Journal of Computer Science in Sport, 5*(1), 4–14.

Pollard, R., & Gómez, M. A. (2012). Re-assessment of home advantage in Spanish handball: Comment on Gutiérrez, et al. *Perceptual and Motor Skills, 115*(3), 937–943.

Póvoas, S., Ascensão, A., Magalhães, J., Seabra, A., Krustrup, P., Soares, J., . . . Rebelo, A. (2014). Physiological demands of elite team handball with special reference to playing position. *Journal of Strength and Conditioning Research, 28*(2), 430–442.

Póvoas, S., Seabra, A., Ascensão, A., Magalhães, J., Soares, J., & Rebelo, A. (2012). Physical and physiological demands of elite team handball. *Journal of Strength and Conditioning Research, 26*(12), 3366–3376.

216

Rogulj, N., Srhoj, V., & Srhoj, L. (2004). The contribution of collective attack tactics in differentiating handball score efficiency. *Collegium Antropologicum, 28*(2), 739–746.

Rogulj, N., Vuleta, D., Milanovic, D., Cavala, M., & Foretic, N. (2011). The efficiency of elements of collective attack tactics in handball. *Kinesiologia Slovenica, 17*(1), 5–14.

Sarmento, H., Marcelino, R., Anguera, M. T., Campaniço, J., Matos, N., & Leitão, J. C. (2014). Match analysis in football: A systematic review. *Journal of Sports Sciences, 32*(20), 1831–1843.

Šibila, M., Vuleta, D., & Pori, P. (2004). Position-related differences in volume and intensity of large-scale cyclic movements of male players in handball. *Kinesiology, 36*(1), 58–68.

Srhoj, V., Rogulj, N., Padovan, M., & Katic, R. (2001). Influence of the attack end conduction on match result in handball. *Collegium Antropologicum, 25*(2), 611–617.

Teles, N., & Volossovitch, A. (2015). The influence of contextual variables on the team performance in the last ten minutes of the handball game. *Revista Brasileira de Educação Física e Esporte, 29*(2), 177–178.

Volossovitch, A. (2013). Handball. In T. McGarry, P. O'Donoghue, & J. Sampaio (Eds.), *Routledge Handbook of Sports Performance Analysis* (pp. 380–392). London: Routledge.

Volossovitch, A., Dumangane, M., & Rosati, N. (2009). Does the relationship between the past teams' performances during the match and the probability of scoring depend on the match quality? *Motricidade, 5*(3), 45.

Volossovitch, A., & Ferreira, A. P. (2013). Da descrição estática à predição dinâmica. A evolução das perspetivas de análise da performance nos jogos desportivos coletivos. In A. Volossovitch & A. P. Ferreira (Eds.), *Fundamentos e aplicações em análise do jogo. (5–32). Lisboa: FMH-Edições* (pp. 5–32). Lisboa: FMH-Edições.

Volossovitch, A., & Gonçalves, I. (2003). *The significance of game indicators for winning and losing team in Handball.* Paper presented at the 8th Annual Congress of European College of Sport Science, Salzburg.

Vuleta, D., Milanovic, D., Grunic, I., & Ohnjec, K. (2007). Influence of the goals scored in the different time periods of the game on the final outcome of matches of the 2003 Men's World Handball Championships, Portugal. *EHF Periodical [Internet].* http://home.eurohandball.com/ehf_files/Publikation/ WP Vuleta-Influence of the gaols scored on final outcomes.pdf

Vuleta, D., Milanovic, D., & Sertic, H. (2003). Relations among variables of shooting for a goal and outcomes of the 2000 men's European handball championship matches. *Kinesiology, 35*(2), 168–183.

Wagner, H., Finkenzeller, T., Würth, S., & van Duvillard, S. P. (2014). Individual and team performance in team-handball: A review. *Journal of Sports Science and Medicine, 13*, 808–816.

CHAPTER 11

RESEARCH TOPICS IN VOLLEYBALL

Leading author: Duarte Araújo

INTRODUCTION

Performance in volleyball is constrained by the characteristics of the game, such as the opposing goals of each team, and the collaboration imposed by the rules of the game within each team. The game is seen as a complex system, where behaviour and performance emerge based on the interaction of the system's components at different levels in time (Davids et al., 2014). In this chapter we start by addressing the volleyball-related research from the last 50 years, and then we explore the implications of a complex systems view on volleyball's coaching, practice environments, performance analysis and research. The aim of this chapter is to identify the key results from research about the constraints that influence individual and team performance in a volleyball match, and provide supported consequences for coaching.

Volleyball is quite different from other traditional team ball sports, like soccer or basketball. Volleyball is a non-invasive, cooperation/opposition–based team sport. Essentially, two teams have opposing goals, as in other traditional team sports, but the fight for ball possession alternates – each team has a limited number of ball contacts (three), as established by the rules; the ball can be touched but not grabbed; the scoring target is the opposing team's playing area, and not a goal or a basket; and the position of each player in the court is rule-dependent ('Official Volleyball Rules', 2013–2016, pp. 23–24). These core features are the basis for the design of training tasks and coaching.

Traditionally in volleyball, there are fundamental skills that are seen as the foundational for performance development (e.g., see Peppler,

2002). The idea is that when these skills are acquired, variability can be added. However, motor variability is always present (there are no two equal movements) as are changes in the way problems are solved (action modes), changes in the definition of the problem (goal) and degrees of goal achievement. Individual and team performance are indeterminate, so they portray a certain amount of behavioural unpredictability. Behaviour is, therefore, not an outcome sustained by a single cause–effect relationship (Passos et al., 2009), but it is potentially non-linear, 'emerging from the system exemplified by small skips, jumps and regressions in motor learning' (Davids, 2010, p. 3).

When coaching volleyball, the tasks may benefit from a focus on the individual-environment interactions, more than on pre-established cause–effect relationships (e.g., single, ready-made solutions). Behaviour emerges from the athlete's exploration of the environmental information available, according to the unique characteristics and state of the athlete and the game. A suggestion for how to design training tasks could be based on representativeness (Chow, 2013; Davids et al., 2012). But before that it is important to know the characteristics of performance.

KEY ISSUES RAISED BY SPORT SCIENTISTS ABOUT PERFORMANCE IN VOLLEYBALL

Players act in order to solve problems presented by the game. In this chapter we approach research on volleyball assuming that the reciprocity of interpersonal interactions in complex social systems, such as a volleyball match, is the proper level of analysis.

In order to complement the narrative review from Mesquita and colleagues (2013), an online-database search (Scopus, Sport Discus, ISI Web of Knowledge and PubMed) was performed to identify volleyball performance–related research in peer-reviewed journals. From this search 1,194 articles were found. These were organised into the following groups, based on their research aims: 'Athlete Typology/Traits Characterization' (341), 'Expertise' (28), 'Injury/Disease/Recovery' (257), 'Instruments and Methodologies' (179), 'Motor Capabilities/Abilities Expression' (85), 'Performance Indicators' (97), 'Performance Constraints' (219) and 'Technique' (30).

This search highlighted that volleyball athletes are seen as a population of interest in the study of certain injuries and injury–intervention/ prevention programs related to the knee (e.g., Voskanian, 2013), ankle (e.g., Petersen et al., 2013) and shoulder and spine (e.g., Seminati & Minetti, 2013); athletes' jumping ability and motor capability were also addressed in relation to injury–prevention/prevention programs (e.g., Wu et al., 2013; Ziv & Lidor, 2010).

The remainder of the research included in this sample focused mainly on the players' characteristics – namely, cognitive ability (e.g., Alves et al., 2013; Gil Arias et al., 2012); physical characteristics (e.g., D'Ascenzi et al., 2013; Ivanovic & Dopsaj, 2012; Santos Silva et al., 2013; Sheppard & Newton, 2012; Un et al., 2013; Zwierko et al., 2010); technique (e.g., Palao et al., 2009); and personality traits (e.g., Lidor & Ziv, 2010; Milavić et al., 2013; Patel et al., 2010; Superlak, 2008).

A bias to see the athlete in isolation and a lack of relation to the match context in the study of volleyball performance is revealed in a detailed analysis of the expertise-related articles. From the 28 articles, 23 related to knowledge-based expression of expertise in laboratory settings (e.g., Tomasino et al., 2013), one of which addressed verbal reports about an in-situ representative task (Afonso et al., 2012); 4 articles reported the evaluation of expertise level through physical and motor non-specific tests or through ability expression in a skill task, like a serve accuracy test (e.g., Lidor et al., 2007). The exception is Hughes and Daniel's (2003) study on playing patterns of elite and non-elite volleyball teams, where game-performance indicators were used to highlight the differences between the two levels of expertise.

Environmental accounts mostly relate to agents, like the coach, or key-moments, like the time out, or contextual variables in relation to individuals' expression of personal characteristics. For instance, research has found that coaches' methodological approach to train-ing is different among competition levels (Sunay, 2013), and also that coaches' leadership styles impact players' competitive anxiety (Rohani et al., 2013). Fernández-Echeverria et al. (2013) found that the use of the time out in formative stages tends to be driven by the opponent's perfor-mance and has an impact on recovering serve possession. Some studies tried to understand the influence of task design in the learning of volley-ball skills, finding that higher contextual interference gets better results (Kalkhoran & Shariati, 2012), as does sequential learning (implicit learn-ing followed by explicit learning), as opposed to only explicit or only implicit learning (Lola et al., 2012). Sheppard et al. (2009) showed, in elite male volleyball, that different playing positions have different

220

physiological demands and characteristics, and also difference demands regarding jumping ability.

Volleyball-related performance research is also associated with match performance indicators such as those related to the following: (i) success at different outcome levels – point (e.g., Marcelino et al., 2012), set (e.g., García-Hermoso et al., 2013; Rodriguez-Ruiz et al., 2011), match (e.g., Patsiaouras et al., 2011; Peña et al., 2013), and competition standings (Drikos et al., 2009; Durkovic et al., 2009); and (ii) the style of play as characterised by gender (e.g., Costa et al., 2012; João et al., 2010) or expertise level (e.g., Nesic et al., 2011; Panfil & Superlak, 2012). In terms of success, the main findings highlight the impact of terminal actions – serve, attack, block and errors – as the ones more associated with success. But importantly, there is growing evidence of the relevance of the performance in Complex II (i.e., the counter-attack) in achieving success at the highest level. When differentiating male from female performance, the female game exhibits a higher continuity and a lower speed, which allows for higher relevance of defensive actions. In terms of playing level, in a sport so clearly dependent on collaboration, it has been shown that more efficiency in these collaborative skills has been related to higher level teams.

At this point, there is an emphasis on the efficacy of a given game-action in another game-action or in team performance. However, there is a question that could be addressed in a near future: '*How* [do] performers use information through the course of action during goal-directed performance' (Correia, Araújo, Vilar, and Davids, 2012)? The ecological dynamics approach can address this, since it's built on performer–environment interactions – 'What were the circumstances that made a given action possible?' (Correia, Araújo, Vilar, and Davids, 2012).

COMPETITIVE ACTIVITY PROFILES AND SPECIFIC POSITION DEMANDS

In volleyball-related research, the study of competitive activity profiles and specific position demands is a recent topic. There is the exception of Bale (1986), who addressed several team sports in terms of physique and performance qualities. In volleyball Bale highlighted height as an essential characteristic, and a slim mobile physique as key in attacking positions, which require speed and agility. Actually his view of position/game-role differences in terms of physical attributes is prevalent for this specific research topic. The focus is on somatotype (e.g., Gualdi-Russo & Zaccagni, 2001), anthropometric measures (e.g., Fattahi et al., 2012), physiologic measures (e.g., Duncan et al., 2006), motor capacity (strength) (e.g., Marques et al., 2009) and motor ability – with jumping ability as the hottest topic in this line of research. Actually it is argued by some researchers that at higher levels of performance, success is mainly determined by speed and jumping ability (Ciccarone et al., 2008). The articles that focus on female athletes at an adult level (Dopsaj et al., 2012) or junior level (Nejić et al., 2013) both find that there aren't any noticeable differences in jumping abilities per position. When addressing male players, there is no consensus in the literature, which could be related to the way the position roles are defined or how the measures are collected – height reached or jump height – with an impact or not of the player's height and/or arm reach on the test performed. For Sattler, Sekulic, Hadzic, Uljevic, and Dervisevic (2012), receivers and liberos have the greatest jumping capacity; for Fattahi et al. (2012), spikers and setters jump higher than liberos; and Sheppard et al. (2009) found that middle hitters have higher block and attack jumps than setters and opposite hitters.

Hurd et al. (2009) found a ratio of the number of hits per game and proposed an intervention program to enhance this ratio.

COACHING AND VOLLEYBALL PERFORMANCE ANALYSIS

Performance analysis aims to result in a better practice for effective future performances (Hughes & Bartlett, 2008). Volleyball performance analysis research has been conducted mainly through notational analysis. This is a method for recording and analysing complex and dynamic situations, such as field games, that allows the gathering of data in an efficient manner, providing an abstract view of the sport in accordance with the researcher's conformity to pre-established scoring criteria (O'Donoghue, 2010). Mesquita et al. (2013) in a recent review of research in volleyball found the following: (i) descriptive and correlational analysis of the game have been crucial to identify that some behaviours are more important than others (e.g., Afonso & Mesquita, 2011); (ii) correlational studies 'have demonstrated high regularity and stability in defensive and offensive patterns' (Mesquita et al., 2013, p. 369) and that attack efficacy is independent from previous game actions (Castro & Mesquita,

222

2010); (iii) predictive studies have highlighted mainly the predictive value of terminal actions, such as attacking, blocking and serving, for set or match outcomes (Drikos & Vagenas, 2011; Marelic et al., 2004; Rocha & Barbanti, 2006), or the predictive value of phases of the game, like Complex I (the attack after the serve) or Complex II (the counter-attack) for the same outcomes (Eom & Schutz, 1992).

Though informative, there's a limitation to this approach to performance analysis. McGarry (2009) argues that this traditional way of doing performance analysis has enabled researchers to answer to the following questions: 'Who' (e.g., player or team) does 'What' (e.g., attack, serve reception, etc.), 'Where' (e.g., player positioned in zone 5; see Figure 11.1) and even 'When' (e.g., instant in time or point with relation to the already-scored/to-be-scored points)? However, there aren't meaningful drawings of such conclusions from sports behaviours to sports outcomes, beyond self-evident associations, even more evident in volleyball due to the highly 'deterministic structure' of the game (Afonso & Mesquita, 2011, p. 70). There is also the need to answer to the question, 'How'? In some performance analysis in volleyball, the 'how' question could relate to the type of action used – for instance, faster *attack tempo* versus slower *attack tempo* (e.g., Castro et al., 2011), but the expression

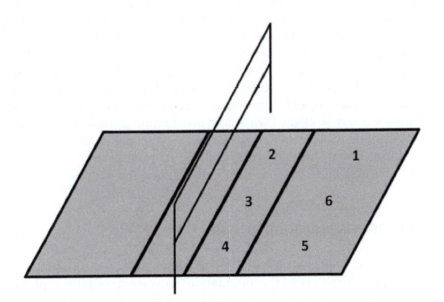

Figure 11.1 Volleyball players' on-court positions according to the rotation rule.

here needs to be broader, not as an action mode expression but relating to the underlying processes. An informed coaching intervention could address all these questions by following the guiding principles of ecological dynamics (Davids et al., 2012).The coach's goal could be seen as a designer of shared affordances to which the players become progressively attuned (Silva et al., 2013). For this, the aim of performance analysis would remain the same, using past performances to improve future performances, but the focus here would be that performance analysis would focus on the circumstances (individual-environment interactions) that prompted a given outcome and not on only the frequencies of the outcome.

When looking at performance analysis for finding answers to practical problems, two intertwined issues could be addressed: the skill level of the team, and the characteristics of the team (e.g., players' physical attributes, playing strengths and weaknesses, etc.). Reference values from the literature tend to be found on elite teams, and, thus, they might not immediately help a non-elite team. Hughes and Daniel (2003), studying the different patterns exhibited by high-level and college-level teams, found the following: (i) the two levels of play did not present differences between the points won when serving, but they differed in the points won and errors made when receiving; and (ii) the serve in the non-elite level was less variable, going to the middle of the court and with less depth, than the serve in the elite level. An interesting question from this study is, Why, in the non-elite level, does receiving a more predictable serve correspond to fewer points won and more errors made? Maybe the action capabilities of the teams influenced their ability to detect and use information relevant to their success; moreover, from an ecological dynamics approach, local information may be aligned with more distal future actions (Araújo et al., 2005; Correia, Araújo, Cummings & Craig, 2012), and consequently, we could suggest that at the non-elite level, the goal was possibly 'to receive' and, at the elite level, the goal was possibly 'to receive in order to attack'.

CONCLUSIONS AND SUGGESTIONS

To focus the analysis of volleyball performance at the individual-environment level, so that the information–movement coupling captured in a setting representative of the performance environment is a promising future avenue. This may be illustrated by some pioneering examples already available in the literature. Handford (2002) studied the volleyball serve as a self-paced extrinsic timing task, to examine implications for the design of practice. When analysing the relationship between the time of the ball's zenith and the initiation of forward hip movement, he found that the occurrence of these two events was extremely invariant and strongly coupled. This relationship holds true despite individual variability, and apparently the relationship between a stable height in ball zenith and the time interval between the initiation of the serving movement at zenith and the point of ball–hand contact for coordinating a successful serve is discovered and adjusted during extensive practice. Jager and Schollhorn (2007) by means of hierarchical cluster analysis based on the positional data of the players (spatial coordinates) found that different teams in the same level of play exhibit different playing patterns – i.e., team-specific behavior. These two studies are examples of capturing how the player–ball, player–court–teammates/opponents interactions are related to performance. When analysing performance, conceiving development programs or planning a practice session, the individual-environment level of analysis is the level of reference. The challenge has been to bring the experiments closer to the performance environment (e.g., Barsingerhorn et al., 2013). But theoretical clarity and technological advances are helpful for this endeavour.

ACKNOWLEDGEMENT

I would like to thank the tremendous help of Ana Paulo, PhD student at the Faculty of Human Kinetics of University of Lisbon, Portugal, for finding the articles for this chapter, organising them and making this text aligned with the key issues of volleyball.

REFERENCES

Afonso, J., Garganta, J., McRobert, A., Williams, A. M., & Mesquita, I. (2012). The perceptual cognitive processes underpinning skilled performance in volley-ball: Evidence from eye-movements and verbal reports of thinking involving an in situ representative task. *Journal of Sports Science and Medicine, 11*(2), 339–345.

Afonso, J., & Mesquita, I. (2011). Determinants of block cohesiveness and attack efficacy in high-level women's volleyball. *European Journal of Sport Science, 11*(1), 69–75. doi: 10.1080/17461391.2010.487114

Alves, H., Voss, M. W., Boot, W. R., Deslandes, A., Cossich, V., Salles, J. I., . . . Kramer, A. F. (2013). Perceptual-cognitive expertise in elite volleyball players. *Front Psychology, 4*, 36. doi: 10.3389/fpsyg.2013.00036

225

Araújo, D., Davids, K., & Serpa, S. (2005). An ecological approach to expertise effects in decision-making in a simulated sailing regatta. *Psychology of Sport and Exercise, 6*(6), 671–692. doi: 10.1016/j.psychsport.2004.12.003

Bale, P. (1986). A review of the physique and performance qualities characteristic of games players in specific positions on the field of play. *Journal of Sports Medicine and Physical Fitness, 26*(2), 109–122.

Barsingerhorn, A. D., Zaal, F. T. J. M., De Poel, H. J., & Pepping, G.-J. (2013). Shaping decisions in volleyball an ecological approach to decision-making in volleyball passing. *International Journal of Sport Psychology, 44*(3), 197–214. doi: 10.7352/ijsp2013.44.197

Castro, J., & Mesquita, I. (2010). Analysis of the attack tempo determinants in volleyball's complex II – a study on elite male teams. *International Journal of Performance Analysis in Sport, 10*(3), 197–206.

Castro, J., Souza, A., & Mesquita, I. (2011). Attack efficacy in volleyball: Elite male teams. *Perceptual and Motor Skills, 113*(2), 395–408. doi: 10.2466/05.25. PMS.113.5.395–408

Chow, J. Y. (2013). Nonlinear learning underpinning pedagogy: Evidence, challenges, and implications. *Quest, 65*(4), 469–484. doi: 10.1080/003362 97.2013.807746

Ciccarone, G., Croisier, J. L., Fontani, G., Martelli, G., Albert, A., Zhang, L., . . . Cloes, M. (2008). Comparison between player specialization, anthropometric characteristics and jumping ability in top-level volleyball players. *Medicina Dello Sport, 61*(1), 29–43.

Correia, V., Araújo, D., Cummins, A., & Craig, C. M. (2012). Perceiving and acting upon spaces in a VR rugby task: Expertise effects in affordance detection and task achievement. *Journal of Sport and Exercise Psychology, 34*(3), 305–321.

Correia, V., Araújo, D., Vilar, L., & Davids, K. (2012). From recording discrete actions to studying continuous goal-directed behaviours in team sports. *Journal of Sports Sciences*, 1–8.

Costa, G., Afonso, J., Brant, E., & Mesquita, I. (2012). Differences in game patterns between male and female youth volleyball. *Kinesiology, 44*(1), 60–66.

D'Ascenzi, F., Alvino, F., Natali, B. M., Cameli, M., Palmitesta, P., Boschetti, G., . . . Mondillo, S. (2013). Precompetitive assessment of heart rate variability in elite female athletes during play offs. *Clinical Physiology and Functional Imaging*. doi: 10.1111/cpf.12088

Davids, K. (2010). The constraints-based approach to motor learning: Implications for non-linear pedagogy in sport and physical education. In I. Renshaw, K. Davids, & G. Savelsbergh (Eds.), *Motor Learning in Practice: A Constraints-Led Approach* (pp. 3–16). Oxfordshire: Routledge.

Davids, K., Araújo, D., Hristovski, R., Passos, P., & Chow, J. Y. (2012). Ecological dynamics and motor learning design in sport. In N. J. Hodges & A. M. Williams (Eds.), *Skill Acquisition in Sport: Research, Theory & Practice* (2nd ed., pp. 112–130). New York: Routledge.

Davids, K., Hristovski, R., Araújo, D., Balague, N., Button, C., & Passos, P. (2014). *Complex Systems in Sport*. London: Routledge.

226

Dopsaj, M., Copić, N., Nešić, G., & Sikimić, M. (2012). Jumping performance in elite female volleyball players relative to playing positions: A practical multidimensional assessment model. *Serbian Journal of Sports Sciences, 6*(2), 61–69.

Drikos, S., Kountouris, P., Laios, A., & Laios, Y. (2009). Correlates of team performance in volleyball. *International Journal of Performance Analysis in Sport, 9*(2), 149–156.

Drikos, S., & Vagenas, G. (2011). Multivariate assessment of selected performance indicators in relation to the type and result of a typical set in Men's Elite Volleyball. *International Journal of Performance Analysis in Sport, 11*(1), 85–95.

Duncan, M. J., Woodfield, L., & Al-Nakeeb, Y. (2006). Anthropometric and physiological characteristics of junior elite volleyball players. *British Journal of Sports Medicine, 40*(7), 649–651. doi: 10.1136/bjsm.2005.021998

Durkovic, T., Marelic, N., & Resetar, T. (2009). Rotation analysis of teams' performances at 2003 youth European volleyball championship. *Kinesiology, 41*(1), 60–66.

Eom, H. J., & Schutz, R. W. (1992). Transition play in team performance of volleyball: A log-linear analysis. *Research Quarterly for Exercise and Sport, 63*(3), 261–269.

Fattahi, A., Ameli, M., Sadeghi, H., & Mahmoodi, B. (2012). Relationship between anthropometric parameters with vertical jump in male elite volleyball players due to game's position. *Journal of Human Sport and Exercise, 7*(3), 714–726. doi: 10.4100/jhse.v7i3.346

Fernández-Echeverría, C., Gil, A., García-González, L., Soares, F. C., Claver, F., & Del Villar, F. (2013). Employment time-out in volleyball formative stages. *Journal of Human Sport and Exercise, 8*(3), S591-S600. doi: 10.4100/jhse.2013.8.Proc3.04

García-Hermoso, A., Dávila-Romero, C., & Saavedra, J. M. (2013). Discriminatory power of game-related statistics in 14–15 year age group male volleyball, according to set. *Perceptual and Motor Skills, 116*(1), 132–143. doi: 10.2466/03.30.pms.116.1.132–143

Gil Arias, A., Moreno, M. P., García-González, L., Moreno, A., & del Villar, F. (2012). Analysis of declarative and procedural knowledge in volleyball according to the level of practice and players' age. *Perceptual and Motor Skills, 115*(2), 632–644. doi: 10.2466/30.10.25.pms.115.5.632–644

Gualdi-Russo, E., & Zaccagni, L. (2001). Somatotype, role and performance in elite volleyball players. *Journal of Sports Medicine and Physical Fitness, 41*(2), 256–262.

Handford, C. (2002). Strategy and practice for acquiring timing in discrete, self-paced interceptive skills. In K. Davids, G. Savelsbergh, S. Bennet, & J. Van der Kamp (Eds.), *Interceptive Actions in Sport: Information and movement* (pp. 288–300). London: Routledge.

Hughes, M., & Bartlett, R. (2008). What is performance analysis? In M. Hughes & I. Franks (Eds.), *Essentials of Performance Analysis: An introduction* (pp. 8–20). London: Routledge.

227

Hughes, M., & Daniel, R. (2003). Playing patterns of elite and non-elite volleyball. *Journal of Sports Sciences, 21*(4), 268–268.

Hurd, W., Hunter-Giordano, A., Axe, M., & Snyder-Mackler, L. (2009). Database interval hitting program for female college volleyball players. *Sports Health, 1*(6), 522–530. doi: 10.1177/1941738109351171

Ivanovic, J., & Dopsaj, M. (2012). Functional dimorphism and characteristics of maximal hand grip force in top level female athletes. *Collegium Antropologicum, 36*(4), 1231–1240.

Jager, J. M., & Schollhorn, W. I. (2007). Situation-orientated recognition of tactical patterns in volleyball. *Journal of Sports Sciences, 25*(12), 1345–1353. doi: 10.1080/02640410701287230

João, P. V., Leite, N., Mesquita, I., & Sampaio, J. (2010). Sex differences in discriminative power of volleyball game-related statistics. *Perceptual and Motor Skills, 111*(3), 893–900. doi: 10.2466/05.11.25.pms.111.6.893–900

Kalkhoran, J. F., & Shariati, A. (2012). The effects of contextual interference on learning volleyball motor skills. *Journal of Physical Education and Sport, 12*(4), 550–556. doi: 10.7752/jpes.2012.04081

Lidor, R., Hershko, Y., Bilkevitz, A., Arnon, M., & Falk, B. (2007). Measurement of talent in volleyball: 15-month follow-up of elite adolescent players. *Journal of Sports Medicine and Physical Fitness, 47*(2), 159–168.

Lidor, R., & Ziv, G. (2010). Physical characteristics and physiological attributes of adolescent volleyball players-a review. *Pediatric Exercise Science, 22*(1), 114–134.

Lola, A. C., Tzetzis, G. C., & Zetou, H. (2012). The effect of implicit and explicit practice in the development of decision making in volleyball serving. *Perceptual and Motor Skills, 114*(2), 665–678.

Marcelino, R. O., Sampaio, J. E., & Mesquita, I. M. (2012). Attack and serve performances according to the match period and quality of opposition in elite volleyball matches. *Journal of Strength and Conditioning Research, 26*(12), 3385–3391. doi: 10.1519/JSC.0b013e3182474269

Marelic, N., Rešetar, T., & Janković, V. (2004). Discriminant analysis of the sets won and the sets lost by one team in A1 Italian volleyball league – a case study. *Kinesiology, 36*(1), 75–82.

Marques, M. C., van den Tillaar, R., Gabbett, T. J., Reis, V. M., & Gonzalez-Badillo, J. J. (2009). Physical fitness qualities of professional volleyball players: Determination of positional differences. *Journal of Strength and Conditioning Research, 23*(4), 1106–1111. doi: 10.1519/JSC.0b013e31819b78c4

McGarry, T. (2009). Applied and theoretical perspectives of performance analysis in sport: Scientific issues and challenges. *International Journal of Performance Analysis in Sport, 9*(1), 128–140.

Mesquita, I., Palao, J. M., Marcelino, R., & Afonso, J. (2013). Indoor volleyball and beach volleyball. In T. McGarry, P. O'Donoghue, & J. Sampaio (Eds.), *Routledge Handbook of Sports Performance Analysis* (pp. 367–379). London: Routledge, Taylor & Francis Group.

Milavić, B., Jurko, D., & Grgantov, Z. (2013). Relations of competitive state anxiety and efficacy of young volleyball players. *Relacije Stanja Natjecateljske Anksioznosti i uspješnosti mladih igrača odbojke, 37*(SUPPL.2), 83–92.

228

Nejić, D., Trajković, N., Stanković, R., Milanović, Z., & Sporiš, G. (2013). A comparison of the jumping performance of female junior volleyball players in terms of their playing positions. *Facta Universitatis: Series Physical Education & Sport, 11*(2), 157–164.

Nesic, G., Sikimic, M., Ilic, V., & Stojanovic, T. (2011). Play structure of top female volleyball players: Explorative factorial approach. *British Journal of Sports Medicine, 45*(6), 541.

O'Donoghue, P. (2010). *Research Methods for Sports Performance Analysis.* London: Routledge.

Official Volleyball Rules (2015–2016).

Palao, J., Manzanares, P., & Ortega, E. (2009). Techniques used and efficacy of volleyball skills in relation to gender. *International Journal of Performance Analysis in Sport, 9*(2), 281–293.

Panfil, R., & Superlak, E. (2012). The relationships between the effectiveness of team play and the sporting level of a team. *Human Movement, 13*(2), 152–160. doi: 10.2478/v10038–012–0017–2

Passos, P., Araújo, D., Davids, K., Gouveia, L., Serpa, S., Milho, J., . . . Fonseca, S. (2009). Interpersonal pattern dynamics and adaptive behavior in multiagent neurobiological systems: Conceptual model and data. *Journal of Motor Behavior, 41*(5), 445–459.

Patel, D. R., Omar, H., & Terry, M. (2010). Sport-related performance anxiety in young female athletes. *Journal of Pediatric and Adolescent Gynecology, 23*(6), 325–335. doi: 10.1016/j.jpag.2010.04.004

Patsiaouras, A., Moustakidis, A., Charitonidis, K., & Kokaridas, D. (2011). Technical skills leading in winning or losing volleyball matches during Beijing Olympic Games. *Journal of Physical Education and Sport, 11*(2), 39–42.

Peña, J., Rodríguez-Guerra, J., Buscá, B., & Serra, N. (2013). Which skills and factors better predict winning and losing in high-level men's volleyball? *Journal of Strength and Conditioning Research, 27*(9), 2487–2493. doi: 10.1519/JSC.0 b013e31827f4dbe10.2202/1559–0410.1234

Peppler, M. J. (2002). Using new and proven teaching techniques. In D. Shondell & C. Reynaud (Eds.), *The Volleyball Coaching Bible* (pp. 113–119). Champaign, IL: Human Kinetics.

Petersen, W., Rembitzki, I. V., Koppenburg, A. G., Ellermann, A., Liebau, C., Brueggemann, G. P., . . . Best, R. (2013). Treatment of acute ankle ligament injuries: A systematic review. *Archives of Orthopaedic and Trauma Surgery, 133*(8), 1129–1141. doi: 10.1007/s00402–013–1742–5

Rocha, C. M., & Barbanti, V. J. (2006). An analysis of the confrontations in the first sequence of game actions in Brazilian volleyball. *Journal of Human Movement Studies, 50*(4), 259–272.

Rodriguez-Ruiz, D., Quiroga, M. E., Miralles, J. A., Sarmiento, S., de Saá, Y., & García-Manso, J. M. (2011). Study of the technical and tactical variables determining set win or loss in top-level European men's volleyball. *Journal of Quantitative Analysis in Sports, 7*(1), Article 7.

Rohani, Z., Janani, H., & Talebian nia, H. (2013). The relationship between coaches leadership styles with athlete's competitive anxiety in the volleyball of medical sciences universities. *Life Science Journal, 10*(SUPPL. 5), 317–322.

Santos Silva, D. A., Petroski, E. L., & Araújo Gaya, A. C. (2013). Anthropometric and physical fitness differences among Brazilian adolescents who practise different team court sports. *Journal of Human Kinetics, 36*, 77–86. doi: 10.2478/hukin-2013–0008

Sattler, T., Sekulic, D., Hadzic, V., Uljevic, O., & Dervisevic, E. (2012). Vertical jumping tests in volleyball: Reliability, validity, and playing-position specifics. *Journal of Strength and Conditioning Research, 26*(6), 1532–1538. doi: 10.1519/JSC.0b013e318234e838

Seminati, E., & Minetti, A. E. (2013). Overuse in volleyball training/practice: A review on shoulder and spine-related injuries. *European Journal of Sport Science, 13*(6), 732–743. doi: 10.1080/17461391.2013.773090

Sheppard, J. M., Gabbett, T. J., & Stanganelli, L. C. R. (2009). An analysis of playing positions in elite men's volleyball: Considerations for competition demands and physiologic characteristics. *Journal of Strength and Conditioning Research, 23*(6), 1858–1866. doi: 10.1519/JSC.0b013e3181b45c6a

Sheppard, J. M., & Newton, R. U. (2012). Long-term training adaptations in elite male volleyball players. *Journal of Strength and Conditioning Research, 26*(8), 2180–2184. doi: 10.1519/JSC.0b013e31823c429a

Silva, P., Garganta, J., Araújo, D., Davids, K., & Aguiar, P. (2013). Shared knowledge or shared affordances? Insights from an ecological dynamics approach to team coordination in sports. *Sports Medicine, 43*(9), 765–772.

Sunay, H. (2013). Coaching practices of first and second league women-men volleyball coaches in Turkey. *Life Science Journal, 10*(SUPPL. 7), 556–561.

Superlak, E. (2008). The structure of ontogenetic dispositions in young volleyball players – European cadet volleyball champions. *Human Movement, 9*(2), 128–133. doi: 10.2478/v10038–008–0017–4

Tomasino, B., Maieron, M., Guatto, E., Fabbro, F., & Rumiati, R. I. (2013). How are the motor system activity and functional connectivity between the cognitive and sensorimotor systems modulated by athletic expertise? *Brain Research, 1540*, 21–41. doi: 10.1016/j.brainres.2013.09.048

Un, C.-P., Lin, K.-H., Shiang, T.-Y., Chang, E.-C., Su, S.-C., & Wang, H.-K. (2013). Comparative and reliability studies of neuromechanical leg muscle performances of volleyball athletes in different divisions. *European Journal of Applied Physiology, 113*(2), 457–466. doi: 10.1007/s00421–012–2454–1

Voskanian, N. (2013). ACL Injury prevention in female athletes: Review of the literature and practical considerations in implementing an ACL prevention program. *Current Reviews in Musculoskeletal Medicine, 6*(2), 158–163. doi: 10.1007/s12178–013–9158-y

Wu, X., Zhang, S., Liu, Y., Zhang, D., & Xie, B. (2013). Do knee concentric and eccentric strength and sagittal-plane knee joint biomechanics differ between jumpers and non-jumpers in landing? *Human Movement Science, 32*(6), 1299–1309. doi: 10.1016/j.humov.2013.03.008

Ziv, G., & Lidor, R. (2010). Vertical jump in female and male volleyball players: a review of observational and experimental studies. *Scand J Med Sci Sports, 20*(4), 556–567. doi: 10.1111/j.1600-0838.2009.01083.x

Zwierko, T., Osiński, W., Lubiński, W., Czepita, D., & Florkiewicz, B. (2010). Speed of visual sensorimotor processes and conductivity of visual pathway in volleyball players. *Journal of Human Kinetics, 23*(1), 21–27. doi: 10.2478/ v10078–010–0003–8

NOTES

1 Issue of the representative learning design is discussed in chapter 4.
2 For more detailed information regarding the variables that can be used with time-motion analysis systems, please see chapter 5.
3 See O'Donoghue (2010) for a particular definition that conceives performance indicators as specific types of variable – namely, those that are valid measures of important aspects of sports performance.
4 For examples of possible coordinative variables, please see chapter 5.
5 For further information on how to measure player's interactive behavior, please see chapter 5.
6 Please see the last section of this chapter.
7 Super 12 (currently known as SuperRugby) is the major professional rugby union competition in the southern hemisphere.
8 Full (or even) strength implies that both teams have five skaters and one goaltender on the ice.
9 A power play is applied to give a team a numerical advantage on the ice.
10 Short-handed refers to having fewer players on the ice, as a result of a penalty.
11 Stefani (2008) suggested the model to calculate the home advantage in terms of the difference in the fraction of games won, with the assumption that the home advantage exists when a team performs better at home than away against the same opponent. This way of quantifying the home advantage is based on team rankings and does not require checking the points won at home and away. For more detailed information about measuring home advantage, see Stefani (2008).
12 Some hockey rules may favour the home team. For example, (1) the last line change is attributed to the home team coach, bringing him or her an advantage in making player substitutions after the visiting team; (2) in the centre ice face-off, the visiting team player must place his or her stick on the ice before the player of the home team; and (3) the home team makes the decision of who shoots first in the shootout in games tied after overtime periods.
13 Total minutes played – the total minutes a given player is on the ice in all games during the entire season (Green, Pivarnik, Carrier, & Womack, 2006).
14 Net scoring chances – the differences between the number of opportunities a player's team has to score and the number of opportunities the opposing team has to score while a given player is on ice (Green et al., 2006).
15 Plus–minus score (+/–, ±, plus/minus) is a statistic used to measure a player's impact on the game, represented by the difference between the goals scored and allowed by team when that player is on ice.

231

16 Linear weights evaluate the average impact an event has towards the scoring process.
17 In a Poisson-like process scoring events occur independently or with little evidence for long-range correlation between successive scores (Gabel & Redner, 2012).
18 A binomial model is characterised by trials, which either end in success (heads) or failure (tails). These are sometimes called Bernoulli trials.
19 Spatial centre is an average of the longitudinal and lateral coordinates of all players of the same team.
20 Stretch index measures the expansion or contraction of space in the longitudinal and lateral directions of a team during the game and represents the mean deviation of each player in a team from the spatial centre.
21 Relative stretch index is calculated from the difference between the stretch indexes of the two teams at any instant of a game
22 Uphill/downhill flux estimates the average change in potential shooting percentage as the ball moves between players in relation to their differential percent shooting success (Fewell et al., 2012).

232

INDEX

233